Writing
Linux Device Drivers

a guide with exercises

LAB SOLUTIONS

Including the 2.6.31 kernel

Jerry Cooperstein

In order to save space the following explanatory comments have been removed from the printed solutions and should be considered as implicitly incorporated:

```
/*
 * The code herein is: Copyright 1998-2009 by Jerry Cooperstein
 *
 * This Copyright is retained for the purpose of protecting free
 * redistribution of source.
 *
 * URL:    http://www.coopj.com
 * email:  coop@coopj.com
 *
 * The primary maintainer for this code is Jerry Cooperstein
 * The CONTRIBUTORS file (distributed with this
 * file) lists those known to have contributed to the source.
 *
 * This code is distributed under Version 2 of the GNU General Public
 * License, which you should have received with the source.
 *
 */
```

The complete text of the GPL v2 and acoompanying documentation can be found at: **http://www.gnu.org/licenses/gpl-2.0.html.**

Contents

Preface

This is a companion volume to *Writing Linux Device Drivers, a guide with exercises*, by Jerry Cooperstein, pub. 2009. (**http://www.coopj.com**)

While the solutions to the exercises in that volume can be obtained from **http://www.coopj.com/LDD**, occasional requests for printed copies of the solutions are sometimes encountered. (Not everyone prefers reading on the screen, even today.) Rather than increasing the length of the book enormously, I've decided to make the solutions themselves available in book form.

There is no exposition here, only the statement of the exercises and then the actual code and necessary scripts.

You should notice there Chapter 27 (Network Drivers IV: Selected Topics) is missing. There were no exercises for this chapter in the original volume and thus none appear here.

Enjoy!

Acknowledgments

First of all I must thank my employer of over 15 years, Axian Inc (**http://www.axian.com**) of Beaverton, Oregon, for giving me permission to use material originally under Axian copyright and which was developed on its dime. In particular, Frank Helle and Steve Bissel have not only been extremely generous in allowing me these rights, but have been true friends and supporters in everything I've done.

In the more than a decade I supervised **Linux** developer classes for Axian (which were most often delivered through **Red Hat**'s training division), I interacted with a large number of instructors who taught from the material I was responsible for. They made many suggestions, fixed errors and in some cases contributed exercises. Colleagues I would like to express a very strong thank you to include

Marc Curry, Dominic Duval, Terry Griffin, George Hacker, Tatsuo Kawasaki, Richard Keech, and Bill Kerr.

I would also like to thank Alessandro Rubini for his warm and generous hospitality when not long after I began teaching about device drivers and **Linux**, I showed up at his home with my whole family. I also thank him for introducing me to the kind folks at O'Reilly publishing who gave me the opportunity to help with the review of their **Linux** kernel books, which has expanded my knowledge enormously and introduced me to a number of key personalities.

The biggest acknowledgment I must give is to the students who have contributed to the material by asking questions, exposing weaknesses, requesting new material and furnishing their real life experiences and needs, which has hopefully kept the material from being pedantic and made it more useful. Without them (and the money they paid to sit in classes and be forced to listen to and interact with me) this presentation would not exist.

I must also thank my family for putting up me with through all of this, especially with my frequent travels.

Finally, I would like to acknowledge the late Hans A. Bethe, who taught me to never be frightened of taking on a task just because other people had more experience on it.

Chapter 1

Preliminaries

1.1 Kernel Versions, Linux Distributions and Procedures

The lab exercise solutions are designed to work with the most recent **Linux** kernels (2.6.31 as of this writing) and with some minor tweaks (which are incorporated in the solutions) as far back as 2.6.26 and even earlier (2.6.18) with a few more tweaks.. They should also work with all major distributor kernels of the same vintage.

The material has been developed primarily on **Red Hat**-based systems, mostly on 64-bit variants with testing also done on 32-bit systems. But it has also been tested on a number of other distributions. Explicitly we have used:

- **Red Hat Enterprise Linux 5.3**
- **Fedora 11**
- **Centos 5.3**
- **Scientific Linux 5.3**
- **Open Suse 11.1**

- **Debian Lenny**

- **Ubuntu 9.04**

- **Gentoo**

You will need a computer installed with a current **Linux** distribution, with the important developer tools (for compiling, etc.) properly deployed.

Where feasible labs will build upon previous lab assignments. The solution set can be retrieved from **http://www.coopj.com/LDD**. As they become available, errata and updated solutions will also be posted on that site.

Lab **solutions** are made available so you can see at least one successful implementation, and have a possible template to begin the next lab exercise if it is a follow up. In addition, **examples** as shown during the exposition are made available as part of the SOLUTIONS package, in the EXAMPLES subdirectory. Once you have obtained the solutions you can unpack it with:

```
tar zxvf LDD*SOLUTIONS*.tar.gz
```

substituting the actual name of the file.

In the main solutions directory, there is a **Makefile** which will recursively compile all subdirectories. It is smart enough to differentiate between kernel code, user applications, and whether multi-threading is used.

There are some tunable features; by default all sub-directories are recursively compiled against the source of the currently running kernel. One can narrow the choice of directories, or use a different kernel source as in the following examples, or even pick a different architecture:

```
make SDIRS=s_22
make KROOT=/lib/modules/2.6.31/build
make SDIRS="s_0* s_23" KROOT=/usr/src/linux-2.6.31/build
make ARCH=i386
```

where KROOT points to the kernel source files. On an **x86_64** platform, specifying ARCH=i386 will compile 32-bit modules. The **genmake** script in the main directory is very useful for automatically generating makefiles, and is worth a perusal.

For this to work, the kernel source has to be suitably prepared; in particular it has to have a **configuration file** (.config in the main kernel source directory) and proper dependencies set up.

One should note that we have emphasized clarity and brevity over rigor in the solutions; e.g., we haven't tried to catch every possible error or take into account every possible kernel configuration option. The code is not bullet-proof; it is meant to be of pedagogical use.

Chapter 2

Device Drivers

2.1   Lab 1: Installing a Basic Character Driver

- In this exercise we are going to compile, load (and unload) and test the a sample character driver (provided). In subsequent sections we will discuss each of these steps in detail.

- **Compiling:** First you have to make sure you have the installed kernel source that you are going to use. The best way to compile kernel modules is to jump inside the kernel source to do it. This requires a simple Makefile, which need have only the line:

  ```
  obj-m += lab1_chrdrv.o
  ```

  If you then type

  ```
  make -C<path to kernel source> M=$PWD modules
  ```

  it will compile your module with all the same options and flags as the kernel modules in that source location.

- **Monitoring Output:** If you are working at a virtual terminal or in non-graphical mode, you'll see the output of your module appear on your screen. Otherwise you'll have to keep an eye on the file `/var/log/messages`, to which the system logging daemons direct kernel print messages. The best way to do this is to open a terminal window, and in it type:

```
tailf /var/log/messages
```

- **Loading and Unloading:** The easiest way to load and unload the module is with:

```
insmod lab1_chrdrv.ko
rmmod lab1_chrdrv
```

  Try and load and unload the module. If you look at **/proc/devices** you should see your driver registered, and if you look at **/proc/modules** (or type **lsmod**) you should see that your module is loaded.

- **Creating a Device Node:** Before you can actually use the module, you'll have to create the `device node` with which applications interact. You do this with the **mknod** command:

```
mknod /dev/mycdrv c 700 0
```

  Note that the **name** of the device node (`/dev/mycdrv`) is irrelevant; the kernel identifies which driver should handle the system calls only by the **major number** (700 in this case.) The **minor number** (0 in this case) is generally used only within the driver.

- **Using the Module**: You should be able to test the module with simple commands like:

```
echo Some Input > /dev/mycdrv
cat somefile > /dev/mycdrv
dd if=/dev/zero of=/dev/mycdrv count=1
dd if=/dev/mycdrv count=1
```

  We've only skimmed the surface; later we will consider the details of each of these steps.

lab1_chrdrv.c

```
/* Copyright 2009, J Cooperstein coop@coopj.com (GPLv2) */

#include <linux/module.h>        /* for modules */
#include <linux/fs.h>            /* file_operations */
#include <linux/uaccess.h>       /* copy_(to,from)_user */
#include <linux/init.h>          /* module_init, module_exit */
#include <linux/slab.h>          /* kmalloc */
#include <linux/cdev.h>          /* cdev utilities */

#define MYDEV_NAME "mycdrv"
#define KBUF_SIZE (size_t) (10*PAGE_SIZE)

static char *kbuf;
static dev_t first;
static unsigned int count = 1;
static int my_major = 700, my_minor = 0;
static struct cdev *my_cdev;

static int mycdrv_open (struct inode *inode, struct file *file)
{
    printk (KERN_INFO " OPENING device: %s:\n\n", MYDEV_NAME);
    return 0;
}
```

```
static int mycdrv_release (struct inode *inode, struct file *file)
{
    printk (KERN_INFO " CLOSING device: %s:\n\n", MYDEV_NAME);
    return 0;
}

static ssize_t
mycdrv_read (struct file *file, char __user * buf, size_t lbuf, loff_t * ppos)
{
    int nbytes = lbuf - copy_to_user (buf, kbuf + *ppos, lbuf);
    *ppos += nbytes;
    printk (KERN_INFO "\n READING function, nbytes=%d, pos=%d\n", nbytes,
            (int)*ppos);
    return nbytes;
}
static ssize_t
mycdrv_write (struct file *file, const char __user * buf, size_t lbuf,
              loff_t * ppos)
{
    int nbytes = lbuf - copy_from_user (kbuf + *ppos, buf, lbuf);
    *ppos += nbytes;
    printk (KERN_INFO "\n WRITING function, nbytes=%d, pos=%d\n", nbytes,
            (int)*ppos);
    return nbytes;
}
static const struct file_operations mycdrv_fops = {
    .owner = THIS_MODULE,
    .read = mycdrv_read,
    .write = mycdrv_write,
    .open = mycdrv_open,
    .release = mycdrv_release,
};
static int __init my_init (void)
{
    kbuf = kmalloc (KBUF_SIZE, GFP_KERNEL);
    first = MKDEV (my_major, my_minor);
    register_chrdev_region (first, count, MYDEV_NAME);
    my_cdev = cdev_alloc ();
    cdev_init (my_cdev, &mycdrv_fops);
    cdev_add (my_cdev, first, count);
    printk (KERN_INFO "\nSucceeded in registering character device %s\n",
            MYDEV_NAME);
    return 0;
}
static void __exit my_exit (void)
{
    cdev_del (my_cdev);
    unregister_chrdev_region (first, count);
    printk (KERN_INFO "\ndevice unregistered\n");
    kfree (kbuf);
}

module_init (my_init);
module_exit (my_exit);
```

```
MODULE_AUTHOR ("Jerry Cooperstein");
MODULE_LICENSE ("GPL v2");
```

Chapter 3

Modules I: Basics

3.1 Lab 1: Module parameters

- Write a module that can take an integer parameter when it is loaded with **insmod**. It should have a default value when none is specified.

- Load it and unload it. While the module is loaded, look at its directory in **/sys/module**, and see if you can change the value of the parameter you established.

`lab1_module.c`

```
/* Copyright 2009, J Cooperstein coop@coopj.com (GPLv2) */

#include <linux/module.h>
#include <linux/init.h>

static int mod_param = 12;
module_param (mod_param, int, S_IRUGO | S_IWUSR);

static int __init my_init (void)
{
```

```
    printk (KERN_INFO "Hello world from modfun \n");
    printk (KERN_INFO " mod_param = %d\n", mod_param);
    return 0;
}

static void __exit my_exit (void)
{
    printk (KERN_INFO "Goodbye world from modfun \n");
}

module_init (my_init);
module_exit (my_exit);

MODULE_AUTHOR ("Jerry Cooperstein");
MODULE_DESCRIPTION ("CLDD 1.0: lab1_module.c");
MODULE_LICENSE ("GPL v2");
```

3.2   Lab 2: Initialization and cleanup functions.

- Take any simple module, and see what happens if instead of having both initialization and cleanup functions, it has:

    - Only an initialization function.
    - Only a cleanup function.
    - Neither an initialization nor a cleanup function.

- In these cases see what happens when you try to load the module, and if that succeeds, when you try to unload it.

lab1_module.c

```
/* Copyright 2009, J Cooperstein coop@coopj.com (GPLv2) */

#include <linux/module.h>
#include <linux/init.h>

static int mod_param = 12;
module_param (mod_param, int, S_IRUGO | S_IWUSR);

static int __init my_init (void)
{
    printk (KERN_INFO "Hello world from modfun \n");
    printk (KERN_INFO " mod_param = %d\n", mod_param);
    return 0;
}

static void __exit my_exit (void)
{
    printk (KERN_INFO "Goodbye world from modfun \n");
}
```

```
module_init (my_init);
module_exit (my_exit);

MODULE_AUTHOR ("Jerry Cooperstein");
MODULE_DESCRIPTION ("CLDD 1.0: lab1_module.c");
MODULE_LICENSE ("GPL v2");
```

Chapter 4

Character Devices

4.1 Lab 1: Improving the Basic Character Driver

- Starting from **sample_driver.c**, extend it to:
  - Keep track of the number of times it has been opened since loading, and print out the counter every time the device is opened.
  - Print the major and minor numbers when the device is opened.

- To exercise your driver, write a program to read (and/or write) from the node, using the standard **Unix** I/O functions (open(), read(), write(), close()).

  After loading the module with **insmod** use this program to access the node.

- Track usage of the module by using **lsmod** (which is equivalent to typing cat /proc/modules.)

```
lab1_char.c
```

```
/* Copyright 2009, J Cooperstein coop@coopj.com (GPLv2) */

#include <linux/module.h>
```

```
#include <linux/fs.h>
#include <linux/uaccess.h>
#include <linux/init.h>
#include <linux/slab.h>
#include <linux/cdev.h>

#define MYDEV_NAME "mycdrv"
#define KBUF_SIZE (size_t)(10*PAGE_SIZE)

static char *kbuf;
static dev_t first;
static unsigned int count = 1;
static int my_major = 700, my_minor = 0;
static struct cdev *my_cdev;

static int mycdrv_open (struct inode *inode, struct file *file)
{
    static int counter = 0;
    printk (KERN_INFO " attempting to open device: %s:\n", MYDEV_NAME);
    printk (KERN_INFO " MAJOR number = %d, MINOR number = %d\n",
            imajor (inode), iminor (inode));
    counter++;

    printk (KERN_INFO " successfully open  device: %s:\n\n", MYDEV_NAME);
    printk (KERN_INFO "I have been opened  %d times since being loaded\n",
            counter);
    printk (KERN_INFO "ref=%d\n", module_refcount (THIS_MODULE));

    return 0;
}

static int mycdrv_release (struct inode *inode, struct file *file)
{
    printk (KERN_INFO " CLOSING device: %s:\n\n", MYDEV_NAME);
    return 0;
}

static ssize_t
mycdrv_read (struct file *file, char __user * buf, size_t lbuf, loff_t * ppos)
{
    int nbytes = lbuf - copy_to_user (buf, kbuf + *ppos, lbuf);
    *ppos += nbytes;
    printk (KERN_INFO "\n READING function, nbytes=%d, pos=%d\n", nbytes,
            (int)*ppos);
    return nbytes;
}

static ssize_t
mycdrv_write (struct file *file, const char __user * buf, size_t lbuf,
              loff_t * ppos)
{
    int nbytes = lbuf - copy_from_user (kbuf + *ppos, buf, lbuf);
    *ppos += nbytes;
    printk (KERN_INFO "\n WRITING function, nbytes=%d, pos=%d\n", nbytes,
            (int)*ppos);
```

```
        return nbytes;
}

static const struct file_operations mycdrv_fops = {
    .owner = THIS_MODULE,
    .read = mycdrv_read,
    .write = mycdrv_write,
    .open = mycdrv_open,
    .release = mycdrv_release,
};

static int __init my_init (void)
{
    first = MKDEV (my_major, my_minor);
    if (register_chrdev_region (first, count, MYDEV_NAME) < 0) {
        printk (KERN_ERR "failed to register character device region\n");
        return -1;
    }
    if (!(my_cdev = cdev_alloc ())) {
        printk (KERN_ERR "cdev_alloc() failed\n");
        unregister_chrdev_region (first, count);
        return -1;
    }
    cdev_init (my_cdev, &mycdrv_fops);
    kbuf = kmalloc (KBUF_SIZE, GFP_KERNEL);
    if (cdev_add (my_cdev, first, count) < 0) {
        printk (KERN_ERR "cdev_add() failed\n");
        cdev_del (my_cdev);
        unregister_chrdev_region (first, count);
        kfree (kbuf);
        return -1;
    }
    printk (KERN_INFO "\nSucceeded in registering character device %s\n",
            MYDEV_NAME);
    return 0;
}

static void __exit my_exit (void)
{
    if (my_cdev)
        cdev_del (my_cdev);
    unregister_chrdev_region (first, count);
    if (kbuf)
        kfree (kbuf);
    printk (KERN_INFO "\ndevice unregistered\n");
}

module_init (my_init);
module_exit (my_exit);

MODULE_AUTHOR ("Jerry Cooperstein");
MODULE_DESCRIPTION ("CLDD 1.0: lab1_char.c");
MODULE_LICENSE ("GPL v2");
```

lab1_char_test.c

```c
/* Copyright 2009, J Cooperstein coop@coopj.com (GPLv2) */

#include <stdio.h>
#include <unistd.h>
#include <fcntl.h>
#include <string.h>
#include <stdlib.h>

int main (int argc, char **argv)
{
    int length, fd1, fd2, rc;
    char *nodename = "/dev/mycdrv";
    char message[] = " *** TESTING CHAR/DRIVER ***\n";

    length = sizeof (message);

    if (argc > 1)
        nodename = argv[1];

    fd1 = open (nodename, O_RDWR);
    printf (" opened file descriptor first time  = %d\n", fd1);
    fd2 = open (nodename, O_RDWR);
    printf (" opened file descriptor second time = %d\n", fd2);

    rc = write (fd1, message, length);
    printf ("return code from write = %d on %d, message=%s\n", rc, fd1,
            message);

    memset (message, 0, length);

    rc = read (fd2, message, length);
    printf ("return code from read  = %d on %d, message=%s\n", rc, fd2,
            message);

    close (fd1);
    exit (0);
}
```

4.2   Lab 2: Private Data for Each Open

- Modify the previous driver so that each opening of the device allocates its own data area, which is freed upon release. Thus data will not be persistent across multiple opens.

lab2_priv.c

```c
/* Copyright 2009, J Cooperstein coop@coopj.com (GPLv2) */

#include <linux/module.h>
#include <linux/fs.h>
#include <linux/uaccess.h>
#include <linux/init.h>
#include <linux/slab.h>
```

```
#include <linux/cdev.h>

#define MYDEV_NAME "mycdrv"
#define KBUF_SIZE (size_t)(10*PAGE_SIZE)

static dev_t first;
static unsigned int count = 1;
static int my_major = 700, my_minor = 0;
static struct cdev *my_cdev;

static int mycdrv_open (struct inode *inode, struct file *file)
{
    static int counter = 0;
    char *kbuf = kmalloc (KBUF_SIZE, GFP_KERNEL);
    file->private_data = kbuf;
    printk (KERN_INFO " attempting to open device: %s:\n", MYDEV_NAME);
    printk (KERN_INFO " MAJOR number = %d, MINOR number = %d\n",
            imajor (inode), iminor (inode));
    counter++;
    printk (KERN_INFO " successfully open  device: %s:\n\n", MYDEV_NAME);
    printk (KERN_INFO "I have been opened  %d times since being loaded\n",
            counter);
    printk (KERN_INFO "ref=%d\n", module_refcount (THIS_MODULE));

    return 0;
}

static int mycdrv_release (struct inode *inode, struct file *file)
{
    char *kbuf = file->private_data;
    printk (KERN_INFO " CLOSING device: %s:\n\n", MYDEV_NAME);
    if (kbuf)
        kfree (kbuf);
    return 0;
}

static ssize_t
mycdrv_read (struct file *file, char __user * buf, size_t lbuf, loff_t * ppos)
{
    char *kbuf = file->private_data;
    int nbytes = lbuf - copy_to_user (buf, kbuf + *ppos, lbuf);
    *ppos += nbytes;
    printk (KERN_INFO "\n READING function, nbytes=%d, pos=%d\n", nbytes,
            (int)*ppos);
    return nbytes;
}

static ssize_t
mycdrv_write (struct file *file, const char __user * buf, size_t lbuf,
              loff_t * ppos)
{
    char *kbuf = file->private_data;
    int nbytes = lbuf - copy_from_user (kbuf + *ppos, buf, lbuf);
    *ppos += nbytes;
    printk (KERN_INFO "\n WRITING function, nbytes=%d, pos=%d\n", nbytes,
```

```
            (int)*ppos);
    return nbytes;
}

static const struct file_operations mycdrv_fops = {
    .owner = THIS_MODULE,
    .read = mycdrv_read,
    .write = mycdrv_write,
    .open = mycdrv_open,
    .release = mycdrv_release,
};

static int __init my_init (void)
{
    first = MKDEV (my_major, my_minor);
    if (register_chrdev_region (first, count, MYDEV_NAME) < 0) {
        printk (KERN_ERR "failed to register character device region\n");
        return -1;
    }
    if (!(my_cdev = cdev_alloc ())) {
        printk (KERN_ERR "cdev_alloc() failed\n");
        unregister_chrdev_region (first, count);
        return -1;
    }
    cdev_init (my_cdev, &mycdrv_fops);
    if (cdev_add (my_cdev, first, count) < 0) {
        printk (KERN_ERR "cdev_add() failed\n");
        cdev_del (my_cdev);
        unregister_chrdev_region (first, count);
        return -1;
    }
    printk (KERN_INFO "\nSucceeded in registering character device %s\n",
            MYDEV_NAME);
    return 0;
}

static void __exit my_exit (void)
{
    if (my_cdev)
        cdev_del (my_cdev);
    unregister_chrdev_region (first, count);
    printk (KERN_INFO "\ndevice unregistered\n");
}

module_init (my_init);
module_exit (my_exit);

MODULE_AUTHOR ("Jerry Cooperstein");
MODULE_DESCRIPTION ("CLDD 1.0: lab2_priv.c");
MODULE_LICENSE ("GPL v2");
```

4.3 Lab 3: Seeking and the End of the Device.

- Adapt one of the previous drivers to have the read and write entries watch out for going off the end of the device

- Implement a lseek() entry point. See the **man** page for lseek() to see how return values and error codes should be specified.

- For an extra exercise, unset the FMODE_LSEEK bit to make any attempt to seek result in an error.

lab3_seek.c

```
/* Copyright 2009, J Cooperstein coop@coopj.com (GPLv2) */

#include <linux/module.h>
#include <linux/fs.h>
#include <linux/uaccess.h>
#include <linux/init.h>
#include <linux/slab.h>
#include <linux/cdev.h>

#define MYDEV_NAME "mycdrv"
#define KBUF_SIZE (size_t)(10*PAGE_SIZE)

static char *kbuf;
static dev_t first;
static unsigned int count = 1;
static int my_major = 700, my_minor = 0;
static struct cdev *my_cdev;

static int mycdrv_open (struct inode *inode, struct file *file)
{
    static int counter = 0;
    printk (KERN_INFO " attempting to open device: %s:\n", MYDEV_NAME);
    printk (KERN_INFO " MAJOR number = %d, MINOR number = %d\n",
            imajor (inode), iminor (inode));
    counter++;

    printk (KERN_INFO " successfully open  device: %s:\n\n", MYDEV_NAME);
    printk (KERN_INFO "I have been opened  %d times since being loaded\n",
            counter);
    printk (KERN_INFO "ref=%d\n", module_refcount (THIS_MODULE));

    /* turn this on to inhibit seeking */
    /* file->f_mode = file->f_mode & ~FMODE_LSEEK; */

    return 0;
}

static int mycdrv_release (struct inode *inode, struct file *file)
{
    printk (KERN_INFO " CLOSING device: %s:\n\n", MYDEV_NAME);
    return 0;
```

```
}

static ssize_t
mycdrv_read (struct file *file, char __user * buf, size_t lbuf, loff_t * ppos)
{
    int nbytes, maxbytes, bytes_to_do;
    maxbytes = KBUF_SIZE - *ppos;
    bytes_to_do = maxbytes > lbuf ? lbuf : maxbytes;
    if (bytes_to_do == 0)
        printk (KERN_INFO "Reached end of the device on a read");
    nbytes = bytes_to_do - copy_to_user (buf, kbuf + *ppos, bytes_to_do);
    *ppos += nbytes;
    printk (KERN_INFO "\n Leaving the   READ function, nbytes=%d, pos=%d\n",
            nbytes, (int)*ppos);
    return nbytes;
}

static ssize_t
mycdrv_write (struct file *file, const char __user * buf, size_t lbuf,
              loff_t * ppos)
{
    int nbytes, maxbytes, bytes_to_do;
    maxbytes = KBUF_SIZE - *ppos;
    bytes_to_do = maxbytes > lbuf ? lbuf : maxbytes;
    if (bytes_to_do == 0)
        printk (KERN_INFO "Reached end of the device on a write");
    nbytes = bytes_to_do - copy_from_user (kbuf + *ppos, buf, bytes_to_do);
    *ppos += nbytes;
    printk (KERN_INFO "\n Leaving the   WRITE function, nbytes=%d, pos=%d\n",
            nbytes, (int)*ppos);
    return nbytes;
}

static loff_t mycdrv_lseek (struct file *file, loff_t offset, int orig)
{
    loff_t testpos;
    switch (orig) {
    case SEEK_SET:
        testpos = offset;
        break;
    case SEEK_CUR:
        testpos = file->f_pos + offset;
        break;
    case SEEK_END:
        testpos = KBUF_SIZE + offset;
        break;
    default:
        return -EINVAL;
    }
    testpos = testpos < KBUF_SIZE ? testpos : KBUF_SIZE;
    testpos = testpos >= 0 ? testpos : 0;
    file->f_pos = testpos;
    printk (KERN_INFO "Seeking to pos=%ld\n", (long)testpos);
    return testpos;
}
```

```
static const struct file_operations mycdrv_fops = {
    .owner = THIS_MODULE,
    .read = mycdrv_read,
    .write = mycdrv_write,
    .open = mycdrv_open,
    .release = mycdrv_release,
    .llseek = mycdrv_lseek
};

static int __init my_init (void)
{
    first = MKDEV (my_major, my_minor);
    if (register_chrdev_region (first, count, MYDEV_NAME) < 0) {
        printk (KERN_ERR "failed to register character device region\n");
        return -1;
    }
    if (!(my_cdev = cdev_alloc ())) {
        printk (KERN_ERR "cdev_alloc() failed\n");
        unregister_chrdev_region (first, count);
        return -1;
    }
    cdev_init (my_cdev, &mycdrv_fops);
    kbuf = kmalloc (KBUF_SIZE, GFP_KERNEL);

    if (cdev_add (my_cdev, first, count) < 0) {
        printk (KERN_ERR "cdev_add() failed\n");
        cdev_del (my_cdev);
        unregister_chrdev_region (first, count);
        kfree (kbuf);
        return -1;
    }

    printk (KERN_INFO "\nSucceeded in registering character device %s\n",
            MYDEV_NAME);
    return 0;
}

static void __exit my_exit (void)
{
    if (my_cdev)
        cdev_del (my_cdev);
    unregister_chrdev_region (first, count);
    if (kbuf)
        kfree (kbuf);
    printk (KERN_INFO "\ndevice unregistered\n");
}

module_init (my_init);
module_exit (my_exit);

MODULE_AUTHOR ("Jerry Cooperstein");
MODULE_DESCRIPTION ("CLDD 1.0: lab3_seek.c");
MODULE_LICENSE ("GPL v2");
```

lab3_seek_test.c

```c
/* Copyright 2009, J Cooperstein coop@coopj.com (GPLv2) */

#include <stdio.h>
#include <unistd.h>
#include <stdlib.h>
#include <fcntl.h>
#include <string.h>

int main (int argc, char *argv[])
{
    int length = 20, position = 0, fd, rc;
    char *message, *nodename = "/dev/mycdrv";

    if (argc > 1)
        nodename = argv[1];

    if (argc > 2)
        position = atoi (argv[2]);

    if (argc > 3)
        length = atoi (argv[3]);

    /* set up the message */
    message = malloc (length);
    memset (message, 'x', length);
    message[length - 1] = '\0'; /* make sure it is null terminated */

    /* open the device node */

    fd = open (nodename, O_RDWR);
    printf (" I opened the device node, file descriptor = %d\n", fd);

    /* seek to position */

    rc = lseek (fd, position, SEEK_SET);
    printf ("return code from lseek = %d\n", rc);

    /* write to the device node twice */

    rc = write (fd, message, length);
    printf ("return code from write = %d\n", rc);
    rc = write (fd, message, length);
    printf ("return code from write = %d\n", rc);

    /* reset the message to null */

    memset (message, 0, length);

    /* seek to position */

    rc = lseek (fd, position, SEEK_SET);
    printf ("return code from lseek = %d\n", rc);
```

```
    /* read from the device node */

    rc = read (fd, message, length);
    printf ("return code from read = %d\n", rc);
    printf ( "the message was: %s\n", message);

    close (fd);
    exit (0);

}
```

4.4   Lab 4: Dynamical Node Creation (I)

- Adapt one of the previous drivers to allocate the device major number dynamically.

- Write loading and unloading scripts that ascertain the major number assigned and make and remove the node as required.

lab4_dynamic.c

```
 /* Copyright 2009, J Cooperstein coop@coopj.com (GPLv2) */

#include <linux/module.h>
#include <linux/fs.h>
#include <linux/uaccess.h>
#include <linux/init.h>
#include <linux/slab.h>
#include <linux/cdev.h>

#define MYDEV_NAME "mycdrv"
#define KBUF_SIZE (size_t)(10*PAGE_SIZE)

static char *kbuf;
static dev_t first;
static unsigned int count = 1;
static struct cdev *my_cdev;

static int mycdrv_open (struct inode *inode, struct file *file)
{
    static int counter = 0;
    printk (KERN_INFO " attempting to open device: %s:\n", MYDEV_NAME);
    printk (KERN_INFO " MAJOR number = %d, MINOR number = %d\n",
            imajor (inode), iminor (inode));
    counter++;

    printk (KERN_INFO " successfully open  device: %s:\n\n", MYDEV_NAME);
    printk (KERN_INFO "I have been opened  %d times since being loaded\n",
            counter);
    printk (KERN_INFO "ref=%d\n", module_refcount (THIS_MODULE));

    return 0;
}
```

```
static int mycdrv_release (struct inode *inode, struct file *file)
{
    printk (KERN_INFO " CLOSING device: %s:\n\n", MYDEV_NAME);
    return 0;
}

static ssize_t
mycdrv_read (struct file *file, char __user * buf, size_t lbuf, loff_t * ppos)
{
    int nbytes, maxbytes, bytes_to_do;
    maxbytes = KBUF_SIZE - *ppos;
    bytes_to_do = maxbytes > lbuf ? lbuf : maxbytes;
    if (bytes_to_do == 0)
        printk (KERN_INFO "Reached end of the device on a read");
    nbytes = bytes_to_do - copy_to_user (buf, kbuf + *ppos, bytes_to_do);
    *ppos += nbytes;
    printk (KERN_INFO "\n Leaving the   READ function, nbytes=%d, pos=%d\n",
            nbytes, (int)*ppos);
    return nbytes;
}

static ssize_t
mycdrv_write (struct file *file, const char __user * buf, size_t lbuf,
              loff_t * ppos)
{
    int nbytes, maxbytes, bytes_to_do;
    maxbytes = KBUF_SIZE - *ppos;
    bytes_to_do = maxbytes > lbuf ? lbuf : maxbytes;
    if (bytes_to_do == 0)
        printk (KERN_INFO "Reached end of the device on a write");
    nbytes = bytes_to_do - copy_from_user (kbuf + *ppos, buf, bytes_to_do);
    *ppos += nbytes;
    printk (KERN_INFO "\n Leaving the   WRITE function, nbytes=%d, pos=%d\n",
            nbytes, (int)*ppos);
    return nbytes;
}

static loff_t mycdrv_lseek (struct file *file, loff_t offset, int orig)
{
    loff_t testpos;
    switch (orig) {
    case 0:                     /* SEEK_SET */
        testpos = offset;
        break;
    case 1:                     /* SEEK_CUR */
        testpos = file->f_pos + offset;
        break;
    case 2:                     /* SEEK_END */
        testpos = KBUF_SIZE + offset;
        break;
    default:
        return -EINVAL;
    }
    testpos = testpos < KBUF_SIZE ? testpos : KBUF_SIZE;
    testpos = testpos >= 0 ? testpos : 0;
```

```
    file->f_pos = testpos;
    printk (KERN_INFO "Seeking to pos=%ld\n", (long)testpos);
    return testpos;
}

static const struct file_operations mycdrv_fops = {
    .owner = THIS_MODULE,
    .read = mycdrv_read,
    .write = mycdrv_write,
    .open = mycdrv_open,
    .release = mycdrv_release,
    .llseek = mycdrv_lseek
};

static int __init my_init (void)
{
    if (alloc_chrdev_region (&first, 0, count, MYDEV_NAME) < 0) {
        printk (KERN_ERR "failed to allocate character device region\n");
        return -1;
    }
    if (!(my_cdev = cdev_alloc ())) {
        printk (KERN_ERR "cdev_alloc() failed\n");
        unregister_chrdev_region (first, count);
        return -1;
    }
    cdev_init (my_cdev, &mycdrv_fops);
    kbuf = kmalloc (KBUF_SIZE, GFP_KERNEL);
    if (cdev_add (my_cdev, first, count) < 0) {
        printk (KERN_ERR "cdev_add() failed\n");
        cdev_del (my_cdev);
        unregister_chrdev_region (first, count);
        kfree (kbuf);
        return -1;
    }

    printk (KERN_INFO "\nSucceeded in registering character device %s\n",
            MYDEV_NAME);
    printk (KERN_INFO "Major number = %d, Minor number = %d\n", MAJOR (first),
            MINOR (first));
    return 0;
}

static void __exit my_exit (void)
{
    if (my_cdev)
        cdev_del (my_cdev);
    unregister_chrdev_region (first, count);
    if (kbuf)
        kfree (kbuf);
    printk (KERN_INFO "\ndevice unregistered\n");
}

module_init (my_init);
module_exit (my_exit);
```

```
MODULE_AUTHOR ("Jerry Cooperstein");
MODULE_DESCRIPTION ("CLDD 1.0: lab4_dynamic.c");
MODULE_LICENSE ("GPL v2");
```

lab4_loadit.sh

```
#!/bin/sh

# 1/2005 J. Cooperstein (coop@coopj.com) License:GPLv2

module=lab3_dynamic.ko
node=/dev/mycdrv
minor=0

[ "$1" != "" ] && module="$1"
[ "$2" != "" ] && node="$2"

echo loading $module
insmod $module

major=$(awk "\$2==\"mycdrv\" {print \$1}" /proc/devices)
echo major number is: $major

echo creating the device node at $node with minor number=0

mknod $node c $major $minor
```

lab4_unloadit.sh

```
#!/bin/sh

# 1/2005 J. Cooperstein (coop@coopj.com) License:GPLv2

module=lab3_dynamic.ko
node=/dev/mycdrv
minor=0

[ "$1" != "" ] && module="$1"
[ "$2" != "" ] && node="$2"


major=$(awk "\$2==\"mycdrv\" {print \$1}" /proc/devices)
echo major number is: $major

echo unloading $module
rmmod $module

echo removing the device node at $node with minor number=0

rm $node
```

4.5 Lab 5: Dynamical Node Creation (II)

- Adapt the previous dynamic registration driver to use **udev** to create the device node on the fly.

lab5_dynamic_udev.c

```
/* Copyright 2009, J Cooperstein coop@coopj.com (GPLv2) */

#include <linux/module.h>
#include <linux/fs.h>
#include <linux/uaccess.h>
#include <linux/init.h>
#include <linux/slab.h>
#include <linux/cdev.h>
#include <linux/device.h>

#define MYDEV_NAME "mycdrv"
#define KBUF_SIZE (size_t)(10*PAGE_SIZE)

static char *kbuf;
static dev_t first;
static unsigned int count = 1;
static struct cdev *my_cdev;

static struct class *foo_class;

static int mycdrv_open (struct inode *inode, struct file *file)
{
    static int counter = 0;
    printk (KERN_INFO " attempting to open device: %s:\n", MYDEV_NAME);
    printk (KERN_INFO " MAJOR number = %d, MINOR number = %d\n",
            imajor (inode), iminor (inode));
    counter++;

    printk (KERN_INFO " successfully open  device: %s:\n\n", MYDEV_NAME);
    printk (KERN_INFO "I have been opened  %d times since being loaded\n",
            counter);
    printk (KERN_INFO "ref=%d\n", module_refcount (THIS_MODULE));

    return 0;
}

static int mycdrv_release (struct inode *inode, struct file *file)
{
    printk (KERN_INFO " CLOSING device: %s:\n\n", MYDEV_NAME);
    return 0;
}

static ssize_t
mycdrv_read (struct file *file, char __user * buf, size_t lbuf, loff_t * ppos)
{
    int nbytes, maxbytes, bytes_to_do;
    maxbytes = KBUF_SIZE - *ppos;
```

```
    bytes_to_do = maxbytes > lbuf ? lbuf : maxbytes;
    if (bytes_to_do == 0)
        printk (KERN_INFO "Reached end of the device on a read");
    nbytes = bytes_to_do - copy_to_user (buf, kbuf + *ppos, bytes_to_do);
    *ppos += nbytes;
    printk (KERN_INFO "\n Leaving the   READ function, nbytes=%d, pos=%d\n",
            nbytes, (int)*ppos);
    return nbytes;
}

static ssize_t
mycdrv_write (struct file *file, const char __user * buf, size_t lbuf,
              loff_t * ppos)
{
    int nbytes, maxbytes, bytes_to_do;
    maxbytes = KBUF_SIZE - *ppos;
    bytes_to_do = maxbytes > lbuf ? lbuf : maxbytes;
    if (bytes_to_do == 0)
        printk (KERN_INFO "Reached end of the device on a write");
    nbytes = bytes_to_do - copy_from_user (kbuf + *ppos, buf, bytes_to_do);
    *ppos += nbytes;
    printk (KERN_INFO "\n Leaving the   WRITE function, nbytes=%d, pos=%d\n",
            nbytes, (int)*ppos);
    return nbytes;
}

static loff_t mycdrv_lseek (struct file *file, loff_t offset, int orig)
{
    loff_t testpos;
    switch (orig) {
    case SEEK_SET:
        testpos = offset;
        break;
    case SEEK_CUR:
        testpos = file->f_pos + offset;
        break;
    case SEEK_END:
        testpos = KBUF_SIZE + offset;
        break;
    default:
        return -EINVAL;
    }
    testpos = testpos < KBUF_SIZE ? testpos : KBUF_SIZE;
    testpos = testpos >= 0 ? testpos : 0;
    file->f_pos = testpos;
    printk (KERN_INFO "Seeking to pos=%ld\n", (long)testpos);
    return testpos;
}

static const struct file_operations mycdrv_fops = {
    .owner = THIS_MODULE,
    .read = mycdrv_read,
    .write = mycdrv_write,
    .open = mycdrv_open,
    .release = mycdrv_release,
```

```
        .llseek = mycdrv_lseek
};

static int __init my_init (void)
{
    if (alloc_chrdev_region (&first, 0, count, MYDEV_NAME) < 0) {
        printk (KERN_ERR "failed to allocate character device region\n");
        return -1;
    }
    if (!(my_cdev = cdev_alloc ())) {
        printk (KERN_ERR "cdev_alloc() failed\n");
        unregister_chrdev_region (first, count);
        return -1;
    }
    cdev_init (my_cdev, &mycdrv_fops);
    kbuf = kmalloc (KBUF_SIZE, GFP_KERNEL);
    if (cdev_add (my_cdev, first, count) < 0) {
        printk (KERN_ERR "cdev_add() failed\n");
        cdev_del (my_cdev);
        unregister_chrdev_region (first, count);
        kfree (kbuf);
        return -1;
    }

    foo_class = class_create (THIS_MODULE, "my_class");
    device_create (foo_class, NULL, first, "%s", "mycdrv");

    printk (KERN_INFO "\nSucceeded in registering character device %s\n",
            MYDEV_NAME);
    printk (KERN_INFO "Major number = %d, Minor number = %d\n", MAJOR (first),
            MINOR (first));
    return 0;
}

static void __exit my_exit (void)
{
    device_destroy (foo_class, first);
    class_destroy (foo_class);

    if (my_cdev)
        cdev_del (my_cdev);
    unregister_chrdev_region (first, count);
    if (kbuf)
        kfree (kbuf);
    printk (KERN_INFO "\ndevice unregistered\n");
}

module_init (my_init);
module_exit (my_exit);

MODULE_AUTHOR ("Jerry Cooperstein");
MODULE_DESCRIPTION ("CLDD 1.0: lab5_dynamic_udev.c");
MODULE_LICENSE ("GPL v2");
```

Chapter 5

Kernel Configuration and Compilation

5.1 Lab 1: Building a Kernel

- In this exercise you will build a **Linux** kernel, tailored to specific needs of hardware/software. You won't actually modify any of the source for the **Linux** kernel; however, you will select features and decide which modules are built.

- Use whatever exact file names and version numbers are appropriate for the sources you have, rather than what is specified below.

5.2 Step 1: Obtain and install the source

- Depending on your **Linux** distribution you may already have the source installed for your currently running kernel. You should be able to do this by looking at the **/lib/modules/kernel-version/** directory and seeing if it has active links to **build** or **source** directories. If not you'll have to obtain the kernel source in the method detailed by your distribution.

- If you are using a vanilla source, then download it from **http://www.kernel.org** and then unpack it with:

```
$ tar jxvf linux-2.6.31.tar.bz2
```

(putting in the proper file and kernel version of course.)

5.3   Step 2: Make sure other ingredients are up to date.

- The file **/usr/src/linux/Documentation/Changes** highlights what versions of various system utilities and libraries are needed to work with the current source.

5.4   Step 3: Configuring the Kernel

- You can use any of the following methods:

   - **make config**
     A purely text-based configuration routine.
   - **make menuconfig**
     An **ncurses** semi-graphical configuration routine.
   - **make xconfig**
     An **X**-based fully-graphical configuration routine, based on the **qt** graphical libraries.
   - **make gconfig**
     Also an **X**-based fully-graphical configuration routine, based on the **GTK** graphical libraries, which has a somewhat different look..

   You'll probably want to use **make xconfig** or **make gconfig**, as these have the nicest interfaces. At any rate, the content and abilities of all the methods are identical. They all produce a file named **.config**, which contains your choices. (It is generally advised not to edit this file directly unless you really know what you are doing!)

- If you have an old configuration, you can speed up the process by doing:

```
$ make oldconfig
```

   which takes your old configuration and asks you only about new choices. If you want to get the default choices as they come out of **kernel.org**, you can obtain the initial configuration with

```
$ make defconfig
```

   Also note that if you are going to a new version through applying a patch, you can use the **patch-kernel** script by going to the source directory and doing:

```
$ scripts/patch-kernel . < patch directory >
```

- The **ketchup** utility, obtainable from **http://www.selenic.com/ketchup**, is very useful for going from one kernel version to another.

- **ketchup** will even download patches and/or full sources as they are needed, and can check source integrity.

- For instance upgrading from 2.6.24 to 2.6.31 would involve going to the source directory and just typing:

```
$ ketchup -G 2.6.31
```

- Take your time configuring the kernel. Read the help items to learn more about the possibilities available. Several choices you should make (for this class) are:

  - Under **Processor type and features:**
    Pick the proper CPU (Choosing too advanced a processor make cause a boot failure.)
  - Under **Loadable module support:**
    Turn **on** "Enable loadable module support."
    Turn **on** "Module unloading."
  - Under **Block Devices:**
    Turn **on** "Loopback device support."
    Turn **on** "RAM disk support"
    Turn **on** "initial RAM disk (initrd) support"
  - Under **Multi-device Support (RAID and LVM):**
    Turn **on** "Device Mapper Support"
  - Under **Instrumentation Support**:
    Turn **on** "Profiling Support" and "Oprofile"
    Turn **on** "Kprobes"
  - Under **Kernel Hacking:**
    Turn **on** "Magic SysRq key".
    Turn **on** "Debug Filesystem".

- Make sure you turn on drivers for your actual hardware; i.e., support for the proper network card and if you have a **SCSI** system the proper disk controller, and your particular sound card.

- You can short circuit this whole procedure by obtaining a `.config` file that should work for most common hardware from **http:/www.coopj.com/LDD** with a name like `config-2.6.31_x86_64`. In this template we turn on the most common network cards etc and pick the options that will provide kernels that can handle the exercises we provide.

- For detailed guidance on configuring kernels an invaluable resource is ***Linux Kernel in a Nutshell***, by Greg Kroah-Hartman, pub. O'Reilly, 2006, the full text of which is available at **http://www.kroah.com/lkn/**.

- In order to compile modules against your kernel source you need more than just a proper `.config` file. Short of running a compilation first, doing `make prepare` or `make oldconfig` will take care of doing the setup for external module compilation, such as making symbolic links to the right architecture.

5.5   Step 4: Configure your boot loader (grub or lilo)

- Before you can reboot, you'll need to reconfigure your boot loader to support the new kernel choice. Use either **grub** or **lilo**; you can't use both as they wipe each other out.

- If you are using **grub**, you'll need to add a section to the configuration file (either **/boot/grub /grub.conf** or **/boot/grub/menu.lst** depending on your distribution) like:

```
title Linux (2.6.31)
        root (hd0,0)
        kernel /vmlinuz-2.6.31 ro root=LABEL=/
        initrd /initrd-2.6.31.img
```

which says the kernel itself is the first partition on the first hard disk (probably mounted as **/boot**) and the root filesystem will be found on partition with the label **/**. (Adjust partitions and labels as needed.)

5.6   Step 5: Compiling and installing the new kernel.

- This involves:

  - Making the **compressed** kernel (**bzImage**) and copying it over to the **/boot** directory with a good name. (On non-**x86** architectures, the kernel may be uncompressed.)
  - Copying over the **System.map** file which is used to resolve kernel addresses mostly for logging and debugging purposes.
  - Making modules and installing them under **/lib/modules/kernel-version/**.
  - Saving the kernel configuration for future reference.
  - Constructing a new **initrd** or **initramfs** image and copying it to the **/boot** directory.
  - Updating your **grub** or **lilo** configuration.

- There is a script (**/sbin/installkernel**) on most distributions which can do these steps for you, and there is also an **install** target for **make**, but we prefer to use our own script over the canned one as it requires fewer arguments and is less rigid. This script is available in the solutions under the name **DO_KERNEL.sh**.

- Thus if you want to use the canned configuration, you can do everything in this manner:

```
$ tar jxvf <pathto>linux-2.6.31.tar.bz2
$ cp <pathto>config-2.6.31_x86_64 linux-2.6.31/.config
$ cd linux-2.6.31
$ <pathto>DO_KERNEL.sh
```

Chapter 6

Kernel Features

6.1   Lab 1: Using strace.

- **strace** is used to trace system calls and signals. In the simplest case you would do:

  ```
  strace [options] command [arguments]
  ```

- Each system call, its arguments and return value are printed. According to the man page:

- *"Arguments are printed in symbolic form with a passion."*

  and indeed they are. There are a lot of options; read the man page!

- As an example, try

  ```
  strace ls -lRF / 2>&1 | less
  ```

  You need the complicated redirection because **strace** puts its output on `stderr` unless you use the `-o` option to redirect it to a file.

- While this is running (paused under **less**), you can examine more details about the **ls** process, by examining the **/proc** filesystem. Do

```
ps aux | grep ls
```

to find out the process ID associated with the process. Then you can look at the pseudo-files

```
/proc/<pid>/fd/*
```

to see how the file descriptors are mapped to the underlying files (or pipes), etc.

Chapter 7

Kernel Style and General Considerations

7.1   Lab 1: Linked Lists

- Write a module that sets up a doubly-linked circular list of data structures. The data structure can be as simple as an integer variable.

- Test inserting and deleting elements in the list.

- Walk through the list (using `list_entry()`) and print out values to make sure the insertion and deletion processes are working.

`lab1_list.c`

```
/* Copyright 2009, J Cooperstein coop@coopj.com (GPLv2) */

#include <linux/module.h>
#include <asm/atomic.h>
#include <linux/errno.h>
```

```
#include <linux/slab.h>
#include <linux/init.h>

/* we're going to do a camel race! */
static LIST_HEAD (camel_list);

struct camel_entry
{
    struct list_head clist;     /* link in camel list */
    int gate;                   /* assigned gate at Camel Derby */
    char name[20];              /* camel's name */
};

static int __init my_init (void)
{
    struct camel_entry *ce;
    int k;

    for (k = 0; k < 5; k++) {

        if (!(ce = kmalloc (sizeof (struct camel_entry), GFP_KERNEL))) {
            printk (KERN_INFO
                    " Camels: failed to allocate memory for camel %d \n", k);
            return -ENOMEM;
        }

        ce->gate = 11 + k;      /* gate number */
        sprintf (ce->name, "Camel_%d", k + 1);
        printk (KERN_INFO " Camels: adding %s at gate %d to camel_list \n",
                ce->name, ce->gate);
        list_add (&ce->clist, &camel_list);
    }
    return 0;
}

static void __exit my_exit (void)
{
    struct list_head *list;     /* pointer to list head object */
    struct list_head *tmp;      /* temporary list head for safe deletion */

    if (list_empty (&camel_list)) {
        printk (KERN_INFO "Camels (exit): camel list is empty! \n");
        return;
    }
    printk (KERN_INFO "Camels: (exit): camel list is NOT empty! \n");

    list_for_each_safe (list, tmp, &camel_list) {
        struct camel_entry *ce = list_entry (list, struct camel_entry, clist);
        list_del (&ce->clist);
        printk (KERN_INFO "Camels (exit): %s at gate %d removed from list \n",
                ce->name, ce->gate);
        kfree (ce);
    }

    /* Now, did we remove the camel manure? */
```

```
    if (list_empty (&camel_list))
        printk (KERN_INFO "Camels (done): camel list is empty! \n");
    else
        printk (KERN_INFO "Camels: (done): camel list is NOT empty! \n");
}

module_init (my_init);
module_exit (my_exit);

MODULE_AUTHOR ("Dave Harris");
/* many modifications by Jerry Cooperstein */
MODULE_DESCRIPTION ("CLDD 1.0: lab1_list.c");
MODULE_LICENSE ("GPL v2");
```

7.2   Lab 2: Finding Tainted Modules

- All modules loaded on the system are linked in a list that can be accessed from any module:

  ```
  struct module {
  ....
  struct list_head modules;
  ....
  char name[MODULE_NAME_LEN];
  ....
  unsigned int taints;
  ....
  }
  ```

- Write a module that walks through this linked list and prints out the value of `taints` and any other values of interest. (The `module` structure is defined in **/usr/src/linux/include/linux /module.h**.)

- You can begin from `THIS_MODULE`.

lab2_taints.c

```
/* Copyright 2009, J Cooperstein coop@coopj.com (GPLv2) */

#include <linux/module.h>
#include <linux/init.h>

static int __init my_init (void)
{
    int j = 0;
    struct list_head *modules;
    struct module *m = THIS_MODULE;
    modules = &m->list;
    printk (KERN_INFO "\n");
    printk (KERN_INFO "%3d MOD:%20s, taints = %d\n", j++, m->name, m->taints);
    list_for_each_entry (m, modules, list) {
        printk (KERN_INFO "%3d MOD:%20s, taints = %d\n", j++, m->name,
                m->taints);
```

```
        if (j > 50)                    /* just here to avoid a runaway, don't need */
            break;
    }
    return 0;
}
static void __exit my_exit (void)
{
    printk (KERN_INFO "Bye: module unloaded from 0x%p\n", my_exit);
}


module_init (my_init);
module_exit (my_exit);

MODULE_AUTHOR ("Jerry Cooperstein");
MODULE_DESCRIPTION ("CLDD 1.0: lab2_taints.c");
MODULE_LICENSE ("GPL v2");
```

7.3   Lab 3: Finding Errors With Sparse

- We give you a minimal module that compiles cleanly, but has at least two errors that show up with the use of **sparse**.

- Install **sparse** according to the description given earlier and correct the errors.

lab3_sparse_errors.c

```
 /* Copyright 2009, J Cooperstein coop@coopj.com (GPLv2) */

#include <linux/module.h>
#include <linux/init.h>
#include <linux/uaccess.h>

static void my_fun (char *buf1, char *buf2, int count, struct task_struct *s)
{
    int rc;
    rc = copy_from_user (buf2, buf1, count);
}
static int __init my_init (void)
{
    int count = 32;
    char buf1[32], buf2[32];
    my_fun (buf1, buf2, count, 0);
    return 0;
}
static void __exit my_exit (void)
{
}

module_init (my_init);
module_exit (my_exit);
MODULE_LICENSE ("GPL v2");
MODULE_AUTHOR ("Jerry Cooperstein");
MODULE_DESCRIPTION ("CLDD 1.0: lab3_sparse_errors.c");
```

lab3_sparse_corrected.c

```c
/* Copyright 2009, J Cooperstein coop@coopj.com (GPLv2) */
#include <linux/module.h>
#include <linux/init.h>
#include <linux/uaccess.h>

static void my_fun (char *buf1, char *buf2, int count, struct task_struct *s)
{
    memcpy (buf2, buf1, count);
}
static int __init my_init (void)
{
    int count = 32;
    char buf1[32], buf2[32];
    my_fun (buf1, buf2, count, NULL);
    return 0;
}
static void __exit my_exit (void)
{
}

module_init (my_init);
module_exit (my_exit);
MODULE_LICENSE ("GPL v2");
MODULE_AUTHOR ("Jerry Cooperstein");
MODULE_DESCRIPTION ("CLDD 1.0: lab3_sparse_corrected.c");
```

Chapter 8

Interrupts and Exceptions

8.1　Lab 1: Shared Interrupts

- Write a module that shares its IRQ with your network card. You can generate some network interrupts either by browsing or pinging. (If you have trouble with the network driver, try using the mouse interrupt.)

- Check /proc/interrupts while it is loaded.

- Have the module keep track of the number of times the interrupt handler gets called.

lab1_interrupt.c

```
/* Copyright 2009, J Cooperstein coop@coopj.com (GPLv2) */

#include <linux/module.h>
#include <linux/init.h>
#include <linux/interrupt.h>

#define SHARED_IRQ 17
```

```
static int irq = SHARED_IRQ, my_dev_id, irq_counter = 0;
module_param (irq, int, S_IRUGO);

static irqreturn_t my_interrupt (int irq, void *dev_id)
{
    irq_counter++;
    printk (KERN_INFO "In the ISR: counter = %d\n", irq_counter);
    return IRQ_NONE;            /* we return IRQ_NONE because we are just observing */
}

static int __init my_init (void)
{
    if (request_irq
        (irq, my_interrupt, IRQF_SHARED, "my_interrupt", &my_dev_id))
        return -1;
    printk (KERN_INFO "Successfully loading ISR handler\n");
    return 0;
}

static void __exit my_exit (void)
{
    synchronize_irq (irq);
    free_irq (irq, &my_dev_id);
    printk (KERN_INFO "Successfully unloading,  irq_counter = %d\n",
            irq_counter);
}

module_init (my_init);
module_exit (my_exit);

MODULE_AUTHOR ("Jerry Cooperstein");
MODULE_DESCRIPTION ("CLDD 1.0: lab1_interrupt.c");
MODULE_LICENSE ("GPL v2");
```

8.2   Lab 2: Sharing All Interrupts

- Extend the previous solution to construct a character driver that shares every possible interrupt with already installed handlers.

- The highest interrupt number you have to consider will depend on your kernel and platform; look at **/proc/interrupts** to ascertain what is necessary.

- Take particular care when you call `free_irq()` as it is very easy to freeze your system if you are not careful.

- The character driver can be very simple; for instance if no `open()` and `release()` methods are specified, success is the default.

- A `read()` on the device should return a brief report on the total number of interrupts handled for each **IRQ**.

- To do this you'll also have to write a short application to retrieve and print out the data. (Don't forget to create the device node before you run the application.)

lab2_interrupt.c

```
 /* Copyright 2009, J Cooperstein coop@coopj.com (GPLv2) */
#include <linux/module.h>
#include <linux/fs.h>
#include <linux/uaccess.h>
#include <linux/init.h>
#include <linux/slab.h>
#include <linux/cdev.h>
#include <linux/interrupt.h>

#define MYDEV_NAME "mycdrv"
#define KBUF_SIZE (size_t)(PAGE_SIZE)
#define MAXIRQS 256
#define NCOPY (MAXIRQS * sizeof(int))

static char *kbuf;
static dev_t first;
static unsigned int count = 1;
static int my_major = 700, my_minor = 0;
static struct cdev *my_cdev;

static int *interrupts;

static irqreturn_t my_interrupt (int irq, void *dev_id)
{
    interrupts[irq]++;
    return IRQ_NONE;              /* we return IRQ_NONE because we are just observing */
}
static void freeup_irqs (void)
{
    int irq;
    for (irq = 0; irq < MAXIRQS; irq++) {
        if (interrupts[irq] >= 0) { /* if greater than 0, was able to share */
            synchronize_irq (irq);
            printk (KERN_INFO "Freeing IRQ= %4d, which had %10d events\n",
                    irq, interrupts[irq]);
            free_irq (irq, interrupts);
        }
    }
}
static ssize_t
mycdrv_read (struct file *file, char __user * buf, size_t lbuf, loff_t * ppos)
{
    int nbytes, maxbytes, bytes_to_do;
    maxbytes = KBUF_SIZE - *ppos;
    bytes_to_do = maxbytes > lbuf ? lbuf : maxbytes;
    if (bytes_to_do == 0)
        printk (KERN_INFO "Reached end of the device on a read");
    nbytes = bytes_to_do - copy_to_user (buf, kbuf + *ppos, bytes_to_do);
    *ppos += nbytes;
    printk (KERN_INFO "\n Leaving the  READ function, nbytes=%d, pos=%d\n",
            nbytes, (int)*ppos);
    return nbytes;
}
```

```
static const struct file_operations mycdrv_fops = {
    .owner = THIS_MODULE,
    .read = mycdrv_read,
};

static int __init my_init (void)
{
    int irq;

    first = MKDEV (my_major, my_minor);

    if (register_chrdev_region (first, count, MYDEV_NAME) < 0) {
        printk (KERN_ERR "failed to register character device region\n");
        return -1;
    }
    if (!(my_cdev = cdev_alloc ())) {
        printk (KERN_ERR "cdev_alloc() failed\n");
        unregister_chrdev_region (first, count);
        return -1;
    }
    cdev_init (my_cdev, &mycdrv_fops);
    kbuf = kmalloc (KBUF_SIZE, GFP_KERNEL);
    if (cdev_add (my_cdev, first, count) < 0) {
        printk (KERN_ERR "cdev_add() failed\n");
        cdev_del (my_cdev);
        unregister_chrdev_region (first, count);
        kfree (kbuf);
        return -1;
    }

    printk (KERN_INFO "\nSucceeded in registering character device %s\n",
            MYDEV_NAME);
    printk (KERN_INFO "Major number = %d, Minor number = %d\n", MAJOR (first),
            MINOR (first));

    interrupts = (int *)kbuf;

    for (irq = 0; irq < MAXIRQS; irq++) {
        interrupts[irq] = -1;   /* set to -1 as a flag */
        if (!request_irq (irq, my_interrupt, IRQF_SHARED, "my_int", interrupts)) {
            interrupts[irq] = 0;
            printk (KERN_INFO "Succeded in registering IRQ=%d\n", irq);
        }
    }

    return 0;
}

static void __exit my_exit (void)
{
    freeup_irqs ();
    cdev_del (my_cdev);
    unregister_chrdev_region (first, count);
    kfree (kbuf);
```

```
    printk (KERN_INFO "\ndevice unregistered\n");
}

module_init (my_init);
module_exit (my_exit);

MODULE_AUTHOR ("Jerry Cooperstein");
MODULE_DESCRIPTION ("CLDD 1.0: lab2_interrupt.c");
MODULE_LICENSE ("GPL v2");
```

lab2_getinterrupts.c

```
 /* Copyright 2009, J Cooperstein coop@coopj.com (GPLv2) */

#include <stdlib.h>
#include <stdio.h>
#include <fcntl.h>
#include <unistd.h>
#include <errno.h>

#define DEATH(mess) { perror(mess); exit(errno); };

#define MAXIRQS 256
#define NB (MAXIRQS * sizeof(int))

int main (int argc, char *argv[])
{
    int fd, j;
    int *interrupts = malloc (NB);
    char *nodename = "/dev/mycdrv";
    if (argc > 1)
        nodename = argv[1];

    if ((fd = open (nodename, O_RDONLY)) < 0)
        DEATH ("opening device node");
    if (read (fd, interrupts, NB) != NB)
        DEATH ("reading interrupts");

    for (j = 0; j < MAXIRQS; j++)
        if (interrupts[j] > 0)
            printf (" %4d %10d\n", j, interrupts[j]);
    exit (0);
}
```

Chapter 9

Modules II: Exporting, Licensing and Dynamic Loading

9.1   Lab 1: Stacked Modules

- Write a pair of modules one of which uses a function defined in the other module.

- Try loading and unloading them, using **insmod** and **modprobe**.

lab1_module1.c

```
/* Copyright 2009, J Cooperstein coop@coopj.com (GPLv2) */

#include <linux/module.h>
#include <linux/init.h>

static int __init my_init (void)
{
    printk (KERN_INFO "Hello world from mod1 \n");
    return 0;
```

```
}

static void __exit my_exit (void)
{
    printk (KERN_INFO "Goodbye world from mod1 \n");
}

static void mod1fun (void)
{
    printk (KERN_INFO " VOILA! I got into mod1fun \n");
}

EXPORT_SYMBOL (mod1fun);

module_init (my_init);
module_exit (my_exit);

MODULE_AUTHOR ("Jerry Cooperstein");
MODULE_DESCRIPTION ("CLDD 1.0: lab1_module1.c");
MODULE_LICENSE ("GPL v2");
```

lab1_module2.c

```
 /* Copyright 2009, J Cooperstein coop@coopj.com (GPLv2) */

#include <linux/module.h>
#include <linux/init.h>

extern void mod1fun (void);

static int __init my_init (void)
{
    printk (KERN_INFO "Hello world from mod2\n");
    mod1fun ();
    return 0;
}

static void __exit my_exit (void)
{
    printk (KERN_INFO "Goodbye world from mod2\n");
}

module_init (my_init);
module_exit (my_exit);

MODULE_AUTHOR ("Jerry Cooperstein");
MODULE_DESCRIPTION ("CLDD 1.0: lab1_module2.c");
MODULE_LICENSE ("GPL v2");
```

9.2   Lab 2 Duplicate Symbols

- Copy your first module to another file, compile and try to load both at the same time:

```
$ cp lab1_module1.c lab1_module1A.c
.... modify Makefile and compile
$ insmod lab1_module1.ko
$ insmod lab1_module1a.ko
```

- Does this succeed?

- Install your modules with `make modules_install`.

  See how **depmod** handles this by. analyzing the `modules.dep` file that results.

9.3 Lab 3: Dynamic Module Loading

- Take your basic character driver from the previous exercise and adapt it to use dynamic loading:

- Construct a trivial second module and have it dynamically loaded during the character driver's `open()` entry point. (Make sure the name of the file that is requested is the same as the name of your file.)

- Add a small function to your character driver and have it referenced by the second module.

- Make sure you place your modules in a place where **modprobe** can find them, (Installing with the target `modules_install` will take care of this for you.)

- You can use either **cat** or the main program from the character driver lab to exercise your module. What happens if you try to request loading more than once?

lab3_module1.c

```
/* Copyright 2009, J Cooperstein coop@coopj.com (GPLv2) */

#include <linux/module.h>
#include <linux/fs.h>
#include <linux/uaccess.h>
#include <linux/init.h>
#include <linux/slab.h>
#include <linux/cdev.h>

#define MYDEV_NAME "mycdrv"
#define KBUF_SIZE (size_t)(10*PAGE_SIZE)

static char *kbuf;
static dev_t first;
static unsigned int count = 1;
static int my_major = 700, my_minor = 0;
static struct cdev *my_cdev;

void mod_fun (void)
{
    printk (KERN_INFO " VOILA! I got into mod_fun \n");
}

EXPORT_SYMBOL (mod_fun);
```

```
static int mycdrv_open (struct inode *inode, struct file *file)
{
    static int counter = 0;
    printk (KERN_INFO " attempting to open device: %s:\n", MYDEV_NAME);
    printk (KERN_INFO " MAJOR number = %d, MINOR number = %d\n",
            imajor (inode), iminor (inode));
    counter++;

    printk (KERN_INFO " successfully open  device: %s:\n\n", MYDEV_NAME);
    printk (KERN_INFO "I have been opened  %d times since being loaded\n",
            counter);
    printk (KERN_INFO "ref=%d\n", module_refcount (THIS_MODULE));

    printk (KERN_INFO "/n rc from requesting module mod_fun is: %d\n",
            request_module ("%s", "lab1_module2"));

    return 0;
}

static int mycdrv_release (struct inode *inode, struct file *file)
{
    printk (KERN_INFO " CLOSING device: %s:\n\n", MYDEV_NAME);
    return 0;
}

static ssize_t
mycdrv_read (struct file *file, char __user * buf, size_t lbuf, loff_t * ppos)
{
    int nbytes = lbuf - copy_to_user (buf, kbuf + *ppos, lbuf);
    *ppos += nbytes;
    printk (KERN_INFO "\n READING function, nbytes=%d, pos=%d\n", nbytes,
            (int)*ppos);
    return nbytes;
}

static ssize_t
mycdrv_write (struct file *file, const char __user * buf, size_t lbuf,
              loff_t * ppos)
{
    int nbytes = lbuf - copy_from_user (kbuf + *ppos, buf, lbuf);
    *ppos += nbytes;
    printk (KERN_INFO "\n WRITING function, nbytes=%d, pos=%d\n", nbytes,
            (int)*ppos);
    return nbytes;
}

static const struct file_operations mycdrv_fops = {
    .owner = THIS_MODULE,
    .read = mycdrv_read,
    .write = mycdrv_write,
    .open = mycdrv_open,
    .release = mycdrv_release,
};
```

```
static int __init my_init (void)
{
    first = MKDEV (my_major, my_minor);
    if (register_chrdev_region (first, count, MYDEV_NAME) < 0) {
        printk (KERN_ERR "failed to register character device region\n");
        return -1;
    }
    if (!(my_cdev = cdev_alloc ())) {
        printk (KERN_ERR "cdev_alloc() failed\n");
        unregister_chrdev_region (first, count);
        return -1;
    }
    cdev_init (my_cdev, &mycdrv_fops);
    kbuf = kmalloc (KBUF_SIZE, GFP_KERNEL);

    if (cdev_add (my_cdev, first, count) < 0) {
        printk (KERN_ERR "cdev_add() failed\n");
        cdev_del (my_cdev);
        unregister_chrdev_region (first, count);
        kfree (kbuf);
        return -1;
    }
    printk (KERN_INFO "\nSucceeded in registering character device %s\n",
            MYDEV_NAME);
    return 0;
}

static void __exit my_exit (void)
{
    if (my_cdev)
        cdev_del (my_cdev);
    unregister_chrdev_region (first, count);
    if (kbuf)
        kfree (kbuf);
    printk (KERN_INFO "\ndevice unregistered\n");
}

module_init (my_init);
module_exit (my_exit);

MODULE_AUTHOR ("Jerry Cooperstein");
MODULE_DESCRIPTION ("CLDD 1.0: lab3_module1.c");
MODULE_LICENSE ("GPL v2");
```

lab3_module2.c

```
 /* Copyright 2009, J Cooperstein coop@coopj.com (GPLv2) */

#include <linux/module.h>
#include <linux/init.h>

extern void mod_fun (void);

static int __init my_init (void)
{
```

```
    printk (KERN_INFO "Hello world from mymod\n");
    mod_fun ();
    return 0;
}

static void __exit my_exit (void)
{
    printk (KERN_INFO "Goodbye world from mymod\n");
}

module_init (my_init);
module_exit (my_exit);

MODULE_AUTHOR ("Jerry Cooperstein");
MODULE_DESCRIPTION ("CLDD 1.0: lab3_module2.c");
MODULE_LICENSE ("GPL v2");
```

9.4   Lab 4: Demand Loading of Drivers

- Make your character driver load upon use of the device; i.e., when you do something like

  `cat file > /dev/mycdrv`

  have the driver load.

- Make the adjustments to `/etc/modprobe.conf` as needed and put the module in the proper place with `make modules_install`.

Chapter 10

Debugging Techniques

10.1 Lab 1: Using kprobes

- Place a **kprobe** at an often executed place in the kernel. A good choice would be the `do_fork()` function, which is executed whenever a child process is born.

- Put in simple handler functions.

- Test the module by loading it and running simple commands which cause the probed instruction to execute, such as starting a new shell with **bash**.

lab1_kprobes.c

```
/* Copyright 2009, J Cooperstein coop@coopj.com (GPLv2) */

#include <linux/module.h>
#include <linux/init.h>
#include <linux/kprobes.h>
#include <linux/kallsyms.h>
```

```
#define PRCUR(t) printk (KERN_INFO "current->comm=%s, current->pid=%d\n", t->comm, t->pid);

static char *name = "do_fork";
module_param (name, charp, S_IRUGO);

static struct kprobe kp;

static int handler_pre (struct kprobe *p, struct pt_regs *regs)
{
    printk (KERN_INFO "pre_handler: p->addr=0x%p\n", p->addr);
    PRCUR (current);
    return 0;
}

static void handler_post (struct kprobe *p, struct pt_regs *regs,
                          unsigned long flags)
{
    printk (KERN_INFO "post_handler: p->addr=0x%p\n", p->addr);
    PRCUR (current);
}

static int handler_fault (struct kprobe *p, struct pt_regs *regs, int trapnr)
{
    printk (KERN_INFO "fault_handler:p->addr=0x%p\n", p->addr);
    PRCUR (current);
    return 0;
}

static int __init my_init (void)
{
    /* set the handler functions */

    kp.pre_handler = handler_pre;
    kp.post_handler = handler_post;
    kp.fault_handler = handler_fault;
    kp.symbol_name = name;

    if (register_kprobe (&kp)) {
        printk (KERN_INFO "Failed to register kprobe, quitting\n");
        return -1;
    }

    printk (KERN_INFO "Hello: module loaded at 0x%p\n", my_init);

    return 0;
}
static void __exit my_exit (void)
{
    unregister_kprobe (&kp);
    printk (KERN_INFO "Bye: module unloaded from 0x%p\n", my_exit);
}

module_init (my_init);
module_exit (my_exit);
MODULE_AUTHOR ("Jerry Cooperstein");
```

```
MODULE_DESCRIPTION ("CLDD 1.0: lab1_kprobes.c");
MODULE_LICENSE ("GPL v2");
```

10.2   Lab 2: Using jprobes

- Test the **jprobes** facility by instrumenting a commonly used kernel function.

- Keep a counter of how many times the function is called. If you print it out each time, be careful not to get overwhelmed with output.

lab2_jprobes.c

```
/* Copyright 2009, J Cooperstein coop@coopj.com (GPLv2) */

#include <linux/module.h>
#include <linux/kprobes.h>
#include <linux/kallsyms.h>

static long mod_timer_count = 0;

static void mod_timer_inst (struct timer_list *timer, unsigned long expires)
{
    mod_timer_count++;
    if (mod_timer_count % 10 == 0)
        printk (KERN_INFO "mod_timer_count=%ld\n", mod_timer_count);
    jprobe_return ();
}

static struct jprobe jp = {
    .kp.addr = (kprobe_opcode_t *) mod_timer,
    .entry = (kprobe_opcode_t *) mod_timer_inst,
};

static int __init my_init (void)
{
    register_jprobe (&jp);
    printk (KERN_INFO "plant jprobe at %p, handler addr %p\n", jp.kp.addr,
            jp.entry);
    return 0;
}
static void __exit my_exit (void)
{

    unregister_jprobe (&jp);
    printk (KERN_INFO "jprobe unregistered\n");
    printk (KERN_INFO "FINAL:mod_timer_count=%ld\n", mod_timer_count);
}

module_init (my_init);
module_exit (my_exit);
MODULE_AUTHOR ("Jerry Cooperstein");
MODULE_DESCRIPTION ("CLDD 1.0: lab2_jprobes.c");
MODULE_LICENSE ("GPL v2");
```

10.3   Lab 3: Probing a module

- Take an earlier module (such as a character driver) and add both **kprobes** and **jprobes** instrumentation to it.

- Does the function you are probing need to be exported to be accessible to the probe utilities?

lab3_probe_module.c

```
/* Copyright 2009, J Cooperstein coop@coopj.com (GPLv2) */

#include <linux/module.h>
#include <linux/kprobes.h>
#include <linux/kallsyms.h>

static int mycdrv_open_probe (struct inode *inode, struct file *file)
{
    printk (KERN_INFO "\n\n ****JPROBE**** in mycdrv_open_debug\n\n");
    jprobe_return ();
    return 0;
}

static struct kprobe kp;

static int handler_pre (struct kprobe *p, struct pt_regs *regs)
{
    printk (KERN_INFO "pre_handler: p->addr=0x%p\n", p->addr);
    return 0;
}

static void handler_post (struct kprobe *p, struct pt_regs *regs,
                          unsigned long flags)
{
    printk (KERN_INFO "post_handler: p->addr=0x%p\n", p->addr);
}

static int handler_fault (struct kprobe *p, struct pt_regs *regs, int trapnr)
{
    printk (KERN_INFO "fault_handler:p->addr=0x%p\n", p->addr);
    return 0;
}

static struct jprobe jp = {
    .kp.symbol_name = "mycdrv_open",
    .entry = (kprobe_opcode_t *) mycdrv_open_probe,
};

static int __init my_init (void)
{
    /* set the handler functions */

    kp.pre_handler = handler_pre;
    kp.post_handler = handler_post;
    kp.fault_handler = handler_fault;
```

```
    kp.symbol_name = "mycdrv_open";

    if (register_kprobe (&kp)) {
        printk (KERN_INFO "Failed to register kprobe, quitting\n");
        return -1;
    }
    register_jprobe (&jp);
    printk (KERN_INFO "plant jprobe at %p, handler addr %p\n", jp.kp.addr,
            jp.entry);
    return 0;
}
static void __exit my_exit (void)
{

    unregister_jprobe (&jp);
    unregister_kprobe (&kp);
    printk (KERN_INFO "k,jprobes unregistered\n");
}

module_init (my_init);
module_exit (my_exit);
MODULE_AUTHOR ("Jerry Cooperstein");
MODULE_DESCRIPTION ("CLDD 1.0: lab3_probe_module.c");
MODULE_LICENSE ("GPL v2");
```

lab3_dynamic_udev.c

```
 /* Copyright 2009, J Cooperstein coop@coopj.com (GPLv2) */

#include <linux/module.h>
#include <linux/fs.h>
#include <linux/uaccess.h>
#include <linux/init.h>
#include <linux/slab.h>
#include <linux/cdev.h>
#include <linux/device.h>

#define MYDEV_NAME "mycdrv"
#define KBUF_SIZE (size_t)(10*PAGE_SIZE)

static char *kbuf;
static dev_t first;
static unsigned int count = 1;
static struct cdev *my_cdev;

static struct class *foo_class;

static int mycdrv_open (struct inode *inode, struct file *file)
{
    static int counter = 0;
    printk (KERN_INFO " attempting to open device: %s:\n", MYDEV_NAME);
    printk (KERN_INFO " MAJOR number = %d, MINOR number = %d\n",
            imajor (inode), iminor (inode));
    counter++;
```

```
    printk (KERN_INFO " successfully open  device: %s:\n\n", MYDEV_NAME);
    printk (KERN_INFO "I have been opened  %d times since being loaded\n",
            counter);
    printk (KERN_INFO "ref=%d\n", module_refcount (THIS_MODULE));

    return 0;
}

static int mycdrv_release (struct inode *inode, struct file *file)
{
    printk (KERN_INFO " CLOSING device: %s:\n\n", MYDEV_NAME);
    return 0;
}

static ssize_t
mycdrv_read (struct file *file, char __user * buf, size_t lbuf, loff_t * ppos)
{
    int nbytes, maxbytes, bytes_to_do;
    maxbytes = KBUF_SIZE - *ppos;
    bytes_to_do = maxbytes > lbuf ? lbuf : maxbytes;
    if (bytes_to_do == 0)
        printk (KERN_INFO "Reached end of the device on a read");
    nbytes = bytes_to_do - copy_to_user (buf, kbuf + *ppos, bytes_to_do);
    *ppos += nbytes;
    printk (KERN_INFO "\n Leaving the   READ function, nbytes=%d, pos=%d\n",
            nbytes, (int)*ppos);
    return nbytes;
}

static ssize_t
mycdrv_write (struct file *file, const char __user * buf, size_t lbuf,
              loff_t * ppos)
{
    int nbytes, maxbytes, bytes_to_do;
    maxbytes = KBUF_SIZE - *ppos;
    bytes_to_do = maxbytes > lbuf ? lbuf : maxbytes;
    if (bytes_to_do == 0)
        printk (KERN_INFO "Reached end of the device on a write");
    nbytes = bytes_to_do - copy_from_user (kbuf + *ppos, buf, bytes_to_do);
    *ppos += nbytes;
    printk (KERN_INFO "\n Leaving the   WRITE function, nbytes=%d, pos=%d\n",
            nbytes, (int)*ppos);
    return nbytes;
}

static loff_t mycdrv_lseek (struct file *file, loff_t offset, int orig)
{
    loff_t testpos;
    switch (orig) {
    case SEEK_SET:
        testpos = offset;
        break;
    case SEEK_CUR:
        testpos = file->f_pos + offset;
        break;
```

```
    case SEEK_END:
        testpos = KBUF_SIZE + offset;
        break;
    default:
        return -EINVAL;
    }
    testpos = testpos < KBUF_SIZE ? testpos : KBUF_SIZE;
    testpos = testpos >= 0 ? testpos : 0;
    file->f_pos = testpos;
    printk (KERN_INFO "Seeking to pos=%ld\n", (long)testpos);
    return testpos;
}

static const struct file_operations mycdrv_fops = {
    .owner = THIS_MODULE,
    .read = mycdrv_read,
    .write = mycdrv_write,
    .open = mycdrv_open,
    .release = mycdrv_release,
    .llseek = mycdrv_lseek
};

static int __init my_init (void)
{
    if (alloc_chrdev_region (&first, 0, count, MYDEV_NAME) < 0) {
        printk (KERN_ERR "failed to allocate character device region\n");
        return -1;
    }
    if (!(my_cdev = cdev_alloc ())) {
        printk (KERN_ERR "cdev_alloc() failed\n");
        unregister_chrdev_region (first, count);
        return -1;
    }
    cdev_init (my_cdev, &mycdrv_fops);
    kbuf = kmalloc (KBUF_SIZE, GFP_KERNEL);
    if (cdev_add (my_cdev, first, count) < 0) {
        printk (KERN_ERR "cdev_add() failed\n");
        cdev_del (my_cdev);
        unregister_chrdev_region (first, count);
        kfree (kbuf);
        return -1;
    }

    foo_class = class_create (THIS_MODULE, "my_class");
    device_create (foo_class, NULL, first, "%s", "mycdrv");

    printk (KERN_INFO "\nSucceeded in registering character device %s\n",
            MYDEV_NAME);
    printk (KERN_INFO "Major number = %d, Minor number = %d\n", MAJOR (first),
            MINOR (first));
    return 0;
}

static void __exit my_exit (void)
{
```

```
        device_destroy (foo_class, first);
        class_destroy (foo_class);

        if (my_cdev)
            cdev_del (my_cdev);
        unregister_chrdev_region (first, count);
        if (kbuf)
            kfree (kbuf);
        printk (KERN_INFO "\ndevice unregistered\n");
}


module_init (my_init);
module_exit (my_exit);


MODULE_AUTHOR ("Jerry Cooperstein");
MODULE_DESCRIPTION ("CLDD 1.0: lab3_dynamic_udev.c");
MODULE_LICENSE ("GPL v2");
```

10.4   Lab 4: Using debugfs.

- Write a module that creates entries in **debugfs**.

- First use one of the convenience functions to make just a simple one variable entry under the root **debugfs** filesystem, of whatever length you desire.

- Next create your own directory and put one or more entries in it.

lab4_debugfs.c

```
 /* Copyright 2009, J Cooperstein coop@coopj.com (GPLv2) */

#include <linux/module.h>
#include <linux/init.h>
#include <linux/fs.h>
#include <linux/debugfs.h>
#include <linux/uaccess.h>
#include <linux/slab.h>

static struct dentry *var32, *parent, *filen;
static u32 val = (u32) 888;
static u32 val32 = (u32) 777;
#define KS 32
static char kstring[KS];         /* should be less sloppy about overflows :) */

static ssize_t
my_read (struct file *file, char __user * buf, size_t lbuf, loff_t * ppos)
{
    int nbytes;
    nbytes = sprintf (kstring, "%d\n", val);
    printk (KERN_INFO "d_inode = %p\n", parent->d_inode);
    return simple_read_from_buffer (buf, lbuf, ppos, kstring, nbytes);
}
```

```
static ssize_t
my_write (struct file *file, const char __user * buf, size_t lbuf,
          loff_t * ppos)
{
    int rc;
    int nbytes = lbuf;
    rc = copy_from_user (&kstring, buf, lbuf);
    sscanf (kstring, "%d", &val);
    printk (KERN_INFO "\n WRITING function, nbytes=%d, val=%d\n", nbytes, val);
    return nbytes;
}

static const struct file_operations fops = {
    .owner = THIS_MODULE,
    .read = my_read,
    .write = my_write,
};

static int __init my_init (void)
{
    var32 = debugfs_create_u32 ("myname", S_IRUGO | S_IWUSR, NULL, &val32);
    parent = debugfs_create_dir ("mydir", NULL);
    filen =
        debugfs_create_file ("filen", S_IRUGO | S_IWUSR, parent, NULL, &fops);
    printk (KERN_INFO "Hello: module loaded at 0x%p\n", my_init);
    return 0;
}
static void __exit my_exit (void)
{
    printk (KERN_INFO "Bye: module unloaded from 0x%p\n", my_exit);
    if (filen)
        debugfs_remove (filen);
    if (parent)
        debugfs_remove (parent);
    if (var32)
        debugfs_remove (var32);
}

module_init (my_init);
module_exit (my_exit);

MODULE_AUTHOR ("Jerry Cooperstein");
MODULE_DESCRIPTION ("CLDD 1.0: lab4_debugfs.c");
MODULE_LICENSE ("GPL v2");
```

Chapter 11

Timing and Timers

11.1 Lab 1: Kernel Timers from a Character Driver

- Write a driver that puts launches a kernel timer whenever a `write()` to the device takes place.

- Pass some data to the driver and have it print out.

- Have it print out the `current->pid` field when the timer function is scheduled, and then again when the function is executed.

lab_char.h

```
#ifndef _LAB_CHAR_H
#define _LAB_CHAR_H

#include <linux/module.h>
#include <linux/fs.h>
#include <linux/uaccess.h>
#include <linux/sched.h>
#include <linux/init.h>
#include <linux/slab.h>
```

```c
#include <linux/cdev.h>
#include <linux/device.h>

/* everything we need for dynamic character device allocation */

static struct class *foo_class;

#define MYDEV_NAME "mycdrv"

static char *ramdisk;
static size_t ramdisk_size = (4 * PAGE_SIZE);
static dev_t first;
static unsigned int count = 1;  /* number of dev_t needed */
static struct cdev *my_cdev;
static const struct file_operations mycdrv_fops;

/* generic entry points */

static inline int mycdrv_generic_open (struct inode *inode, struct file *file)
{
    static int counter = 0;
    printk (KERN_INFO " attempting to open device: %s:\n", MYDEV_NAME);
    printk (KERN_INFO " MAJOR number = %d, MINOR number = %d\n",
            imajor (inode), iminor (inode));
    counter++;

    printk (KERN_INFO " successfully open  device: %s:\n\n", MYDEV_NAME);
    printk (KERN_INFO "I have been opened  %d times since being loaded\n",
            counter);
    printk (KERN_INFO "ref=%d\n", module_refcount (THIS_MODULE));

    return 0;
}
static inline int mycdrv_generic_release (struct inode *inode,
                                          struct file *file)
{
    printk (KERN_INFO " closing character device: %s:\n\n", MYDEV_NAME);
    return 0;
}
static inline ssize_t
mycdrv_generic_read (struct file *file, char __user * buf, size_t lbuf,
                     loff_t * ppos)
{
    int nbytes, maxbytes, bytes_to_do;
    maxbytes = ramdisk_size - *ppos;
    bytes_to_do = maxbytes > lbuf ? lbuf : maxbytes;
    if (bytes_to_do == 0)
        printk (KERN_WARNING "Reached end of the device on a read");

    nbytes = bytes_to_do - copy_to_user (buf, ramdisk + *ppos, bytes_to_do);
    *ppos += nbytes;
    printk (KERN_INFO "\n Leaving the   READ function, nbytes=%d, pos=%d\n",
            nbytes, (int)*ppos);
    return nbytes;
}
```

```
static inline ssize_t
mycdrv_generic_write (struct file *file, const char __user * buf, size_t lbuf,
                      loff_t * ppos)
{
    int nbytes, maxbytes, bytes_to_do;
    maxbytes = ramdisk_size - *ppos;
    bytes_to_do = maxbytes > lbuf ? lbuf : maxbytes;
    if (bytes_to_do == 0)
        printk (KERN_WARNING "Reached end of the device on a write");
    nbytes = bytes_to_do - copy_from_user (ramdisk + *ppos, buf, bytes_to_do);
    *ppos += nbytes;
    printk (KERN_INFO "\n Leaving the  WRITE function, nbytes=%d, pos=%d\n",
            nbytes, (int)*ppos);
    return nbytes;
}


static inline loff_t mycdrv_generic_lseek (struct file *file, loff_t offset,
                                           int orig)
{
    loff_t testpos;
    switch (orig) {
    case SEEK_SET:
        testpos = offset;
        break;
    case SEEK_CUR:
        testpos = file->f_pos + offset;
        break;
    case SEEK_END:
        testpos = ramdisk_size + offset;
        break;
    default:
        return -EINVAL;
    }
    testpos = testpos < ramdisk_size ? testpos : ramdisk_size;
    testpos = testpos >= 0 ? testpos : 0;
    file->f_pos = testpos;
    return testpos;
}

static inline int __init my_generic_init (void)
{
    if (alloc_chrdev_region (&first, 0, count, MYDEV_NAME) < 0) {
        printk (KERN_ERR "failed to allocate character device region\n");
        return -1;
    }
    if (!(my_cdev = cdev_alloc ())) {
        printk (KERN_ERR "cdev_alloc() failed\n");
        unregister_chrdev_region (first, count);
        return -1;
    }
    cdev_init (my_cdev, &mycdrv_fops);

    ramdisk = kmalloc (ramdisk_size, GFP_KERNEL);
```

```
    if (cdev_add (my_cdev, first, count) < 0) {
        printk (KERN_ERR "cdev_add() failed\n");
        cdev_del (my_cdev);
        unregister_chrdev_region (first, count);
        kfree (ramdisk);
        return -1;
    }

    foo_class = class_create (THIS_MODULE, "my_class");
    device_create (foo_class, NULL, first, "%s", "mycdrv");
    printk (KERN_INFO "\nSucceeded in registering character device %s\n",
            MYDEV_NAME);
    printk (KERN_INFO "Major number = %d, Minor number = %d\n", MAJOR (first),
            MINOR (first));

    return 0;
}

static inline void __exit my_generic_exit (void)
{
    device_destroy (foo_class, first);
    class_destroy (foo_class);

    if (my_cdev)
        cdev_del (my_cdev);
    unregister_chrdev_region (first, count);
    kfree (ramdisk);
    printk (KERN_INFO "\ndevice unregistered\n");
}

MODULE_AUTHOR ("Jerry Cooperstein");
MODULE_DESCRIPTION ("CLDD 1.0: lab_char.h");
MODULE_LICENSE ("GPL v2");
#endif
```

lab1_timer.c

```
 /* Copyright 2009, J Cooperstein coop@coopj.com (GPLv2) */

#include <linux/module.h>
#include "lab_char.h"
#include <linux/timer.h>

static struct timer_list my_timer;

static void my_timer_function (unsigned long ptr)
{
    printk (KERN_INFO "I am in my_timer_fun, jiffies = %ld\n", jiffies);
    printk (KERN_INFO " I think my current task pid is %d\n",
            (int)current->pid);
    printk (KERN_INFO " my data is: %d\n", (int)ptr);
}

static ssize_t
mycdrv_write (struct file *file, const char __user * buf, size_t lbuf,
```

```
                loff_t * ppos)
{
    static int len = 100;
    printk (KERN_INFO " Entering the WRITE function\n");
    printk (KERN_INFO " my current task pid is %d\n", (int)current->pid);
    init_timer (&my_timer);      /* intialize */
    my_timer.function = my_timer_function;
    my_timer.expires = jiffies + HZ;     /* one second delay */
    /*  my_timer.data = (void *) len; */
    my_timer.data = len;
    printk (KERN_INFO "Adding timer at jiffies = %ld\n", jiffies);
    add_timer (&my_timer);
    len += 100;
    return lbuf;
}

static const struct file_operations mycdrv_fops = {
    .owner = THIS_MODULE,
    .read = mycdrv_generic_read,
    .write = mycdrv_write,
    .open = mycdrv_generic_open,
    .release = mycdrv_generic_release,
};

static void __exit my_exit (void)
{
    /* delete any running timers */
    printk (KERN_INFO "Deleted time,r rc = %d\n", del_timer_sync (&my_timer));
    my_generic_exit ();
}

module_init (my_generic_init);
module_exit (my_exit);

MODULE_AUTHOR ("Jerry Cooperstein");
MODULE_DESCRIPTION ("CLDD 1.0: lab1_timer.c");
MODULE_LICENSE ("GPL v2");
```

11.2   Lab 2: Multiple Kernel Timers

- Make the period in the first lab long enough so you can issue multiple writes before the timer function run. (Hint: you may want to save your data before running this lab.)

- How many times does the function get run?

- Fix the solution so multiple timers work properly.

lab2_multitimer.c

```
/* Copyright 2009, J Cooperstein coop@coopj.com (GPLv2) */

#include <linux/module.h>
#include "lab_char.h"
```

```c
#include <linux/timer.h>
#include <linux/delay.h>

/* you probably don't need the ntimers variable, and it is a
   forward reference because we haven't done atomic variables
   but it is here to avoid unloading while there are still
   timers to unload.  It is also used sloppily on the exit :)
*/
static atomic_t ntimers;

struct my_dat
{
    int l;
    struct timer_list *tl;
};

static void my_timer_function (unsigned long ptr)
{
    struct my_dat *tl = (struct my_dat *)ptr;
    printk (KERN_INFO "I am in my_timer_fun, jiffies = %ld\n", jiffies);
    printk (KERN_INFO " I think my current task pid is %d\n",
            (int)current->pid);
    printk (KERN_INFO " my data is: %d\n", tl->l);
    kfree (tl->tl);
    kfree (tl);
    atomic_dec (&ntimers);
    printk (KERN_INFO "ntimers deced to %d\n", atomic_read (&ntimers));
}


static ssize_t
mycdrv_write (struct file *file, const char __user * buf, size_t lbuf,
             loff_t * ppos)
{
    struct timer_list *tl;
    struct my_dat *mdata;
    static int len = 100;
    atomic_inc (&ntimers);
    printk (KERN_INFO "ntimers upped to %d\n", atomic_read (&ntimers));
    tl = (struct timer_list *)kmalloc (sizeof (struct timer_list), GFP_KERNEL);
    printk (KERN_INFO " Entering the WRITE function\n");
    printk (KERN_INFO " my current task pid is %d\n", (int)current->pid);
    init_timer (tl);              /* intialize */
    tl->function = my_timer_function;
    tl->expires = jiffies + 4 * HZ; /* four second delay */
    mdata = (struct my_dat *)kmalloc (sizeof (struct my_dat), GFP_KERNEL);
    tl->data = (unsigned long)mdata;
    mdata->l = len;
    mdata->tl = tl;
    /*  my_timer.data = (void *) len; */

    printk (KERN_INFO "Adding timer at jiffies = %ld\n", jiffies);
    add_timer (tl);
    len += 100;
    return lbuf;
}
```

```
static const struct file_operations mycdrv_fops = {
    .owner = THIS_MODULE,
    .read = mycdrv_generic_read,
    .write = mycdrv_write,
    .open = mycdrv_generic_open,
    .release = mycdrv_generic_release,
};

static int __init my_init (void)
{
    atomic_set (&ntimers, 0);
    return my_generic_init ();
}

static void __exit my_exit (void)
{
    /* wait for all timers to finish ; pretty crummy */
    printk (KERN_INFO "ntimers in remove routine to %d\n",
            atomic_read (&ntimers));
    while (atomic_read (&ntimers)) {
        printk (KERN_INFO "sleeping, ntimers still %d\n",
                atomic_read (&ntimers));
        msleep (1000);            /* wait a second, ugly */
    }
    my_generic_exit ();
}

module_init (my_init);
module_exit (my_exit);

MODULE_AUTHOR ("Jerry Cooperstein");
MODULE_DESCRIPTION ("CLDD 1.0: lab2_multitimer.c");
MODULE_LICENSE ("GPL v2");
```

11.3 Lab 3: Periodic Kernel Timers

- Write a module that launches a periodic kernel timer function; i.e., it should re-install itself.

lab3_periodic_timer.c

```
/* Copyright 2009, J Cooperstein coop@coopj.com (GPLv2) */

#include <linux/module.h>
#include <linux/timer.h>
#include <linux/jiffies.h>
#include <linux/init.h>

static struct timer_list timer;
static struct kt_data
{
    unsigned long period;
```

```
    unsigned long start_time;    /* jiffies value when we first started the timer */
    unsigned long timer_start;   /* jiffies when timer was queued */
    unsigned long timer_end;     /* jiffies when timer is executed */
} data;

static void ktfun (unsigned long var)
{
    struct kt_data *tdata = (struct kt_data *)var;

    printk (KERN_INFO "ktimer: period = %ld  elapsed = %ld\n",
            tdata->period, jiffies - tdata->start_time);
    /* resubmit */
    mod_timer (&timer, tdata->period + jiffies);
}
static int __init my_init (void)
{

    data.period = 2 * HZ;        /* short period,   2 secs */

    init_timer (&timer);
    timer.function = ktfun;
    timer.data = (unsigned long)&data;
    timer.expires = jiffies + data.period;
    data.start_time = jiffies;
    add_timer (&timer);

    return 0;
}
static void __exit my_exit (void)
{
    /* delete any running timers */
    printk (KERN_INFO "Deleted time,r rc = %d\n", del_timer_sync (&timer));
    printk (KERN_INFO "Module successfully unloaded \n");
}

module_init (my_init);
module_exit (my_exit);

MODULE_AUTHOR ("Jerry Cooperstein");
MODULE_DESCRIPTION ("CLDD 1.0: lab3_periodic_timer.c");
MODULE_LICENSE ("GPL v2");
```

11.4   Lab 4: Multiple Periodic Kernel Timers

- Write a module that launches two periodic kernel timer functions; i.e., they should re-install themselves.

- One periodic sequence should be for less than 256 ticks (so it falls in the tv1 vector), and the other should be for less than 16 K ticks (so it falls in the tv2 vector.)

- Each time the timer functions execute, print out the total elapsed time since the module was loaded (in jiffies).

- For one of the functions, also read the **TSC** and calibrate with the CPU frequency (as read from /proc/cpuinfo or the cpu_khz variable) to print out the elapsed time (hopefully) more accurately.

lab4_periodic_timers.c

```
/* Copyright 2009, J Cooperstein coop@coopj.com (GPLv2) */

#include <linux/module.h>
#include <linux/timer.h>
#include <asm/msr.h>              /* needed for Time Stamp Counter functions */
#include <linux/init.h>
#include <linux/jiffies.h>

static unsigned long speed;       /* MHZ of CPU */

static struct timer_list timer_a, timer_b;

static struct kt_data
{
    unsigned long period;
    unsigned long start_time;    /* jiffies value when we first started the timer */
    u64 tsc_start;               /* TSC when timer was queued */
    u64 tsc_end;                 /* TSC when timer is executed */
} *data_a, *data_b;

static void ktfun_a (unsigned long var)
{
    u64 ticks;
    int msecs;
    struct kt_data *tdata = (struct kt_data *)var;

    rdtscll (tdata->tsc_end);
    ticks = tdata->tsc_end - tdata->tsc_start;
    msecs = (unsigned long)ticks / (speed * 1000);
    printk (KERN_INFO
            "A: period = %ld  elapsed = %ld TSC ticks: %lld msecs = %d\n",
            tdata->period, jiffies - tdata->start_time, ticks, msecs);

    /* read the TSC for start time for the next cycle and resubmit */
    rdtscll (tdata->tsc_start);
    mod_timer (&timer_a, tdata->period + jiffies);
}
static void ktfun_b (unsigned long var)
{
    struct kt_data *tdata = (struct kt_data *)var;

    printk (KERN_INFO "   B: period = %ld  elapsed = %ld \n", tdata->period,
            jiffies - tdata->start_time);

    /* resubmit */
    mod_timer (&timer_b, tdata->period + jiffies);
}
static int __init my_init (void)
```

```
{
    speed = cpu_khz / 1000;
    printk (KERN_INFO "CPU MHZ is found to be: %ld \n", speed);

    init_timer (&timer_a);
    init_timer (&timer_b);

    timer_a.function = ktfun_a;
    timer_b.function = ktfun_b;

    data_a = kmalloc (sizeof (*data_a), GFP_KERNEL);
    data_b = kmalloc (sizeof (*data_b), GFP_KERNEL);

    timer_a.data = (unsigned long)data_a;
    timer_b.data = (unsigned long)data_b;

    data_a->period = 1 * HZ;     /* short period, 1 second  */
    data_b->period = 10 * HZ;    /* longer period, 10 seconds */

    data_a->start_time = jiffies;
    data_b->start_time = jiffies;

    timer_a.expires = jiffies + data_a->period;
    timer_b.expires = jiffies + data_b->period;

    rdtscll (data_a->tsc_start);

    add_timer (&timer_a);
    add_timer (&timer_b);

    return 0;
}
static void __exit my_exit (void)
{
    /* delete any running timers */
    printk (KERN_INFO "Deleted timer A: rc = %d\n", del_timer_sync (&timer_a));
    printk (KERN_INFO "Deleted timer B: rc = %d\n", del_timer_sync (&timer_b));
    kfree (data_a);
    kfree (data_b);
    printk (KERN_INFO "Module successfully unloaded \n");
}

module_init (my_init);
module_exit (my_exit);

MODULE_AUTHOR ("Jerry Cooperstein");
MODULE_DESCRIPTION ("CLDD 1.0: lab4_periodic_timers.c");
MODULE_LICENSE ("GPL v2");
```

11.5   Lab 5: High Resolution Timers

- Do the same things as in the previous exercise, setting up two periodic timers, but this time use the **hrtimer** interface.

lab5_hrtimer.c

```
/* Copyright 2009, J Cooperstein coop@coopj.com (GPLv2) */

#include <linux/module.h>
#include <linux/timer.h>
#include <asm/msr.h>              /* needed for Time Stamp Counter functions */
#include <linux/init.h>
#include <linux/ktime.h>
#include <linux/hrtimer.h>

static unsigned long speed;       /* MHZ of CPU */

static struct kt_data
{
    struct hrtimer timer;
    ktime_t period;
    unsigned long start_time;     /* jiffies value when we first started the timer */
    u64 tsc_start;                /* TSC when timer was queued */
    u64 tsc_end;                  /* TSC when timer is executed */
} *data_a, *data_b;

static void resubmit_it (struct hrtimer *var, struct kt_data *data)
{
    ktime_t now = var->base->get_time ();
    data->start_time = jiffies;
    hrtimer_forward (var, now, data->period);
}

static enum hrtimer_restart ktfun_a (struct hrtimer *var)
{
    u64 ticks;
    int msecs;
    rdtscll (data_a->tsc_end);
    ticks = data_a->tsc_end - data_a->tsc_start;
    msecs = (unsigned long)ticks / (speed * 1000);
    /* read the TSC for start time for the next cycle and resubmit */
    rdtscll (data_a->tsc_start);
    printk (KERN_INFO
            "A: period = %lld  elapsed = %ld TSC ticks: %lld msecs = %d\n",
            ktime_to_ns (data_a->period), jiffies - data_a->start_time, ticks,
            msecs);
    resubmit_it (var, data_a);
    return HRTIMER_NORESTART;
}

static enum hrtimer_restart ktfun_b (struct hrtimer *var)
{
    printk (KERN_INFO "   B: period = %lld  elapsed = %ld \n",
            ktime_to_ns (data_b->period), jiffies - data_b->start_time);
    /* resubmit */
    resubmit_it (var, data_b);
    return HRTIMER_NORESTART;
}
```

```
static int __init my_init (void)
{

    data_a = kmalloc (sizeof (*data_a), GFP_KERNEL);
    data_b = kmalloc (sizeof (*data_b), GFP_KERNEL);

    speed = cpu_khz / 1000;
    printk (KERN_INFO "CPU MHZ is found to be: %ld \n", speed);

    data_a->period = ktime_set (1, 0);  /* short period, 1 second  */
    data_b->period = ktime_set (10, 0); /* longer period, 10 seconds */

    hrtimer_init (&data_a->timer, CLOCK_REALTIME, HRTIMER_MODE_REL);
    hrtimer_init (&data_b->timer, CLOCK_REALTIME, HRTIMER_MODE_REL);

    data_a->timer.function = ktfun_a;
    data_b->timer.function = ktfun_b;

    /* initial timing info */
    data_a->start_time = jiffies;
    data_b->start_time = jiffies;
    rdtscll (data_a->tsc_start);

    hrtimer_start (&data_a->timer, data_a->period, HRTIMER_MODE_REL);
    hrtimer_start (&data_b->timer, data_b->period, HRTIMER_MODE_REL);

    return 0;
}
static void __exit my_exit (void)
{
    /* delete any running timers */
    printk (KERN_INFO "Deleted timer A: rc = %d\n",
            hrtimer_cancel (&data_a->timer));
    printk (KERN_INFO "Deleted timer B: rc = %d\n",
            hrtimer_cancel (&data_b->timer));
    kfree (data_a);
    kfree (data_b);
    printk (KERN_INFO "Module successfully unloaded \n");
}

module_init (my_init);
module_exit (my_exit);

MODULE_AUTHOR ("Jerry Cooperstein");
MODULE_DESCRIPTION ("CLDD 1.0: lab5_hrtimer.c");
MODULE_LICENSE ("GPL v2");
```

11.6   Lab 6: Using kprobes to get statistics.

- Using **kprobes**, find out how often kernel timers are deleted before they are run.

- Examination of the kernel source discloses that the exported function `__mod_timer()` is called every time either `add_timer()` or `mod_timer()` is called.

- You can see how often timers are deleted by monitoring `del_timer()` and `del_timer_sync()`; however, on single processor systems, `del_timer_sync()` is not defined.

- Timers are frequent so you'll probably won't want to print out every time they are scheduled or deleted, but say every 100 times plus final statistics.

- Is it possible that timer deletion can be more frequent than timer scheduling?

lab6_kprobes.c

```
/* Copyright 2009, J Cooperstein coop@coopj.com (GPLv2) */

#include <linux/module.h>
#include <linux/init.h>
#include <linux/kprobes.h>
#include <linux/kallsyms.h>

static struct kprobe kp_mod_timer, kp_del_timer;
static int count_mod_timer = 0, count_del_timer = 0, count_del_timer_sync = 0;

static int do_count (int *count, char *name)
{
    (*count)++;
    if ((*count) % 100 == 1) {
        printk (KERN_INFO "count_%s=%8d    ", name, *count);
        printk (KERN_INFO "current->comm=%s, current->pid=%d\n", current->comm,
                current->pid);
    }
    return 0;
}
static int h_mod_timer (struct kprobe *p, struct pt_regs *regs)
{
    return do_count (&count_mod_timer, "mod_timer");
}
static int h_del_timer (struct kprobe *p, struct pt_regs *regs)
{
    return do_count (&count_del_timer, "del_timer");
}

#ifdef CONFIG_SMP
static struct kprobe kp_del_timer_sync;
static int h_del_timer_sync (struct kprobe *p, struct pt_regs *regs)
{
    return do_count (&count_del_timer_sync, "del_timer_sync");
}
#endif

static int __init setup_probe (struct kprobe *kp, const char *name,
                               int (*h_pre) (struct kprobe * kp,
                                             struct pt_regs * regs))
{
    kp->pre_handler = h_pre;
    kp->symbol_name = (char *)name;
    printk (KERN_INFO "handler for %s at loaded\n", name);
```

```
    if (register_kprobe (kp)) {
        printk (KERN_INFO "Failed to register kprobe, quitting\n");
        return -1;
    }
    return 0;
}

static int __init my_init (void)
{
    /* set the handler functions */

    if (setup_probe (&kp_mod_timer, "__mod_timer", h_mod_timer))
        return -1;
    if (setup_probe (&kp_del_timer, "del_timer", h_del_timer)) {
        unregister_kprobe (&kp_mod_timer);
        return -1;
    }
#ifdef CONFIG_SMP
    if (setup_probe (&kp_del_timer_sync, "del_timer_sync", h_del_timer_sync)) {
        unregister_kprobe (&kp_mod_timer);
        unregister_kprobe (&kp_del_timer);
        return -1;
    }
#endif

    printk (KERN_INFO "Hello: module loaded at 0x%p\n", my_init);

    return 0;
}

static void __exit my_exit (void)
{
    unregister_kprobe (&kp_mod_timer);
    unregister_kprobe (&kp_del_timer);
#ifdef CONFIG_SMP
    unregister_kprobe (&kp_del_timer_sync);
#endif
    printk (KERN_INFO "\n\n FINAL STATISTICS:\n\n");
    printk (KERN_INFO "count_mod_timer = %d\n", count_mod_timer);
    printk (KERN_INFO "count_del_timer = %d\n", count_del_timer);
    printk (KERN_INFO "count_del_timer_sync = %d\n", count_del_timer_sync);
    printk (KERN_INFO "Bye: module unloaded from 0x%p\n", my_exit);
}

module_init (my_init);
module_exit (my_exit);
MODULE_AUTHOR ("Jerry Cooperstein");
MODULE_DESCRIPTION ("CLDD 1.0: lab6_kprobes.c");
MODULE_LICENSE ("GPL v2");
```

11.7 Lab 7: Mutex Locking from a Timer.

- Write a simple module that loads a timer and takes out a mutex and then releases it when the timer runs.

- Doing this in an interrupt handler is supposed to be illegal. Here we have a softirq context; is that illegal too? Is this ignored, enforced, or warned against?

lab7_unlock.c

```
/* Copyright 2009, J Cooperstein coop@coopj.com (GPLv2) */
#include <linux/module.h>
#include <linux/init.h>
#include <linux/timer.h>
static DEFINE_MUTEX (my_mutex);

static struct timer_list timr;
static void ktfun (unsigned long var)
{
    printk (KERN_INFO "timer executing at jiffies=%ld\n", jiffies);
    mutex_lock (&my_mutex);
    printk (KERN_INFO "\nInit mutex in locked state, count=%d:\n",
            atomic_read (&my_mutex.count));
    mutex_unlock (&my_mutex);
    printk (KERN_INFO "\n mutex unlocked in timer, count=%d:\n",
            atomic_read (&my_mutex.count));
}

static int __init my_init (void)
{
    init_timer (&timr);
    timr.expires = jiffies + 3 * HZ;     /*3 seconds */
    timr.function = ktfun;
    add_timer (&timr);
    return 0;
}
static void __exit my_exit (void)
{
    /* delete any running timers */
    printk (KERN_INFO "Deleted timer A: rc = %d\n", del_timer_sync (&timr));
    printk (KERN_INFO "\nExiting with  mutex having count=%d:\n",
            atomic_read (&my_mutex.count));
}

module_init (my_init);
module_exit (my_exit);

MODULE_AUTHOR ("Jerry Cooperstein");
MODULE_DESCRIPTION ("CLDD 1.0: lab7_unlock.c");
MODULE_LICENSE ("GPL v2");
```

11.8   Lab 8: Executing a process from a timer.

- Modify your first lab so the long period timer executes a user process, such as **wall**.

lab8_exec.c

```
/* Copyright 2009, J Cooperstein coop@coopj.com (GPLv2) */

#include <linux/module.h>
#include <linux/timer.h>
#include <asm/msr.h>              /* needed for Time Stamp Counter functions */
#include <linux/init.h>
#include <linux/jiffies.h>

static char *str;                /* string to pass to module */
module_param (str, charp, S_IRUGO);

static unsigned long speed;      /* MHZ of CPU */

static struct timer_list timer_a, timer_b;

static struct kt_data
{
    unsigned long period;
    unsigned long start_time;   /* jiffies value when we first started the timer */
    u64 tsc_start;              /* TSC when timer was queued */
    u64 tsc_end;               /* TSC when timer is executed */
} *data_a, *data_b;

static void ktfun_a (unsigned long var)
{
    u64 ticks;
    int msecs;
    struct kt_data *tdata = (struct kt_data *)var;

    rdtscll (tdata->tsc_end);
    ticks = tdata->tsc_end - tdata->tsc_start;
    msecs = (unsigned long)ticks / (speed * 1000);
    printk (KERN_INFO
            "A: period = %ld  elapsed = %ld TSC ticks: %lld msecs = %d\n",
            tdata->period, jiffies - tdata->start_time, ticks, msecs);

    /* read the TSC for start time for the next cycle and resubmit */
    rdtscll (tdata->tsc_start);
    mod_timer (&timer_a, tdata->period + jiffies);
}
static void ktfun_b (unsigned long var)
{
    int rc;
    char *argv[] = { "wall", "This is a message from the Kernel", NULL };
    static char *envp[] = { NULL };
    struct kt_data *tdata = (struct kt_data *)var;

    printk (KERN_INFO "   B: period = %ld  elapsed = %ld \n", tdata->period,
```

```
                    jiffies - tdata->start_time);

    if (str)
        argv[1] = str;
    printk (KERN_INFO "Trying to execute %s %s \n", argv[0], argv[1]);
    rc = call_usermodehelper ("/usr/bin/wall", argv, envp, 0);
    if (rc)
        printk (KERN_INFO "Failed to execute %s %s\n", argv[0], argv[1]);

    /* resubmit */
    mod_timer (&timer_b, tdata->period + jiffies);
}

static int __init my_init (void)
{
    speed = cpu_khz / 1000;
    printk (KERN_INFO "CPU MHZ is found to be: %ld \n", speed);

    init_timer (&timer_a);
    init_timer (&timer_b);

    timer_a.function = ktfun_a;
    timer_b.function = ktfun_b;

    data_a = kmalloc (sizeof (*data_a), GFP_KERNEL);
    data_b = kmalloc (sizeof (*data_b), GFP_KERNEL);

    timer_a.data = (unsigned long)data_a;
    timer_b.data = (unsigned long)data_b;

    data_a->period = 1 * HZ;    /* short period, 1 second  */
    data_b->period = 10 * HZ;   /* longer period, 10 seconds */

    data_a->start_time = jiffies;
    data_b->start_time = jiffies;

    timer_a.expires = jiffies + data_a->period;
    timer_b.expires = jiffies + data_b->period;

    rdtscll (data_a->tsc_start);

    add_timer (&timer_a);
    add_timer (&timer_b);

    return 0;
}
static void __exit my_exit (void)
{
    /* delete any running timers */
    printk (KERN_INFO "Deleted timer A: rc = %d\n", del_timer_sync (&timer_a));
    printk (KERN_INFO "Deleted timer B: rc = %d\n", del_timer_sync (&timer_b));
    kfree (data_a);
    kfree (data_b);
    printk (KERN_INFO "Module successfully unloaded \n");
}
```

```
module_init (my_init);
module_exit (my_exit);

MODULE_AUTHOR ("Jerry Cooperstein");
MODULE_DESCRIPTION ("CLDD 1.0: lab8_exec.c");
MODULE_LICENSE ("GPL v2");
```

Chapter 12

Race Conditions and Synchronization Methods

12.1 Lab 1: Semaphore Contention

- Write three simple modules where the second and third one use a variable exported from the first one. The second and third one can be identical; just give them different names.

  Hint: You can use the macro `__stringify(KBUILD_MODNAME)` to print out the module name.

- You can implement this by making small modifications to your results from the modules exercise.

- The exported variable should be a semaphore. Have the first module initialize it in the unlocked state.

- The second (third) module should attempt to lock the semaphore, and if it is locked, fail to load; make sure you return the appropriate value from your initialization function.

- Make sure you release the semaphore in your cleanup function.

- Test by trying to load both modules simultaneously, and see if it is possible. Make sure you can load one of the modules after the other has been unloaded, to make sure you released the semaphore properly.

lab1_sem1.c

```
/* Copyright 2009, J Cooperstein coop@coopj.com (GPLv2) */

#include <linux/module.h>
#include <linux/init.h>
#include <asm/atomic.h>
#include <linux/version.h>
#if LINUX_VERSION_CODE < KERNEL_VERSION(2,6,27)
#include <asm/semaphore.h>
#else
#include <linux/semaphore.h>
#endif

DECLARE_MUTEX (my_sem);
EXPORT_SYMBOL (my_sem);

#if LINUX_VERSION_CODE < KERNEL_VERSION(2,6,26)
#define PRINT_COUNT(a) printk(KERN_INFO "semaphore_count=%d\n", atomic_read(&a));
#else
#define PRINT_COUNT(a) printk(KERN_INFO "semaphore_count=%u\n", a);
#endif

static int __init my_init (void)
{
    printk (KERN_INFO "\nInitializing semaphore, ");
    PRINT_COUNT (my_sem.count);
    return 0;
}

static void __exit my_exit (void)
{
    printk (KERN_INFO "\nExiting semaphore, ");
    PRINT_COUNT (my_sem.count);
}

module_init (my_init);
module_exit (my_exit);

MODULE_AUTHOR ("Jerry Cooperstein");
MODULE_DESCRIPTION ("CLDD 1.0: lab1_sem1.c");
MODULE_LICENSE ("GPL v2");
```

lab1_sem2.c

```
/* Copyright 2009, J Cooperstein coop@coopj.com (GPLv2) */

#include <linux/module.h>
#include <linux/init.h>
#include <asm/atomic.h>
```

```
#include <linux/errno.h>
#include <linux/version.h>
#if LINUX_VERSION_CODE < KERNEL_VERSION(2,6,27)
#include <asm/semaphore.h>
#else
#include <linux/semaphore.h>
#endif

static char *modname = __stringify (KBUILD_BASENAME);

extern struct semaphore my_sem;

#if LINUX_VERSION_CODE < KERNEL_VERSION(2,6,26)
#define PRINT_COUNT(a) printk(KERN_INFO "sempaphore_count=%d\n", atomic_read(&a));
#else
#define PRINT_COUNT(a) printk(KERN_INFO "sempaphore_count=%u\n", a);
#endif

static int __init my_init (void)
{
    printk (KERN_INFO "Trying to load module %s\n", modname);
    PRINT_COUNT (my_sem.count);

    if (down_trylock (&my_sem)) {
        printk (KERN_WARNING "Not loading the module; down_trylock() failed\n");
        return -EBUSY;
    }
    printk (KERN_INFO "\nGrabbed semaphore in %s, ", modname);
    PRINT_COUNT (my_sem.count);

    return 0;
}

static void __exit my_exit (void)
{
    up (&my_sem);
    printk (KERN_INFO "\nExiting semaphore in %s, ", modname);
    PRINT_COUNT (my_sem.count);
}

module_init (my_init);
module_exit (my_exit);

MODULE_AUTHOR ("Jerry Cooperstein");
MODULE_DESCRIPTION ("CLDD 1.0: lab1_sem2.c");
MODULE_LICENSE ("GPL v2");
```

lab1_sem3.c

```
 /* Copyright 2009, J Cooperstein coop@coopj.com (GPLv2) */

#include <linux/module.h>
#include <linux/init.h>
#include <asm/atomic.h>
#include <linux/errno.h>
```

```
#include <linux/version.h>
#if LINUX_VERSION_CODE < KERNEL_VERSION(2,6,27)
#include <asm/semaphore.h>
#else
#include <linux/semaphore.h>
#endif

static char *modname = __stringify (KBUILD_BASENAME);

extern struct semaphore my_sem;

#if LINUX_VERSION_CODE < KERNEL_VERSION(2,6,26)
#define PRINT_COUNT(a) printk(KERN_INFO "sempaphore_count=%d\n", atomic_read(&a));
#else
#define PRINT_COUNT(a) printk(KERN_INFO "sempaphore_count=%u\n", a);
#endif

static int __init my_init (void)
{
    printk (KERN_INFO "Trying to load module %s\n", modname);
    PRINT_COUNT (my_sem.count);

    if (down_trylock (&my_sem)) {
        printk (KERN_WARNING "Not loading the module; down_trylock() failed\n");
        return -EBUSY;
    }
    printk (KERN_INFO "\nGrabbed semaphore in %s, ", modname);
    PRINT_COUNT (my_sem.count);

    return 0;
}

static void __exit my_exit (void)
{
    up (&my_sem);
    printk (KERN_INFO "\nExiting semaphore in %s, ", modname);
    PRINT_COUNT (my_sem.count);
}

module_init (my_init);
module_exit (my_exit);

MODULE_AUTHOR ("Jerry Cooperstein");
MODULE_DESCRIPTION ("CLDD 1.0: lab1_sem3.c");
MODULE_LICENSE ("GPL v2");
```

12.2   Lab 2: Mutex Contention

- Now do the same thing using **mutexes** instead of semaphores.

lab2_mutex1.c

```
/* Copyright 2009, J Cooperstein coop@coopj.com (GPLv2) */
```

```
#include <linux/module.h>
#include <linux/init.h>

DEFINE_MUTEX (my_mutex);
EXPORT_SYMBOL (my_mutex);

static int __init my_init (void)
{
    printk (KERN_INFO "\nInit mutex in unlocked state, count=%d:\n",
            atomic_read (&my_mutex.count));
    return 0;
}
static void __exit my_exit (void)
{
    printk (KERN_INFO "\nExiting with  mutex having count=%d:\n",
            atomic_read (&my_mutex.count));
}

module_init (my_init);
module_exit (my_exit);

MODULE_AUTHOR ("Tatsuo Kawasaki");
MODULE_DESCRIPTION ("CLDD 1.0: lab2_mutex1.c");
MODULE_LICENSE ("GPL v2");
```

lab2_mutex2.c

```
/* Copyright 2009, J Cooperstein coop@coopj.com (GPLv2) */

#include <linux/module.h>
#include <linux/init.h>
#include <linux/mutex.h>
#include <asm/atomic.h>
#include <linux/errno.h>

extern struct mutex my_mutex;

static char *modname = __stringify (KBUILD_BASENAME);

static int __init my_init (void)
{
    printk (KERN_INFO "Trying to load module %s\n", modname);
    printk (KERN_INFO "\n%s start count=%d:\n", modname,
            atomic_read (&my_mutex.count));
#if 1
    if (mutex_lock_interruptible (&my_mutex)) {
        printk (KERN_INFO "mutex unlocked - wake up \n");
        return -1;
    }
#else
    mutex_lock (&my_mutex);
#endif
    printk (KERN_INFO "\n%s mutex put mutex, count=%d:\n",
            modname, atomic_read (&my_mutex.count));
```

```
    return 0;
}

static void __exit my_exit (void)
{
    mutex_unlock (&my_mutex);
    printk (KERN_INFO "\n%s mutex end count=%d:\n",
            modname, atomic_read (&my_mutex.count));
}

module_init (my_init);
module_exit (my_exit);

MODULE_AUTHOR ("Tatsuo Kawasaki");
MODULE_DESCRIPTION ("CLDD 1.0: lab2_mutex2.c");
MODULE_LICENSE ("GPL v2");
```

lab2_mutex3.c

```
 /* Copyright 2009, J Cooperstein coop@coopj.com (GPLv2) */

#include <linux/module.h>
#include <linux/init.h>
#include <linux/mutex.h>
#include <asm/atomic.h>
#include <linux/errno.h>

extern struct mutex my_mutex;

static char *modname = __stringify (KBUILD_BASENAME);

static int __init my_init (void)
{
    printk (KERN_INFO "Trying to load module %s\n", modname);
    printk (KERN_INFO "\n%s start count=%d:\n", modname,
            atomic_read (&my_mutex.count));
#if 1
    if (mutex_lock_interruptible (&my_mutex)) {
        printk (KERN_INFO "mutex unlocked - wake up \n");
        return -1;
    }
#else
    mutex_lock (&my_mutex);
#endif
    printk (KERN_INFO "\n%s mutex put mutex, count=%d:\n",
            modname, atomic_read (&my_mutex.count));

    return 0;
}

static void __exit my_exit (void)
{
    mutex_unlock (&my_mutex);
    printk (KERN_INFO "\n%s mutex end count=%d:\n",
```

```
                    modname, atomic_read (&my_mutex.count));
}

module_init (my_init);
module_exit (my_exit);

MODULE_AUTHOR ("Tatsuo Kawasaki");
MODULE_DESCRIPTION ("CLDD 1.0: lab2_mutex3.c");
MODULE_LICENSE ("GPL v2");
```

12.3   Lab 3: Mutex Unlocking from an Interrupt.

- Modify the simple interrupt sharing lab to have a mutex taken out and then released in the interrupt handler.

- This is supposed to be illegal. Is this ignored, enforced, or warned against? Why?

lab3_unlock.c

```
/* Copyright 2009, J Cooperstein coop@coopj.com (GPLv2) */

#include <linux/module.h>
#include <linux/init.h>
#include <linux/interrupt.h>

static DEFINE_MUTEX (my_mutex);
#define SHARED_IRQ 19
static int irq = SHARED_IRQ, my_dev_id, irq_counter = 0;
module_param (irq, int, S_IRUGO);

static irqreturn_t my_interrupt (int irq, void *dev_id)
{
    irq_counter++;
    mutex_lock (&my_mutex);
    printk (KERN_INFO "\nInit mutex in locked state, count=%d:\n",
            atomic_read (&my_mutex.count));
    printk (KERN_INFO "In the ISR: counter = %d\n", irq_counter);
    mutex_unlock (&my_mutex);
    return IRQ_NONE;            /* we return IRQ_NONE because we are just observing */
}
static int __init my_init (void)
{
    if (request_irq
        (irq, my_interrupt, IRQF_SHARED, "my_interrupt", &my_dev_id))
        return -1;
    printk (KERN_INFO "Successfully loading ISR handler\n");

    return 0;
}
static void __exit my_exit (void)
{
    printk (KERN_INFO "\nExiting with  mutex having count=%d:\n",
            atomic_read (&my_mutex.count));
```

```
    synchronize_irq (irq);
    free_irq (irq, &my_dev_id);
    printk (KERN_INFO "Successfully unloading,  irq_counter = %d\n",
            irq_counter);
}

module_init (my_init);
module_exit (my_exit);

MODULE_AUTHOR ("Jerry Cooperstein");
MODULE_DESCRIPTION ("CLDD 1.0: lab3_unlock.c");
MODULE_LICENSE ("GPL v2");
```

Chapter 13

ioctls

13.1 Lab 1: Using ioctl's to pass data

- Write a simple module that uses the **ioctl** directional information to pass a data buffer of fixed size back and forth between the driver and the user-space program.

- The size and direction(s) of the data transfer should be encoded in the command number.

- You'll need to write a user-space application to test this.

lab_char.h

lab1_ioctl_data.c

```
/* Copyright 2009, J Cooperstein coop@coopj.com (GPLv2) */

#include <linux/module.h>
#include "lab_char.h"

struct my_data
{
```

```
    int i;
    long x;
    char s[256];
};

static struct my_data my_data = {
    .i = -100,
    .x = 100,
    .s = "original string",
};

#define MYIOC_TYPE 'k'

static long
mycdrv_unlocked_ioctl (struct file *fp, unsigned int cmd, unsigned long arg)
{
    int size, rc, direction;
    void __user *ioargp = (void __user *)arg;

    if (_IOC_TYPE (cmd) != MYIOC_TYPE) {
        printk (KERN_INFO " got invalid case, CMD=%d\n", cmd);
        return -EINVAL;
    }

    direction = _IOC_DIR (cmd);
    size = _IOC_SIZE (cmd);

    switch (direction) {

    case _IOC_WRITE:
        printk
            (KERN_INFO
             " reading = %d bytes from user-space and writing to device\n",
             size);
        rc = copy_from_user (&my_data, ioargp, size);
        printk
            (KERN_INFO
             "    my_data.i = %d\n    (int)my_data.x = %ld\n    my_data.s = %s\n",
             my_data.i, my_data.x, my_data.s);
        return rc;
        break;

    case _IOC_READ:
        printk (KERN_INFO
                " reading device and writing = %d bytes to user-space\n", size);
        printk
            (KERN_INFO
             "    my_data.i = %d\n    (int)my_data.x = %ld\n    my_data.s = %s\n",
             my_data.i, my_data.x, my_data.s);
        rc = copy_to_user (ioargp, &my_data, size);
        return rc;
        break;

    default:
        printk (KERN_INFO " got invalid case, CMD=%d\n", cmd);
```

```
            return -EINVAL;
    }
}


static const struct file_operations mycdrv_fops = {
    .owner = THIS_MODULE,
    .unlocked_ioctl = mycdrv_unlocked_ioctl,
    .open = mycdrv_generic_open,
    .release = mycdrv_generic_release
};

module_init (my_generic_init);
module_exit (my_generic_exit);

MODULE_AUTHOR ("Jerry Cooperstein");
MODULE_DESCRIPTION ("CLDD 1.0: lab1_ioctl_data.c");
MODULE_LICENSE ("GPL v2");
```

lab1_ioctl_data_test.c

```
/*
 * Using ioctl's to pass data (User-space application)
 */

#include <stdio.h>
#include <stdlib.h>
#include <unistd.h>
#include <fcntl.h>
#include <sys/ioctl.h>
#include <string.h>

struct my_data
{
    int i;
    long x;
    char s[256];
} my_data;

#define MYIOC_TYPE 'k'

int main (int argc, char *argv[])
{
    int fd, rc;
    int MY_IOCTL;
    char *nodename = "/dev/mycdrv";

    /* open the device node */

    if (argc > 1)
        nodename = argv[1];
    fd = open (nodename, O_RDWR);
    printf (" I opened the device node, file descriptor = %d\n", fd);

    /* retrieve the original values; */
```

```
MY_IOCTL = (int)_IOR (MYIOC_TYPE, 1, struct my_data);
rc = ioctl (fd, MY_IOCTL, &my_data);
printf ("\n rc from ioctl reading = %d \n\n", rc);
printf
    ("    my_data.i = %d\n    my_data.x = %ld\n    my_data.s = %s\n",
     my_data.i, my_data.x, my_data.s);

/* fill up the data structure */

strcpy (my_data.s, "a string");
my_data.i = 10;
my_data.x = -700;
printf ("\n Sending from user-space:\n");
printf
    ("    my_data.i = %d\n    my_data.x = %ld\n    my_data.s = %s\n",
     my_data.i, my_data.x, my_data.s);

/* send to the device */

MY_IOCTL = (int)_IOW (MYIOC_TYPE, 1, struct my_data);
rc = ioctl (fd, MY_IOCTL, &my_data);
printf ("\n rc from ioctl = %d \n\n", rc);

/* reread device and see if it got through */

MY_IOCTL = (int)_IOR (MYIOC_TYPE, 1, struct my_data);
rc = ioctl (fd, MY_IOCTL, &my_data);
printf ("\n rc from ioctl reading = %d \n\n", rc);
printf
    ("    my_data.i = %d\n    my_data.x = %ld\n    my_data.s = %s\n",
     my_data.i, my_data.x, my_data.s);

close (fd);
exit (0);

}
```

13.2   Lab 2: Using ioctl's to pass data of variable length.

- Extend the previous exercise to send a buffer whose length is determined at run time. You will probably need to use the _IOC macro directly in the user-space program. (See linux/ioctl.h.)

lab_char.h

lab2_ioctl_vardata.c

```
/* Copyright 2009, J Cooperstein coop@coopj.com (GPLv2) */

#include <linux/module.h>
#include "lab_char.h"

#define MYIOC_TYPE 'k'
```

```
static inline long
mycdrv_unlocked_ioctl (struct file *fp, unsigned int cmd, unsigned long arg)
{
    int i, rc, direction;
    int size;
    char *buffer;
    void __user *ioargp = (void __user *)arg;

    /* make sure it is a valid command */

    if (_IOC_TYPE (cmd) != MYIOC_TYPE) {
        printk (KERN_WARNING " got invalid case, CMD=%d\n", cmd);
        return -EINVAL;
    }

    /* get the size of the buffer and kmalloc it */

    size = _IOC_SIZE (cmd);
    buffer = kmalloc ((size_t) size, GFP_KERNEL);
    if (!buffer) {
        printk (KERN_ERR "Kmalloc failed for buffer\n");
        return -ENOMEM;
    }

    /* fill it with X */

    memset (buffer, 'X', size);

    direction = _IOC_DIR (cmd);

    switch (direction) {

    case _IOC_WRITE:
        printk
            (KERN_INFO
             " reading = %d bytes from user-space and writing to device\n",
             size);
        rc = copy_from_user (buffer, ioargp, size);
        printk (KERN_INFO "rc from copy_from_user = %d\n", rc);
        break;

    case _IOC_READ:
        printk (KERN_INFO
                " reading device and writing = %d bytes to user-space\n", size);
        rc = copy_to_user (ioargp, buffer, size);
        printk (KERN_INFO "rc from copy_to_user = %d\n", rc);
        break;

    default:
        printk (KERN_WARNING " got invalid case, CMD=%d\n", cmd);
        return -EINVAL;
    }
    for (i = 0; i < size; i++)
        printk (KERN_INFO "%c", buffer[i]);
    printk (KERN_INFO "\n");
```

```
    if (buffer)
        kfree (buffer);
    return rc;
}

static const struct file_operations mycdrv_fops = {
    .owner = THIS_MODULE,
    .unlocked_ioctl = mycdrv_unlocked_ioctl,
    .open = mycdrv_generic_open,
    .release = mycdrv_generic_release
};

module_init (my_generic_init);
module_exit (my_generic_exit);

MODULE_AUTHOR ("Jerry Cooperstein");
MODULE_DESCRIPTION ("CLDD 1.0: lab2_ioctl_vardata.c");
MODULE_LICENSE ("GPL v2");
```

lab2_ioctl_vardata_test.c

```
 /* Copyright 2009, J Cooperstein coop@coopj.com (GPLv2) */

#include <stdio.h>
#include <stdlib.h>
#include <unistd.h>
#include <fcntl.h>
#include <sys/ioctl.h>
#include <malloc.h>
#include <string.h>

#define MYIOC_TYPE 'k'
#define MY_IOW(type,nr,size) _IOC(_IOC_WRITE,(type),(nr),size)
#define MY_IOR(type,nr,size) _IOC(_IOC_READ, (type),(nr),size)

int main (int argc, char *argv[])
{
    int fd, rc, i, lbuf;
    char *buffer, *nodename = "/dev/mycdrv";
    int MYIOC_X;

    /* open the device node */

    if (argc > 1)
        nodename = argv[1];
    fd = open (nodename, O_RDWR);
    printf (" I opened the device node, file descriptor = %d\n", fd);

    /* how big should the buffer be? */
    lbuf = 1000;
    if (argc > 2)
        lbuf = atoi (argv[1]);
    printf (" I am going to send back and forth a buffer of %d bytes\n", lbuf);
```

```
/* malloc the buffer */
buffer = malloc (lbuf);

/* send the IOCTL and read the contents from the kernel */
printf ("\n Getting data from the kernel:\n");
MYIOC_X = (int)MY_IOR (MYIOC_TYPE, 1, lbuf);
rc = ioctl (fd, MYIOC_X, buffer);
printf ("\n rc from ioctl = %d \n\n", rc);

printf (" buffer in user-space is =\n    ");
for (i = 0; i < lbuf; i++)
    printf ("%c", buffer[i]);
printf ("\n");

/*  clear it and send it back */

memset (buffer, '0', lbuf);

printf ("\n Sending data to the kernel:\n");
MYIOC_X = (int)MY_IOW (MYIOC_TYPE, 1, lbuf);
rc = ioctl (fd, MYIOC_X, buffer);
printf ("\n rc from ioctl = %d \n\n", rc);

printf (" buffer in user-space is =\n    ");
for (i = 0; i < lbuf; i++)
    printf ("%c", buffer[i]);
printf ("\n");

close (fd);
exit (0);
}
```

13.3   Lab 3: Using ioctl's to send signals.

- It is sometimes desirable to send a signal to an application from within the kernel. The function for doing this is:

  ```
  int send_sig (int signal, struct task_struct *tsk, int priv);
  ```

  where **signal** is the signal to send, **tsk** points to the task structure corresponding to the process to which the signal should be sent, and **priv** indicates the privilege level (0 for user applications, 1 for the kernel.)

- Write a character driver that has three **ioctl** commands:

  - Set the process ID to which signals should be sent.
  - Set the signal which should be sent.
  - Send the signal.

- You'll also have to develop the sending program.

  - If given no arguments it should send **SIGKILL** to the current process.

  – If given one argument it should set the process ID to send signals to.

  – If given two arguments it should also set the signal.

lab_char.h
lab3_ioctl_signal.c

```
 /* Copyright 2009, J Cooperstein coop@coopj.com (GPLv2) */

#include <linux/module.h>
#include "lab_char.h"

#define MYIOC_TYPE 'k'
#define MYIOC_SETPID   _IO(MYIOC_TYPE,1)
#define MYIOC_SETSIG   _IO(MYIOC_TYPE,2)
#define MYIOC_SENDSIG  _IO(MYIOC_TYPE,3)

static int sig_pid = 0;
static struct task_struct *sig_tsk = NULL;
static int sig_tosend = SIGKILL;

static inline long
mycdrv_unlocked_ioctl (struct file *fp, unsigned int cmd, unsigned long arg)
{
    int retval;
    switch (cmd) {
    case MYIOC_SETPID:
        sig_pid = (int)arg;
        printk (KERN_INFO " Setting pid to send signals to, sigpid = %d\n",
                sig_pid);
        /*      sig_tsk = find_task_by_vpid (sig_pid); */
        sig_tsk = pid_task (find_vpid(sig_pid),PIDTYPE_PID);
        break;
    case MYIOC_SETSIG:
        sig_tosend = (int)arg;
        printk (KERN_INFO " Setting signal to send as: %d \n", sig_tosend);
        break;
    case MYIOC_SENDSIG:
        if (!sig_tsk) {
            printk (KERN_INFO "You haven't set the pid; using current\n");
            sig_tsk = current;
            sig_pid = (int)current->pid;
        }
        printk (KERN_INFO " Sending signal %d to process ID %d\n", sig_tosend,
                sig_pid);
        retval = send_sig (sig_tosend, sig_tsk, 0);
        printk (KERN_INFO "retval = %d\n", retval);

        break;
    default:
        printk (KERN_INFO " got invalid case, CMD=%d\n", cmd);
        return -EINVAL;
    }
    return 0;
```

```
}

static const struct file_operations mycdrv_fops = {
    .owner = THIS_MODULE,
    .unlocked_ioctl = mycdrv_unlocked_ioctl,
    .open = mycdrv_generic_open,
    .release = mycdrv_generic_release
};

module_init (my_generic_init);
module_exit (my_generic_exit);

MODULE_AUTHOR ("Jerry Cooperstein");
MODULE_DESCRIPTION ("CLDD 1.0: lab3_ioctl_signal.c");
MODULE_LICENSE ("GPL v2");
```

lab3_ioctl_signal_test.c

```
 /* Copyright 2009, J Cooperstein coop@coopj.com (GPLv2) */

#include <stdio.h>
#include <stdlib.h>
#include <unistd.h>
#include <fcntl.h>
#include <sys/ioctl.h>
#include <string.h>
#include <signal.h>

#define MYIOC_TYPE 'k'
#define MYIOC_SETPID   (int)_IO(MYIOC_TYPE,1)
#define MYIOC_SETSIG   (int)_IO(MYIOC_TYPE,2)
#define MYIOC_SENDSIG  (int)_IO(MYIOC_TYPE,3)
#define SIGDEFAULT SIGKILL

int main (int argc, char *argv[])
{
    int fd, rc;
    unsigned long pid, sig;
    char *nodename = "/dev/mycdrv";

    /* set up the message */
    pid = getpid ();
    sig = SIGDEFAULT;

    if (argc > 1)
        pid = atoi (argv[1]);

    if (argc > 2)
        sig = atoi (argv[2]);

    if (argc > 3)
        nodename = argv[3];

    /* open the device node */
```

```
    fd = open (nodename, O_RDWR);
    printf (" I opened the device node, file descriptor = %d\n", fd);

    /* send the IOCTL to set the PID */

    rc = ioctl (fd, MYIOC_SETPID, pid);
    printf ("\n\n rc from ioctl setting pid is = %d \n\n", rc);

    /* send the IOCTL to set the signal */

    rc = ioctl (fd, MYIOC_SETSIG, sig);
    printf ("\n\n rc from ioctl setting signal is = %d \n\n", rc);

    /* send the IOCTL to send the signal */

    rc = ioctl (fd, MYIOC_SENDSIG, "anything");
    printf ("\n\n rc from ioctl sending signal is = %d \n\n", rc);

    /* ok go home */
    close (fd);
    printf ("\n\n FINISHED, TERMINATING NORMALLY\n");

    exit (0);
}
```

Chapter 14

The proc Filesystem

14.1 Lab 1: /proc/kcore

- Try to remove /proc/kcore. Is there is a permissions problem? If so try to reset them with chmod 666 /proc/kcore and try again.

- If it doesn't work, explain what this file is, and why it is difficult (if not impossible) to remove.

If you use **cat** to test your read entries in the following labs, you may find the unexpected behaviour that the entry point is always called twice, even when you signal end of file. (You can use **strace** to verify this happens with **all** proc entries and is not an error in your module.) This is due to the way **cat** is written and is nothing to worry about.

14.2   Lab 2: Using the /proc filesystem.

- Write a module that creates a **/proc** filesystem entry and can read and write to it.

- When you read from the entry, you should obtain the value of some parameter set in your module.

- When you write to the entry, you should modify that value, which should then be reflected in a subsequent read.

- Make sure you remove the entry when you unload your module. What happens if you don't and you try to access the entry after the module has been removed?

- The solution shows how to create the entry in the /proc directory and also in the /proc/driver directory.

lab2_proc.c

```
/* Copyright 2009, J Cooperstein coop@coopj.com (GPLv2) */

#include <linux/module.h>
#include <linux/proc_fs.h>
#include <linux/uaccess.h>
#include <linux/init.h>

#if 0
#define NODE "my_proc"
#else
#define NODE "driver/my_proc"
#endif

static int param = 100;
static struct proc_dir_entry *my_proc;

static int
my_proc_read (char *page, char **start, off_t off, int count,
              int *eof, void *data)
{
    *eof = 1;
    return sprintf (page, "%d\n", param);
}

static int
my_proc_write (struct file *file, const char __user * buffer,
              unsigned long count, void *data)
{
    char *str;
    str = kmalloc ((size_t) count, GFP_KERNEL);
    if (copy_from_user (str, buffer, count)) {
        kfree (str);
        return -EFAULT;
    }
    sscanf (str, "%d", &param);
    printk (KERN_INFO "param has been set to %d\n", param);
```

```
        kfree (str);
        return count;
}

static int __init my_init (void)
{
    my_proc = create_proc_entry (NODE, S_IRUGO | S_IWUSR, NULL);
    if (!my_proc) {
        printk (KERN_ERR "I failed to make %s\n", NODE);
        return -1;
    }
    printk (KERN_INFO "I created %s\n", NODE);
    my_proc->read_proc = my_proc_read;
    my_proc->write_proc = my_proc_write;
    return 0;
}

static void __exit my_exit (void)
{
    if (my_proc) {
        remove_proc_entry (NODE, NULL);
        printk (KERN_INFO "Removed %s\n", NODE);
    }
}

module_init (my_init);
module_exit (my_exit);

MODULE_AUTHOR ("Jerry Cooperstein");
MODULE_DESCRIPTION ("CLDD 1.0: lab2_proc.c");
MODULE_LICENSE ("GPL v2");
```

14.3   Lab 3: Making your own subdirectory in /proc.

- Write a module that creates your own **proc** filesystem subdirectory and creates at least two entries under it.

- As in the first exercise, reading an entry should obtain a parameter value, and writing it should reset it.

- You may use the `data` element in the `proc_dir_entry` structure to use the same callback functions for multiple entries.

lab3_proc_solA.c

```
/* Copyright 2009, J Cooperstein coop@coopj.com (GPLv2) */

#include <linux/module.h>
#include <linux/proc_fs.h>
#include <linux/uaccess.h>
#include <linux/init.h>

#define NODE_DIR "my_proc_dir"
```

```
#define NODE_1 "param_1"
#define NODE_2 "param_2"

static int param_1 = 100, param_2 = 200;
static struct proc_dir_entry *my_proc_dir, *my_proc_1, *my_proc_2;

static int
my_proc_read (char *page, char **start, off_t off, int count,
              int *eof, void *data)
{
    *eof = 1;
    if (data == my_proc_1)
        return sprintf (page, "%d\n", param_1);
    if (data == my_proc_2)
        return sprintf (page, "%d\n", param_2);
    return -EINVAL;
}
static int
my_proc_write (struct file *file, const char __user * buffer,
               unsigned long count, void *data)
{
    char *str = kmalloc ((size_t) count, GFP_KERNEL);

    if (copy_from_user (str, buffer, count)) {
        kfree (str);
        return -EFAULT;
    }

    if (data == my_proc_1) {
        sscanf (str, "%d", &param_1);
        printk (KERN_INFO "param_1 has been set to %d\n", param_1);
        kfree (str);
        return count;
    }

    if (data == my_proc_2) {
        sscanf (str, "%d", &param_2);
        printk (KERN_INFO "param_2 has been set to %d\n", param_2);
        kfree (str);
        return count;
    }
    kfree (str);
    return -EINVAL;
}
static int __init my_init (void)
{
    my_proc_dir = proc_mkdir (NODE_DIR, NULL);
    if (!my_proc_dir) {
        printk (KERN_ERR "I failed to make %s\n", NODE_DIR);
        return -1;
    }
    printk (KERN_INFO "I created %s\n", NODE_DIR);

    my_proc_1 = create_proc_entry (NODE_1, S_IRUGO | S_IWUSR, my_proc_dir);
    if (!my_proc_1) {
```

```
            printk (KERN_ERR "I failed to make %s\n", NODE_1);
            remove_proc_entry (NODE_DIR, NULL);
            return -1;
    }
    printk (KERN_INFO "I created %s\n", NODE_1);
    my_proc_1->read_proc = my_proc_read;
    my_proc_1->write_proc = my_proc_write;
    my_proc_1->data = my_proc_1;

    my_proc_2 = create_proc_entry (NODE_2, S_IRUGO | S_IWUSR, my_proc_dir);
    if (!my_proc_2) {
            printk (KERN_ERR "I failed to make %s\n", NODE_2);
            remove_proc_entry (NODE_1, my_proc_dir);
            remove_proc_entry (NODE_DIR, NULL);
            return -1;
    }
    printk (KERN_INFO "I created %s\n", NODE_2);
    my_proc_2->read_proc = my_proc_read;
    my_proc_2->write_proc = my_proc_write;
    my_proc_2->data = my_proc_2;
    return 0;
}

static void __exit my_exit (void)
{
    if (my_proc_1) {
            remove_proc_entry (NODE_1, my_proc_dir);
            printk (KERN_INFO "Removed %s\n", NODE_1);
    }
    if (my_proc_2) {
            remove_proc_entry (NODE_2, my_proc_dir);
            printk (KERN_INFO "Removed %s\n", NODE_2);
    }
    if (my_proc_dir) {
            remove_proc_entry (NODE_DIR, NULL);
            printk (KERN_INFO "Removed %s\n", NODE_DIR);
    }
}

module_init (my_init);
module_exit (my_exit);

MODULE_AUTHOR ("Jerry Cooperstein");
MODULE_DESCRIPTION ("CLDD 1.0: lab3_proc_solA.c");
MODULE_LICENSE ("GPL v2");
```

lab3_proc_solB.c

```
/* Copyright 2009, J Cooperstein coop@coopj.com (GPLv2) */

#include <linux/module.h>
#include <linux/proc_fs.h>
#include <linux/uaccess.h>
#include <linux/init.h>
```

```
#define NODE_DIR "my_proc_dir"
#define NODE_1 "param_1"
#define NODE_2 "param_2"

static int param_1 = 100, param_2 = 200;
static struct proc_dir_entry *my_proc_dir, *my_proc_1, *my_proc_2;

static int
my_proc_read1 (char *page, char **start, off_t off, int count,
                int *eof, void *data)
{
    *eof = 1;
    return sprintf (page, "%d\n", param_1);
}
static int
my_proc_read2 (char *page, char **start, off_t off, int count,
                int *eof, void *data)
{
    *eof = 1;
    return sprintf (page, "%d\n", param_2);
}
static int
my_proc_write1 (struct file *file, const char __user * buffer,
                unsigned long count, void *data)
{
    char *str = kmalloc ((size_t) count, GFP_KERNEL);

    if (copy_from_user (str, buffer, count)) {
        kfree (str);
        return -EFAULT;
    }

    sscanf (str, "%d", &param_1);
    printk (KERN_INFO "param_1 has been set to %d\n", param_1);
    kfree (str);
    return count;
}

static int
my_proc_write2 (struct file *file, const char __user * buffer,
                unsigned long count, void *data)
{
    char *str = kmalloc ((size_t) count, GFP_KERNEL);
    if (copy_from_user (str, buffer, count))
        return -EFAULT;
    sscanf (str, "%d", &param_2);
    printk (KERN_INFO "param_2 has been set to %d\n", param_2);
    kfree (str);
    return count;
}
static int __init my_init (void)
{
    my_proc_dir = proc_mkdir (NODE_DIR, NULL);
    if (!my_proc_dir) {
        printk (KERN_ERR "I failed to make %s\n", NODE_DIR);
```

```
            return -1;
        }
        printk (KERN_INFO "I created %s\n", NODE_DIR);

        my_proc_1 = create_proc_entry (NODE_1, S_IRUGO | S_IWUSR, my_proc_dir);
        if (!my_proc_1) {
            printk (KERN_ERR "I failed to make %s\n", NODE_1);
            remove_proc_entry (NODE_DIR, NULL);
            return -1;
        }
        printk (KERN_INFO "I created %s\n", NODE_1);
        my_proc_1->read_proc = my_proc_read1;
        my_proc_1->write_proc = my_proc_write1;

        my_proc_2 = create_proc_entry (NODE_2, S_IRUGO | S_IWUSR, my_proc_dir);
        if (!my_proc_2) {
            printk (KERN_ERR "I failed to make %s\n", NODE_2);
            remove_proc_entry (NODE_1, my_proc_dir);
            remove_proc_entry (NODE_DIR, NULL);
            return -1;
        }
        printk (KERN_INFO "I created %s\n", NODE_2);
        my_proc_2->read_proc = my_proc_read2;
        my_proc_2->write_proc = my_proc_write2;
        return 0;
}

static void __exit my_exit (void)
{
        if (my_proc_1) {
            remove_proc_entry (NODE_1, my_proc_dir);
            printk (KERN_INFO "Removed %s\n", NODE_1);
        }
        if (my_proc_2) {
            remove_proc_entry (NODE_2, my_proc_dir);
            printk (KERN_INFO "Removed %s\n", NODE_2);
        }
        if (my_proc_dir) {
            remove_proc_entry (NODE_DIR, NULL);
            printk (KERN_INFO "Removed %s\n", NODE_DIR);
        }
}

module_init (my_init);
module_exit (my_exit);

MODULE_AUTHOR ("Jerry Cooperstein");
MODULE_DESCRIPTION ("CLDD 1.0: lab3_proc_solB.c");
MODULE_LICENSE ("GPL v2");
```

14.4   Lab 4: Using /proc to send signals.

- It is sometimes desirable to send a signal to an application from within the kernel. The function for doing this is:

  ```
  int send_sig (int signal, struct task_struct *tsk, int priv);
  ```

  where `signal` is the signal to send, `tsk` points to the task structure corresponding to the process to which the signal should be sent, and `priv` indicates the privilege level (0 for user applications, 1 for the kernel.)

- Write a module that opens up two entries in the `proc` file system.

  - When the first entry is written to, it sets the process ID of the process which is registered to receive signals via this mechanism.

  - When the second entry is written to, it gets the signal to be delivered and then sends it.

  - Reading either entry simply shows the current values of these parameters.

lab4_proc_sig_solA.c

```
/* Copyright 2009, J Cooperstein coop@coopj.com (GPLv2) */

#include <linux/module.h>
#include <linux/proc_fs.h>
#include <linux/uaccess.h>
#include <linux/init.h>
#include <linux/signal.h>
#include <linux/sched.h>

#define NODE_DIR "my_sig_dir"
#define NODE_1 "pid"
#define NODE_2 "signal"

static int sig_pid = -1, sig_tosend = SIGUSR1;
static struct task_struct *sig_tsk = NULL;
static struct proc_dir_entry *proc_sigdir, *proc_pid, *proc_signal;

static int
my_proc_read (char *page, char **start, off_t off, int count,
              int *eof, void *data)
{
    *eof = 1;
    if (data == proc_pid)
        return sprintf (page, "%d\n", sig_pid);
    if (data == proc_signal)
        return sprintf (page, "%d\n", sig_tosend);
    return -EINVAL;
}
static int
my_proc_write (struct file *file, const char __user * buffer,
               unsigned long count, void *data)
{
    int retval;
```

```
    char *str = kmalloc ((size_t) count, GFP_KERNEL);

    /* copy the string from user-space to kernel-space */

    if (copy from user (str, buffer, count)) {
        kfree (str);
        return -EFAULT;
    }

    /* convert the string into a long */

    if (data == proc_pid) {
        /*        sig_pid = simple_strtol (str, NULL, 10); */
        sscanf (str, "%d", &sig_pid);
        printk (KERN_INFO "sig_pid has been set to %d\n", sig_pid);
        /* sig_tsk = find_task_by_vpid (sig_pid);*/
        sig_tsk = pid_task (find_vpid(sig_pid),PIDTYPE_PID);
        kfree (str);
        return count;
    }

    if (data == proc_signal) {
        /*        sig_tosend = simple_strtol (str, NULL, 10); */
        sscanf (str, "%d", &sig_tosend);
        printk (KERN_INFO "sig_tosend has been set to %d\n", sig_tosend);
        if (!sig_tsk) {
            printk (KERN_INFO "You haven't set the pid; using current\n");
            sig_tsk = current;
            sig_pid = (int)current->pid;
        }
        printk (KERN_INFO " Sending signal %d to process ID %d\n", sig_tosend,
                sig_pid);
        retval = send_sig (sig_tosend, sig_tsk, 0);
        printk (KERN_INFO "retval = %d\n", retval);
        kfree (str);
        return count;
    }
    kfree (str);
    return -EINVAL;
}
static int __init my_init (void)
{
    proc_sigdir = proc_mkdir (NODE_DIR, NULL);
    if (!proc_sigdir) {
        printk (KERN_ERR "I failed to make %s\n", NODE_DIR);
        return -1;
    }
    printk (KERN_INFO "I created %s\n", NODE_DIR);

    proc_pid = create_proc_entry (NODE_1, S_IRUGO | S_IWUSR, proc_sigdir);
    if (!proc_pid) {
        printk (KERN_ERR "I failed to make %s\n", NODE_1);
        remove_proc_entry (NODE_DIR, NULL);
        return -1;
    }
```

```
        printk (KERN_INFO "I created %s\n", NODE_1);
        proc_pid->read_proc = my_proc_read;
        proc_pid->write_proc = my_proc_write;
        proc_pid->data = proc_pid;

        proc_signal = create_proc_entry (NODE_2, S_IRUGO | S_IWUSR, proc_sigdir);
        if (!proc_signal) {
            printk (KERN_ERR "I failed to make %s\n", NODE_2);
            remove_proc_entry (NODE_1, proc_sigdir);
            remove_proc_entry (NODE_DIR, NULL);
            return -1;
        }
        printk (KERN_INFO "I created %s\n", NODE_2);
        proc_signal->read_proc = my_proc_read;
        proc_signal->write_proc = my_proc_write;
        proc_signal->data = proc_signal;
        return 0;
}

static void __exit my_exit (void)
{
        if (proc_pid) {
            remove_proc_entry (NODE_1, proc_sigdir);
            printk (KERN_INFO "Removed %s\n", NODE_1);
        }
        if (proc_signal) {
            remove_proc_entry (NODE_2, proc_sigdir);
            printk (KERN_INFO "Removed %s\n", NODE_2);
        }
        if (proc_sigdir) {
            remove_proc_entry (NODE_DIR, NULL);
            printk (KERN_INFO "Removed %s\n", NODE_DIR);
        }
}

module_init (my_init);
module_exit (my_exit);

MODULE_AUTHOR ("Jerry Cooperstein");
MODULE_DESCRIPTION ("CLDD 1.0: lab4_proc_sig_solA.c");
MODULE_LICENSE ("GPL v2");
```

lab4_proc_sig_solB.c

```
 /* Copyright 2009, J Cooperstein coop@coopj.com (GPLv2) */

#include <linux/module.h>
#include <linux/proc_fs.h>
#include <linux/uaccess.h>
#include <linux/init.h>
#include <linux/signal.h>
#include <linux/sched.h>

#define NODE_DIR "my_sig_dir"
#define NODE_1 "pid"
```

```
#define NODE_2 "signal"

static int sig_pid = -1, sig_tosend = SIGUSR1;
static struct task_struct *sig_tsk = NULL;
static struct proc_dir_entry *proc_sigdir, *proc_pid, *proc_signal;

static int
my_proc_read1 (char *page, char **start, off_t off, int count,
               int *eof, void *data)
{
    *eof = 1;
    return sprintf (page, "%d\n", sig_pid);
}

static int
my_proc_read2 (char *page, char **start, off_t off, int count,
               int *eof, void *data)
{
    *eof = 1;
    return sprintf (page, "%d\n", sig_tosend);
}

static int
my_proc_write1 (struct file *file, const char __user * buffer,
                unsigned long count, void *data)
{
    char *str = kmalloc ((size_t) count, GFP_KERNEL);

    /* copy the string from user-space to kernel-space */

    if (copy_from_user (str, buffer, count)) {
        kfree (str);
        return -EFAULT;
    }

    /* convert the string into a long */

    /*       sig_pid = simple_strtol (str, NULL, 10); */
    sscanf (str, "%d", &sig_pid);
    printk (KERN_INFO "sig_pid has been set to %d\n", sig_pid);
    /* sig_tsk = find_task_by_vpid (sig_pid);*/
    sig_tsk = pid_task (find_vpid(sig_pid),PIDTYPE_PID);
    kfree (str);
    return count;
}

static int
my_proc_write2 (struct file *file, const char __user * buffer,
                unsigned long count, void *data)
{
    int retval;
    char *str = kmalloc ((size_t) count, GFP_KERNEL);

    /* copy the string from user-space to kernel-space */
```

```
    if (copy_from_user (str, buffer, count))
        return -EFAULT;

    /* convert the string into a long */

    /*        sig_tosend = simple_strtol (str, NULL, 10); */
    sscanf (str, "%d", &sig_tosend);
    printk (KERN_INFO "sig_tosend has been set to %d\n", sig_tosend);
    if (!sig_tsk) {
        printk (KERN_INFO "You haven't set the pid; using current\n");
        sig_tsk = current;
        sig_pid = (int)current->pid;
    }
    printk (KERN_INFO " Sending signal %d to process ID %d\n", sig_tosend,
            sig_pid);
    retval = send_sig (sig_tosend, sig_tsk, 0);
    printk (KERN_INFO "retval = %d\n", retval);
    kfree (str);
    return count;
}

static int __init my_init (void)
{
    proc_sigdir = proc_mkdir (NODE_DIR, NULL);
    if (!proc_sigdir) {
        printk (KERN_ERR "I failed to make %s\n", NODE_DIR);
        return -1;
    }
    printk (KERN_INFO "I created %s\n", NODE_DIR);

    proc_pid = create_proc_entry (NODE_1, S_IRUGO | S_IWUSR, proc_sigdir);
    if (!proc_pid) {
        printk (KERN_ERR "I failed to make %s\n", NODE_1);
        remove_proc_entry (NODE_DIR, NULL);
        return -1;
    }
    printk (KERN_INFO "I created %s\n", NODE_1);
    proc_pid->read_proc = my_proc_read1;
    proc_pid->write_proc = my_proc_write1;

    proc_signal = create_proc_entry (NODE_2, S_IRUGO | S_IWUSR, proc_sigdir);
    if (!proc_signal) {
        printk (KERN_ERR "I failed to make %s\n", NODE_2);
        remove_proc_entry (NODE_1, proc_sigdir);
        remove_proc_entry (NODE_DIR, NULL);
        return -1;
    }
    printk (KERN_INFO "I created %s\n", NODE_2);
    proc_signal->read_proc = my_proc_read2;
    proc_signal->write_proc = my_proc_write2;
    return 0;
}

static void __exit my_exit (void)
{
```

```
    if (proc_pid) {
        remove_proc_entry (NODE_1, proc_sigdir);
        printk (KERN_INFO "Removed %s\n", NODE_1);
    }
    if (proc_signal) {
        remove_proc_entry (NODE_2, proc_sigdir);
        printk (KERN_INFO "Removed %s\n", NODE_2);
    }
    if (proc_sigdir) {
        remove_proc_entry (NODE_DIR, NULL);
        printk (KERN_INFO "Removed %s\n", NODE_DIR);
    }
}

module_init (my_init);
module_exit (my_exit);

MODULE_AUTHOR ("Jerry Cooperstein");
MODULE_DESCRIPTION ("CLDD 1.0: lab4_proc_sig_solB.c");
MODULE_LICENSE ("GPL v2");
```

lab4_proc_sig_test.c

```
/* Copyright 2009, J Cooperstein coop@coopj.com (GPLv2) */

#include <stdio.h>
#include <stdlib.h>
#include <unistd.h>
#include <fcntl.h>
#include <sys/ioctl.h>
#include <string.h>
#include <signal.h>

void print_and_rewind (FILE * fp_pid, FILE * fp_tosend)
{
    unsigned long pid, sig;

    /* read current values and print */
    fscanf (fp_pid, "%lud", &pid);
    fscanf (fp_tosend, "%lud", &sig);
    printf ("pid = %ld, signal = %ld\n\n", pid, sig);

    /* set back to the beginning */
    fseek (fp_pid, 0, SEEK_SET);
    fseek (fp_tosend, 0, SEEK_SET);
}

int main (int argc, char *argv[])
{
    FILE *fp_pid, *fp_tosend;
    unsigned long pid, sig;

    /* set up the values if on the command line */

    pid = getpid ();
```

```
    sig = SIGKILL;

    if (argc > 1)
        pid = atoi (argv[1]);

    if (argc > 2)
        sig = atoi (argv[2]);

    /* open the proc files node */

    fp_pid = fopen ("/proc/my_sig_dir/pid", "w+");
    fp_tosend = fopen ("/proc/my_sig_dir/signal", "w+");
    printf ("\n I opened /proc/my_sig_dir/pid and /proc/my_sig_dir/signal\n\n");

    printf (" \nValues read from /proc before doing anything:\n");
    print_and_rewind (fp_pid, fp_tosend);

    /* set the pid */

    fprintf (fp_pid, "%ld", pid);
    fseek (fp_pid, 0, SEEK_SET);

    printf (" \nValues read from /proc after setting pid:\n");
    print_and_rewind (fp_pid, fp_tosend);

    printf ("\n Sending the signal:\n");
    fprintf (fp_tosend, "%ld", sig);
    fseek (fp_tosend, 0, SEEK_SET);

    printf (" \nValues read from /proc after sending signal:\n");
    print_and_rewind (fp_pid, fp_tosend);
    /* ok go home */
    fclose (fp_pid);
    fclose (fp_tosend);

    printf ("\n\n FINISHED, TERMINATING NORMALLY\n");

    exit (0);
}
```

14.5   Lab 5: Using seq_file for the /proc filesystem.

* Take the simple x_busy **proc** entry discussed earlier, and re-implement it using the seq_file interface.

* As a parameter, input the number of lines to print out.

lab5_seqfile.c

```
/* Copyright 2009, J Cooperstein coop@coopj.com (GPLv2) */

#include <linux/module.h>
#include <linux/sched.h>        /* Get "jiffies" from here */
```

```
#include <linux/proc_fs.h>
#include <linux/init.h>
#include <linux/seq_file.h>

static int items = 1;
static int x_delay = 1;
static unsigned long future;

static char const my_proc[] = { "x_busy" };

/* Sequential file iterator                                                  */

static void *x_busy_seq_start (struct seq_file *sf, loff_t * pos)
{
    void *results;

    if (*pos < items) {
        future = jiffies + x_delay * HZ;
        while (time_before (jiffies, future)) ;
        results = (void *)&jiffies;
    } else {
        results = NULL;
    }
    return results;
}

static void *x_busy_seq_next (struct seq_file *sf, void *v, loff_t * pos)
{
    void *results;

    (*pos)++;
    if (*pos < items) {
        future = jiffies + x_delay * HZ;
        while (time_before (jiffies, future)) ;
        results = (void *)&jiffies;
    } else {
        results = NULL;
    }
    return results;
}

static void x_busy_seq_stop (struct seq_file *sf, void *v)
{
    /* Nothing to do here */
}

static int x_busy_seq_show (struct seq_file *sf, void *v    /* jiffies in disquise */
    )
{
    volatile unsigned long *const jp = (volatile unsigned long *)v;
    int results;

    seq_printf (sf, "jiffies = %lu.\n", *jp);
    results = 0;
    return results;
```

```
}

static struct seq_operations proc_x_busy_seq_ops = {
    .start = x_busy_seq_start,
    .next = x_busy_seq_next,
    .stop = x_busy_seq_stop,
    .show = x_busy_seq_show,
};

static int proc_x_busy_open (struct inode *inode, struct file *file)
{
    return seq_open (file, &proc_x_busy_seq_ops);
}

static const struct file_operations proc_x_busy_operations = {
    .open = proc_x_busy_open,
    .read = seq_read,
    .llseek = seq_lseek,
    .release = seq_release
};

static struct proc_dir_entry *x_proc_busy;

static int __init my_init (void)
{
    int results;

    results = -1;
    do {
        x_proc_busy = create_proc_entry (my_proc, 0, NULL);
        if (!x_proc_busy) {
            break;
        }
        x_proc_busy->proc_fops = &proc_x_busy_operations;
        results = 0;
    } while (0);
    return results;
}

static void __exit my_exit (void)
{
    if (x_proc_busy) {
        remove_proc_entry (my_proc, NULL);
    }
}

module_init (my_init);
module_exit (my_exit);

MODULE_AUTHOR ("Tommy Reynolds");
/* minor reformatting etc., 4/21/2002, J. Cooperstein */
MODULE_DESCRIPTION ("CLDD 1.0: lab5_seqfile.c");
MODULE_LICENSE ("GPL v2");
module_param (items, int, S_IRUGO);
MODULE_PARM_DESC (items, "How many items to simulate");
```

Chapter 15

Unified Device Model and sysfs

15.1 Lab 1: Using libsysfs and sysfsutils.

- The **systool** multipurpose utility gives an easy interface for examining the /sys device tree, and is part of the **sysfstools** package. Currently it uses **libsysfs**, which is being deprecated in favor of **libhal**.

- Do **man systool** and run the **systool** command without arguments. It should portray all bus types, devices classes, and root devices. Do `systool -h` to see how to use some of the additional arguments and options.

- Explore!

Chapter 16

Firmware

16.1   Lab 1: Loading Firmware

- Write a module that loads some firmware from the filesystem. It should print out the contents.

- In order to do this you'll need to place a firmware file under **/lib/firmware**. You can use just a text file for the purpose of this demonstration.

- Since this is a pseudo device, you will have to declare and initialize a `device` structure. Minimally you must set the `void (*release)(struct device *dev)` field in this structure, and call

  ```
  int dev_set_name (struct device *dev, const char *fmt, ...);
  ```

  to set the device name, which can be read out with:

  ```
  const char *dev_name(const struct device *dev);
  ```

  (You may want to see what happens if you neglect setting one of these quantities.)

- Make sure you call

```
device_register  (struct device *dev);
device_unregister(struct device *dev);
```

before requesting and after releasing the firmware.

lab1_firmware.c

```
/* Copyright 2009, J Cooperstein coop@coopj.com (GPLv2) */

#include <linux/module.h>
#include <linux/init.h>
#include <linux/device.h>
#include <linux/firmware.h>

#define FWFILE "my_fwfile"
static const struct firmware *fw;

static void my_release (struct device *dev)
{
    printk (KERN_INFO "releasing firmware device\n");
}

static struct device dev = {
    .release = my_release
};

static int __init my_init (void)
{
    dev_set_name (&dev, "my0");
    device_register (&dev);
    printk (KERN_INFO "firmware_example: my device inserted\n");

    if (request_firmware (&fw, FWFILE, &dev)) {
        printk (KERN_ERR "requesting firmware failed\n");
        device_unregister (&dev);
        return -1;
    }
    printk (KERN_INFO "firmware contents=\n%s\n", fw->data);
    return 0;
}
static void __exit my_exit (void)
{
    release_firmware (fw);
    device_unregister (&dev);
    printk (KERN_INFO "release firwmare and unregistered device\n");
}

module_init (my_init);
module_exit (my_exit);

MODULE_LICENSE ("GPL");
```

Chapter 17

Memory Management and Allocation

17.1   Lab 1: Memory Caches

- Extend your character driver to allocate the driver's internal buffer by using your own memory cache. Make sure you free any slabs you create.

- For extra credit create more than one object (perhaps every time you do a read or write) and make sure you release them all before destroying the cache.

```
lab_char.h
lab1_cache.c
```

```
/* Copyright 2009, J Cooperstein coop@coopj.com (GPLv2) */

#include <linux/module.h>
#include "lab_char.h"
```

```
static int size = PAGE_SIZE;
static struct kmem_cache *my_cache;
module_param (size, int, S_IRUGO);

static int mycdrv_open (struct inode *inode, struct file *file)
{
    /* allocate a memory cache object */

    if (!(ramdisk = kmem_cache_alloc (my_cache, GFP_ATOMIC))) {
        printk (KERN_ERR " failed to create a cache object\n");
        return -ENOMEM;
    }
    printk (KERN_INFO " successfully created a cache object\n");
    return mycdrv_generic_open (inode, file);
}

static int mycdrv_release (struct inode *inode, struct file *file)
{
    /* destroy a memory cache object */
    kmem_cache_free (my_cache, ramdisk);
    printk (KERN_INFO "destroyed a memory cache object\n");
    printk (KERN_INFO " closing character device: %s:\n\n", MYDEV_NAME);
    return 0;
}

static const struct file_operations mycdrv_fops = {
    .owner = THIS_MODULE,
    .read = mycdrv_generic_read,
    .write = mycdrv_generic_write,
    .open = mycdrv_open,
    .release = mycdrv_release
};

static int __init my_init (void)
{
    if (alloc_chrdev_region (&first, 0, count, MYDEV_NAME) < 0) {
        printk (KERN_ERR "failed to allocate character device region\n");
        return -1;
    }
    if (!(my_cdev = cdev_alloc ())) {
        printk (KERN_ERR "cdev_alloc() failed\n");
        unregister_chrdev_region (first, count);
        return -1;
    }
    cdev_init (my_cdev, &mycdrv_fops);
    if (cdev_add (my_cdev, first, count) < 0) {
        printk (KERN_ERR "cdev_add() failed\n");
        cdev_del (my_cdev);
        unregister_chrdev_region (first, count);
        return -1;
    }
    foo_class = class_create (THIS_MODULE, "my_class");
    device_create (foo_class, NULL, first, "%s", "mycdrv");
    printk (KERN_INFO "\nSucceeded in registering character device %s\n",
            MYDEV_NAME);
```

```
    printk (KERN_INFO "Major number = %d, Minor number = %d\n", MAJOR (first),
           MINOR (first));

    /* create a memory cache */

    if (size > (32 * PAGE_SIZE)) {
        printk
            (KERN_INFO " size=%d is too large; you can't have more than 32 pages!\n",
             size);
        return -1;
    }
    /* before 2.6.23 there was a destuctor method also */
    if (!(my_cache = kmem_cache_create ("mycache", size, 0,
                                        SLAB_HWCACHE_ALIGN, NULL))) {
        printk (KERN_ERR "kmem_cache_create failed\n");
        return -ENOMEM;
    }
    printk (KERN_INFO "allocated memory cache correctly\n");
    ramdisk_size = size;

    return 0;
}

static void __exit my_exit (void)
{
    device_destroy (foo_class, first);
    class_destroy (foo_class);

    if (my_cdev)
        cdev_del (my_cdev);
    unregister_chrdev_region (first, count);
    printk (KERN_INFO "\ndevice unregistered\n");

    (void)kmem_cache_destroy (my_cache);
}

module_init (my_init);
module_exit (my_exit);

MODULE_AUTHOR ("Jerry Cooperstein");
MODULE_DESCRIPTION ("CLDD 1.0: lab1_cache.c");
MODULE_LICENSE ("GPL v2");
```

17.2 Lab 2: Testing Maximum Memory Allocation

- See how much memory you can obtain dynamically, using both `kmalloc()` and `__get_free_pages()`.

- Start with requesting 1 page of memory, and then keep doubling until your request fails for each type fails.

- Make sure you free any memory you receive.

- You'll probably want to use `GFP_ATOMIC` rather than `GFP_KERNEL`. (Why?)

- If you have trouble getting enough memory due to memory fragmentation trying writing a poor-man's de-fragmenter, and then running again. The de-fragmenter can just be an application that grabs all available memory, uses it, and then releases it when done, thereby clearing the caches. You can also try the command sync; echo 3 > /proc/sys/vm/drop_caches .

- Try the same thing with vmalloc(). Rather than doubling allocations, start at 4 MB and increase in 4 MB increments until failure results. Note this may hang while loading. (Why?)

lab2_maxmem.c

```
 /* Copyright 2009, J Cooperstein coop@coopj.com (GPLv2) */

#include <linux/module.h>
#include <linux/slab.h>
#include <linux/init.h>

static int __init my_init (void)
{
    static char *kbuff;
    static unsigned long order;
    int size;

    /* try __get_free_pages__ */

    for (size = PAGE_SIZE, order = 0; order < MAX_ORDER; order++, size *= 2) {
        printk (KERN_INFO " order=%2ld, pages=%5ld, size=%8d ", order,
                size / PAGE_SIZE, size);
        if (!(kbuff = (char *)__get_free_pages (GFP_ATOMIC, order))) {
            printk (KERN_ERR "... __get_free_pages failed\n");
            break;
        }
        printk (KERN_INFO "... __get_free_pages OK\n");
        free_pages ((unsigned long)kbuff, order);
    }

    /* try kmalloc */

    for (size = PAGE_SIZE, order = 0; order < MAX_ORDER; order++, size *= 2) {
        printk (KERN_INFO " order=%2ld, pages=%5ld, size=%8d ", order,
                size / PAGE_SIZE, size);
        if (!(kbuff = (char *)kmalloc ((size_t) size, GFP_ATOMIC))) {
            printk (KERN_ERR "... kmalloc failed\n");
            break;
        }
        printk (KERN_INFO "... kmalloc OK\n");
        kfree (kbuff);
    }
    return 0;
}
static void __exit my_exit (void)
{
    printk (KERN_INFO "Module Unloading\n");
}
```

```
module_init (my_init);
module_exit (my_exit);

MODULE_AUTHOR ("Jerry Cooperstein");
MODULE_DESCRIPTION ("CLDD 1.0: lab2_maxmem.c");
MODULE_LICENSE ("GPL v2");
```

lab2_maxvmalloc.c

```
/* Copyright 2009, J Cooperstein coop@coopj.com (GPLv2) */

#include <linux/module.h>
#include <linux/init.h>
#include <linux/vmalloc.h>

static int mem = 64;
module_param (mem, int, S_IRUGO);

#define MB (1024*1024)

static int __init my_init (void)
{
    static char *vm_buff;
    int size;

    /* try vmalloc */

    for (size = 4 * MB; size <= mem * MB; size += 4 * MB) {
        printk (KERN_INFO " pages=%6ld, size=%8d ", size / PAGE_SIZE,
                size / MB);
        if (!(vm_buff = (char *)vmalloc (size))) {
            printk (KERN_ERR "... vmalloc failed\n");
            break;
        }
        printk (KERN_INFO "... vmalloc OK\n");
        vfree (vm_buff);
    }

    return 0;
}
static void __exit my_exit (void)
{
    printk (KERN_INFO "Module Unloading\n");
}

module_init (my_init);
module_exit (my_exit);

MODULE_AUTHOR ("Jerry Cooperstein");
MODULE_DESCRIPTION ("CLDD 1.0: lab2_maxvmalloc.c");
MODULE_LICENSE ("GPL v2");
```

lab2_wastemem.c

```
/* Copyright 2009, J Cooperstein coop@coopj.com (GPLv2) */
```

```c
#include <stdio.h>
#include <stdlib.h>
#include <unistd.h>
#include <string.h>

int main (int argc, char **argv)
{
    int j;
    char *c;
    int m = atoi (argv[1]);
    c = malloc (m * 1024 * 1024);
    for (j = 0; j < m; j++) {
        memset (c + 1024 * 1024 * j, j, 1024 * 1024);
        printf ("%5d", j);
        fflush (stdout);
    }
    printf ("Quitting and releasing memory\n");
    exit (0);
}
```

Chapter 18

Transferring Between User and Kernel Space

18.1   Lab 1: Using get_user() and put_user().

- Adapt your character driver to use get_user() and put_user().

lab_char.h

lab1_copytofrom.c

```
/* Copyright 2009, J Cooperstein coop@coopj.com (GPLv2) */

#include <linux/module.h>
#include "lab_char.h"

static const struct file_operations mycdrv_fops = {
    .owner = THIS_MODULE,
    .read = mycdrv_generic_read,
    .write = mycdrv_generic_write,
```

```
    .open = mycdrv_generic_open,
    .release = mycdrv_generic_release,
};

module_init (my_generic_init);
module_exit (my_generic_exit);

MODULE_AUTHOR ("Jerry Cooperstein");
MODULE_DESCRIPTION ("CLDD 1.0: lab1_copytofrom.c");
MODULE_LICENSE ("GPL v2");
```

lab1_putget.c

```
 /* Copyright 2009, J Cooperstein coop@coopj.com (GPLv2) */

#include <linux/module.h>
#include "lab_char.h"

static inline ssize_t
mycdrv_read (struct file *file, char __user * buf, size_t lbuf, loff_t * ppos)
{
    int nbytes = 0, maxbytes, bytes_to_do;
    char *tmp = ramdisk + *ppos;
    maxbytes = ramdisk_size - *ppos;
    bytes_to_do = maxbytes > lbuf ? lbuf : maxbytes;
    if (bytes_to_do == 0)
        printk (KERN_INFO "Reached end of the device on a read");
    while ((nbytes < bytes_to_do) && !put_user (*tmp, (buf + nbytes))) {
        nbytes++;
        tmp++;
    }
    *ppos += nbytes;
    printk (KERN_INFO "\n Leaving the   READ function, nbytes=%d, pos=%d\n",
            nbytes, (int)*ppos);
    return nbytes;
}

static inline ssize_t
mycdrv_write (struct file *file, const char __user * buf, size_t lbuf,
              loff_t * ppos)
{
    int nbytes = 0, maxbytes, bytes_to_do;
    char *tmp = ramdisk + *ppos;
    maxbytes = ramdisk_size - *ppos;
    bytes_to_do = maxbytes > lbuf ? lbuf : maxbytes;
    if (bytes_to_do == 0)
        printk (KERN_INFO "Reached end of the device on a write");
    while ((nbytes < bytes_to_do) && !get_user (*tmp, (buf + nbytes))) {
        nbytes++;
        tmp++;
    }
    *ppos += nbytes;
    printk (KERN_INFO "\n Leaving the   WRITE function, nbytes=%d, pos=%d\n",
            nbytes, (int)*ppos);
    return nbytes;
```

```
}

static const struct file_operations mycdrv_fops = {
    .owner = THIS_MODULE,
    .read = mycdrv_read,
    .write = mycdrv_write,
    .open = mycdrv_generic_open,
    .release = mycdrv_generic_release,
};

module_init (my_generic_init);
module_exit (my_generic_exit);

MODULE_AUTHOR ("Jerry Cooperstein");
MODULE_DESCRIPTION ("CLDD 1.0: lab1_putget.c");
MODULE_LICENSE ("GPL v2");
```

lab1_read_write.c

```
/* Copyright 2009, J Cooperstein coop@coopj.com (GPLv2) */

#include <stdio.h>
#include <unistd.h>
#include <stdlib.h>
#include <fcntl.h>
#include <string.h>

int main (int argc, char *argv[])
{
    int length = 20, fd, rc;
    char *message, *nodename = "/dev/mycdrv";

    if (argc > 1)
        nodename = argv[1];

    if (argc > 2)
        length = atoi (argv[2]);

    /* set up the message */
    message = malloc (length);
    memset (message, 'x', length);
    message[length - 1] = '\0'; /* make sure it is null terminated */

    /* open the device node */

    fd = open (nodename, O_RDWR);
    printf (" I opened the device node, file descriptor = %d\n", fd);

    /* write to the device node */

    rc = write (fd, message, length);
    printf ("return code from write = %d\n", rc);

    /* reset the message to null */
```

```
    memset (message, 0, length);

    /* go back to the beginning */

    lseek (fd, 0, SEEK_SET);

    /* read from the device node */

    rc = read (fd, message, length);
    printf ("return code from read = %d\n", rc);
    printf (" the message was: %s\n", message);

    close (fd);
    exit (0);

}
```

18.2   Lab 2: Mapping User Pages

- Use the character device driver, adapt it to use `get_user_pages()` for the `read()` and `write()` entry points.

- To properly exercise this you'll need to use a page-aligned utility such as **dd**, or write page-aligned reading and writing programs.

lab_char.h
lab2_usermap.c

```
/* Copyright 2009, J Cooperstein coop@coopj.com (GPLv2) */

#include <linux/module.h>
#include "lab_char.h"
#include <linux/mm.h>
#include <linux/pagemap.h>

static ssize_t
mycdrv_rw (struct file *file, unsigned long buf, size_t lbuf, loff_t * ppos,
          int rw)
{
    int j, nb, rc, npages;
    struct page **pages;
    char *uaddr, *ktmp;

    /* get the total number of pages of memory needed */
    npages = (lbuf - 1) / PAGE_SIZE + 1;

    /* allocate space for array of page structures */

    printk (KERN_INFO "npages = %d for %ld bytes\n", npages, (long)lbuf);
    if (!(pages = kmalloc (npages * sizeof (pages), GFP_KERNEL))) {
        printk (KERN_ERR "allocating pages failed\n");
        return -ENOMEM;
```

```
    }

    /* get the page structures, protect with a lock */

    down_read (&current->mm->mmap_sem);
    rc = get_user_pages (current, current->mm,
                         (unsigned long)buf, npages, 1, 0, pages, NULL);
    up_read (&current->mm->mmap_sem);
    printk (KERN_INFO " I received %d pages from the user \n", rc);

    for (j = 0, nb = PAGE_SIZE, ktmp = ramdisk; j < npages;
         j++, ktmp += PAGE_SIZE) {

        /* remap the page address; could also use page_address(page) */

        uaddr = kmap (pages[j]);

        if (j == npages - 1)
            nb = (lbuf - 1) % PAGE_SIZE + 1;

        /* do the actual i/o operation ; for now just to a kernel buffer */

        /* should put the switch outside the loop; for now live with it */

        switch (rw) {
        case 0:                /* read */
            memcpy (uaddr, ktmp, nb);
            //          printk (KERN_INFO " kernel sees on a read:\n%s\n", uaddr);
            break;
        case 1:                /* write */
            memcpy (ktmp, uaddr, nb);
            //          printk (KERN_INFO " kernel sees on a write:uaddr:\n%s\n", uaddr);
            break;
        default:                   /* should never hit here */
            printk (KERN_INFO "Error in rw routine, rw=%d\n", rw);
            break;
        }

        /* release the page cache -- no surprises to apps */
        lock_page (pages[j]);
        set_page_dirty (pages[j]);  /* make sure it is flushed */
        unlock_page (pages[j]);

        //set_page_dirty_lock(pages[j]);
        page_cache_release (pages[j]);  /* make sure it is released from cache */

        /* release the remap; don't need to do if use page_address() */
        kunmap (pages[j]);
    }

    kfree (pages);

    printk (KERN_INFO "\n Leaving the READ  function, nbytes=%ld\n",
            (long)lbuf);
    return lbuf;
```

```
}
static ssize_t
mycdrv_read (struct file *file, char __user * buf, size_t lbuf, loff_t * ppos)
{
    int rw = 0;
    return mycdrv_rw (file, (unsigned long)buf, lbuf, ppos, rw);
}
static ssize_t
mycdrv_write (struct file *file, const char __user * buf, size_t lbuf,
            loff_t * ppos)
{
    int rw = 1;
    return mycdrv_rw (file, (unsigned long)buf, lbuf, ppos, rw);
}

static const struct file_operations mycdrv_fops = {
    .owner = THIS_MODULE,
    .read = mycdrv_read,
    .write = mycdrv_write,
    .open = mycdrv_generic_open,
    .release = mycdrv_generic_release,
};

module_init (my_generic_init);
module_exit (my_generic_exit);

MODULE_AUTHOR ("Jerry Cooperstein");
MODULE_DESCRIPTION ("CLDD 1.0: lab2_usermap.c");
MODULE_LICENSE ("GPL v2");
```

lab2_read_aligned.c

```
/* Copyright 2009, J Cooperstein coop@coopj.com (GPLv2) */

#include <stdio.h>
#include <unistd.h>
#include <fcntl.h>
#include <stdlib.h>
#include <string.h>
#include <stdlib.h>
#include <malloc.h>

int main (int argc, char *argv[])
{
    int fd, rc = 0, nbytes, pagesize;
    void *buffer;
    char *filename = "/dev/mycdrv";

    pagesize = getpagesize ();
    nbytes = pagesize;

    if (argc > 1)
        filename = argv[1];
    if (argc > 2)
        nbytes = atoi (argv[2]) * pagesize;
```

```
    rc = posix_memalign (&buffer, pagesize, nbytes);
    /*    buffer = (char *)memalign (pagesize, nbytes);  */

    printf ("rc=%d, buffer=%p, mod pagesize = %ld\n", rc, buffer,
            (unsigned long)buffer % pagesize);

    fd = open (filename, O_RDONLY);
    printf ("opened file: %s,  with file descriptor = %d\n", filename, fd);
    rc = read (fd, buffer, nbytes);
    printf ("read %d bytes which were:\n%s\n", rc, (char *)buffer);
    close (fd);
    exit (EXIT_SUCCESS);
}
```

lab2_write_aligned.c

```
 /* Copyright 2009, J Cooperstein coop@coopj.com (GPLv2) */

#include <stdio.h>
#include <unistd.h>
#include <fcntl.h>
#include <stdlib.h>
#include <string.h>
#include <stdlib.h>
#include <malloc.h>
#include <sys/stat.h>

#define STRING "TESTING DRIVER WITH A WRITE"

int main (int argc, char *argv[])
{
    int fd, rc = 0, size, pagesize;
    void *buffer;
    char *filename = "/dev/mycdrv";
    size = strlen (STRING) + 1; /* leave room for \0 */
    pagesize = getpagesize ();
    rc = posix_memalign (&buffer, pagesize, size);
    /*    buffer = (char *)memalign (pagesize, size); */
    printf ("rc=%d, buffer=%p, mod pagesize = %ld\n", rc, buffer,
            (unsigned long)buffer % pagesize);
    strcpy (buffer, STRING);

    if (argc > 1)
        filename = argv[1];

    fd = open (filename, O_RDWR | O_CREAT | O_TRUNC, S_IRUSR | S_IWUSR);
    printf ("opened file: %s,  with file descriptor = %d\n", filename, fd);
    rc = write (fd, buffer, strlen (buffer) + 1);
    printf ("wrote %d bytes which were:\n%s\n", rc, (char *)buffer);
    close (fd);
    exit (EXIT_SUCCESS);
}
```

18.3   Lab 3: Memory Mapping an Allocated Region

- Write a character driver that implements a `mmap()` entry point that memory maps a kernel buffer, allocated dynamically (probably during initialization).

- There should also be `read()` and `write()` entry points.

- Optionally, you may want to use an `ioctl()` command to tell user-space the size of the kernel buffer being memory mapped.

- Note: This is not an easy exercise to do properly, so if time is lacking you may merely experiment with the solutions.

lab3_mmap.c

```
/* Copyright 2009, J Cooperstein coop@coopj.com (GPLv2) */

#include <linux/module.h>
#include <linux/mm.h>
#include <linux/io.h>            /* for virt_to_phys() */
#include "lab_char.h"

#define MMAP_DEV_CMD_GET_BUFSIZE 1  /* defines our IOCTL cmd */

static int mycdrv_mmap (struct file *filp, struct vm_area_struct *vma)
{
    unsigned long pfn;
    unsigned long offset = vma->vm_pgoff << PAGE_SHIFT;
    unsigned long len = vma->vm_end - vma->vm_start;

    if (offset >= ramdisk_size)
        return -EINVAL;
    if (len > (ramdisk_size - offset))
        return -EINVAL;
    printk (KERN_INFO "%s: mapping %ld bytes of ramdisk at offset %ld\n",
            __stringify (KBUILD_BASENAME), len, offset);

    /* need to get the pfn for remap_pfn_range -- either of these two
       follwoing methods will work */

    /*    pfn = page_to_pfn (virt_to_page (ramdisk + offset)); */
    pfn = virt_to_phys (ramdisk + offset) >> PAGE_SHIFT;

    if (remap_pfn_range (vma, vma->vm_start, pfn, len, vma->vm_page_prot)) {
        return -EAGAIN;
    }
    return 0;
}

/*
 *  mycdrv_ioctl() --- give the user the value ramdisk_size
 */
static int
mycdrv_ioctl (struct inode *ino, struct file *filp,
```

```
                    unsigned int cmd, unsigned long arg)
{
    unsigned long tbs = ramdisk_size;
    void __user *ioargp = (void __user *)arg;

    switch (cmd) {
    default:
        return -EINVAL;

    case MMAP_DEV_CMD_GET_BUFSIZE:
        if (copy_to_user (ioargp, &tbs, sizeof (tbs)))
            return -EFAULT;
        return 0;
    }
}

static const struct file_operations mycdrv_fops = {
    .owner = THIS_MODULE,
    .read = mycdrv_generic_read,
    .write = mycdrv_generic_write,
    .mmap = mycdrv_mmap,
    .ioctl = mycdrv_ioctl,
};

module_init (my_generic_init);
module_exit (my_generic_exit);

MODULE_AUTHOR ("Bill Kerr");
MODULE_AUTHOR ("Jerry Cooperstein");
MODULE_DESCRIPTION ("CLDD 1.0: lab3_mmap.c");
MODULE_LICENSE ("GPL v2");
```

lab3_mmap_test.c

```
/* Copyright 2009, J Cooperstein coop@coopj.com (GPLv2) */
#include <stdio.h>
#include <stdlib.h>
#include <unistd.h>
#include <sys/mman.h>
#include <string.h>
#include <errno.h>
#include <fcntl.h>
#include <sys/ioctl.h>
#include <malloc.h>

#define MMAP_DEV_CMD_GET_BUFSIZE 1   /* defines our IOCTL cmd */

void read_and_compare (int fd, char *read_buf, char *mmap_buf,
                       unsigned long len)
{
    /* Read the file and compare with mmap_buf[] */

    if (read (fd, read_buf, len) != len) {
        fprintf (stderr, "read problem:  %s\n", strerror (errno));
        exit (1);
```

```
    }
    if (memcmp (read_buf, mmap_buf, len) != 0) {
        fprintf (stderr, "buffer miscompare\n");
        exit (1);
    }
}

int main (int argc, char **argv)
{
    unsigned long j, len;
    int fd;
    char *read_buf, *mmap_buf, *filename = "/dev/mycdrv";

    srandom (getpid ());

    if (argc > 1)
        filename = argv[1];

    if ((fd = open (filename, O_RDWR)) < 0) {
        fprintf (stderr, "open of %s failed:  %s\n", filename,
                strerror (errno));
        exit (1);
    }
    /* have the driver tell us the buffer size */
    if (ioctl (fd, MMAP_DEV_CMD_GET_BUFSIZE, &len) < 0) {
        fprintf (stderr, "ioctl failed:  %s\n", strerror (errno));
        exit (1);
    }
    printf ("driver's ioctl says buffer size is %ld\n", len);

    read_buf = malloc (len);
    mmap_buf = mmap (NULL, len, PROT_READ | PROT_WRITE, MAP_SHARED, fd, 0);
    if (mmap_buf == (char *)MAP_FAILED) {
        fprintf (stderr, "mmap of %s failed:  %s\n", filename,
                strerror (errno));
        exit (1);
    }
    printf ("mmap succeeded: %p\n", mmap_buf);

    /* modify the mmaped buffer */
    for (j = 0; j < len; j++)
        *(mmap_buf + j) = (char)j;

    /* Read the file and compare with mmap_buf[] */
    read_and_compare (fd, read_buf, mmap_buf, len);
    printf ("comparison of same data via read() and mmap() successful\n");

    /* Change one randomly chosen byte in the mmap region */

    j = random () % len;
    *(mmap_buf + j) = random () % j;

    /*  repeat the read-back comparison. */
    (void)lseek (fd, 0, SEEK_SET);
    read_and_compare (fd, read_buf, mmap_buf, len);
```

```
    printf ("comparison of modified data via read() and mmap() successful\n");

    return 0;
}
```

18.4   Lab 4: Using Relay Channels.

- Write a kernel module that opens up a relay channel and makes the associated files visible in the **debugfs** filesystem.

- Make sure you mount the filesystem (if necessary) with

  ```
  mount -t debugfs none /sys/kernel/debug
  ```

- Have the initialization routine write a series of entries into the channel. While the kernel module is loaded, try reading from it using **read()** and **mmap()**.

- If you read more than once on the open file descriptor what do you see?

- For more advanced exercises, you might try making sure your kernel client writes over sub-buffer boundaries, or writes into the channel from other functions such as an interrupt routine, or other entry points.

lab4_relay_module.c

```c
 /* Copyright 2009, J Cooperstein coop@coopj.com (GPLv2) */

#include <linux/module.h>
#include <linux/init.h>
#include <linux/relay.h>
#include <linux/debugfs.h>

/* 16 page sized sub-buffers, total buffer size = 16 pages */

#define SB_SIZE PAGE_SIZE
#define N_SB 16

static struct rchan *mychan;
static char *fname = "my_rc_file";

static struct dentry
    *create_buf_file_handler (const char *filename,
                        struct dentry *parent,
                        int mode, struct rchan_buf *buf, int *is_global)
{
    //    *is_global=1; /* turn on if you want only one file on SMP */
    return debugfs_create_file (filename, mode, parent, buf,
                        &relay_file_operations);
}

static int remove_buf_file_handler (struct dentry *dentry)
{
    debugfs_remove (dentry);
```

```
        return 0;
}

static struct rchan_callbacks relay_callbacks = {
    .create_buf_file = create_buf_file_handler,
    .remove_buf_file = remove_buf_file_handler,
};

static int __init my_init (void)
{
    int j, k;
    char data[64];
    mychan = relay_open (fname, NULL, SB_SIZE, N_SB, &relay_callbacks, NULL);

    /* can't use smp_processor_id() properly otherwise */
    for (k = 0; k < 10; k++) {   /* do this for a minute */
        preempt_disable ();
        for (j = 0; j < 10; j++) {
            memset (data, 0, 64);
            sprintf (data, "data=%d\n", j * k);
            relay_write (mychan, data, 64);
        }
        printk (KERN_INFO "Relay Channel %s loaded on cpu=%d.\n", fname,
                smp_processor_id ());
        preempt_enable ();
        msleep (6000);
    }
    return 0;
}

static void __exit my_exit (void)
{
    relay_close (mychan);
    printk (KERN_INFO "Relay Channel %s unloaded.\n", fname);
}

module_init (my_init);
module_exit (my_exit);

MODULE_AUTHOR ("Jerry Cooperstein");
MODULE_DESCRIPTION ("CLDD 1.0: lab4_relay_module.c");
MODULE_LICENSE ("GPL v2");
```

lab4_relay_read.c

```
 /* Copyright 2009, J Cooperstein coop@coopj.com (GPLv2) */
#include <stdio.h>
#include <unistd.h>
#include <stdlib.h>
#include <fcntl.h>

int main (int argc, char **argv)
{
    int fd, j, rc;
    char buf[64];
```

```
    char *fname = "/sys/kernel/debug/my_rc_file0";
    if (argc > 1)
        fname = argv[1];
    fd = open (fname, O_RDONLY);
    printf ("opening %s, fd=%d\n", fname, fd);

    for (j = 1; j < 20; j++) {
        rc = read (fd, buf, 64);
        printf ("rc=%d    %s::", rc, buf);
    }
    exit (0);
}
```

lab4_relay_mmap.c

```
/* Copyright 2009, J Cooperstein coop@coopj.com (GPLv2) */

#include <stdlib.h>
#include <stdio.h>
#include <unistd.h>
#include <string.h>
#include <fcntl.h>
#include <errno.h>
#include <sys/mman.h>

#define N_SB 16

int main (int argc, char **argv)
{
    int fd, size;
    char *area, *fname = "/sys/kernel/debug/my_rc_file0";

    if (argc > 1)
        fname = argv[1];

    size = N_SB * getpagesize ();    /* make sure this agrees with module! */

    if (argc > 2)
        size = atoi (argv[2]);

    printf (" Memory Mapping %s, size %d bytes\n", fname, size);

    if ((fd = open (fname, O_RDONLY)) < 0) {
        perror ("problems opening the file ");
        exit (errno);
    }
    area = mmap (NULL, size, PROT_READ, MAP_SHARED, fd, 0);
    if (area == MAP_FAILED) {
        perror ("error mmaping");
        exit (errno);
    }
    write (STDOUT_FILENO, area, 64 * 20);   /* may want to write out more */
    close (fd);
    exit (0);
}
```

Chapter 19

Sleeping and Wait Queues

19.1   Lab 1: Using Wait Queues

- Generalize the previous character driver to use wait queues,

- Have the read() function go to sleep until woken by a write() function. (You could also try reversing read and write.)

- You may want to open up two windows and read in one window and then write in the other window.

- Try putting more than one process to sleep, i.e., run your test read program more than once simultaneously before running the write program to awaken them. If you keep track of the **pid**'s you should be able to detect in what order processes are woken.

- There are several solutions given:

    - Using wait_event_interruptible(). You may want to use **atomic** functions for any global variables used in the logical condition.
    There are two solutions with this interface; one that wakes up only one sleeper, one that wakes up all sleepers.

- Using `wait_for_completion()`.
- Using **semaphores**.
- Using **read/write semaphores**.
- Using exclusive waiting on the many readers solution.. How many processes wake up?

- If you test with **cat**, **echo**, or **dd**, you may see different results than if you use the supplied simple read/write programs. Why?

lab_char.h
lab1_read.c

```
 /* Copyright 2009, J Cooperstein coop@coopj.com (GPLv2) */

#include <stdio.h>
#include <unistd.h>
#include <fcntl.h>
#include <stdlib.h>
#include <string.h>
#include <stdlib.h>

int main (int argc, char *argv[])
{
    int fd, rc, nbytes = 32;
    char *buffer, *filename = "/dev/mycdrv";

    if (argc > 1)
        filename = argv[1];
    if (argc > 2)
        nbytes = atoi (argv[2]);
    buffer = malloc (nbytes);

    fd = open (filename, O_RDONLY);
    printf ("opened file: %s,  with file descriptor = %d\n", filename, fd);
    rc = read (fd, buffer, nbytes);
    printf ("read %d bytes which were:\n%s\n", rc, buffer);
    close (fd);
    exit (EXIT_SUCCESS);
}
```

lab1_write.c

```
 /* Copyright 2009, J Cooperstein coop@coopj.com (GPLv2) */

#include <stdio.h>
#include <unistd.h>
#include <fcntl.h>
#include <stdlib.h>
#include <string.h>
#include <stdlib.h>
#include <sys/stat.h>

int main (int argc, char *argv[])
```

```
{
    int fd, rc;
    char *buffer = "TESTING CHAR DRIVER WITH A WRITE", *filename =
        "/dev/mycdrv";

    if (argc > 1)
        filename = argv[1];

    fd = open (filename, O_RDWR | O_CREAT | O_TRUNC, S_IRUSR | S_IWUSR);
    rc = write (fd, buffer, strlen (buffer));
    printf ("process %d wrote %d bytes to %s\n", getpid (), rc, filename);
    close (fd);
    exit (EXIT_SUCCESS);
}
```

lab1_wait_event_1.c

```
/* Copyright 2009, J Cooperstein coop@coopj.com (GPLv2) */

#include <linux/module.h>
#include "lab_char.h"

static DECLARE_WAIT_QUEUE_HEAD (wq);

static atomic_t data_ready;

static ssize_t
mycdrv_read (struct file *file, char __user * buf, size_t lbuf, loff_t * ppos)
{
    printk (KERN_INFO "process %i (%s) going to sleep\n", current->pid,
            current->comm);
    wait_event_interruptible (wq, (atomic_read (&data_ready)));
    printk (KERN_INFO "process %i (%s) awakening\n", current->pid,
            current->comm);
    atomic_set (&data_ready, 0);
    return mycdrv_generic_read (file, buf, lbuf, ppos);
}

static ssize_t
mycdrv_write (struct file *file, const char __user * buf, size_t lbuf,
              loff_t * ppos)
{
    int nbytes = mycdrv_generic_write (file, buf, lbuf, ppos);
    printk (KERN_INFO "process %i (%s) awakening the readers...\n",
            current->pid, current->comm);
    atomic_set (&data_ready, 1);
    wake_up_interruptible (&wq);
    return nbytes;
}

static const struct file_operations mycdrv_fops = {
    .owner = THIS_MODULE,
    .read = mycdrv_read,
    .write = mycdrv_write,
    .open = mycdrv_generic_open,
```

```
        .release = mycdrv_generic_release,
};

static int __init my_init (void)
{
    atomic_set (&data_ready, 0);
    return my_generic_init ();
}

module_init (my_init);
module_exit (my_generic_exit);

MODULE_AUTHOR ("Jerry Cooperstein");
MODULE_DESCRIPTION ("CLDD 1.0: lab1_wait_event_1.c");
MODULE_LICENSE ("GPL v2");
```

lab1_wait_event_many.c

```
 /* Copyright 2009, J Cooperstein coop@coopj.com (GPLv2) */

#include <linux/module.h>
#include "lab_char.h"

static DECLARE_WAIT_QUEUE_HEAD (wq);

static atomic_t data_ready, nsleepers;
static spinlock_t nsleepers_lock;

static ssize_t
mycdrv_read (struct file *file, char __user * buf, size_t lbuf, loff_t * ppos)
{
    printk (KERN_INFO "process %i (%s) going to sleep\n", current->pid,
            current->comm);
    atomic_inc (&nsleepers);
    wait_event_interruptible (wq, (atomic_read (&data_ready)));
    printk (KERN_INFO "process %i (%s) awakening\n", current->pid,
            current->comm);

    /* need to take spin lock to avoid preemption */

    spin_lock (&nsleepers_lock);
    if (atomic_dec_and_test (&nsleepers))
        atomic_set (&data_ready, 0);
    spin_unlock (&nsleepers_lock);

    return mycdrv_generic_read (file, buf, lbuf, ppos);
}

static ssize_t
mycdrv_write (struct file *file, const char __user * buf, size_t lbuf,
              loff_t * ppos)
{
    int nbytes = mycdrv_generic_write (file, buf, lbuf, ppos);

    printk (KERN_INFO "process %i (%s) awakening the readers...\n",
```

```
                    current->pid, current->comm);
        atomic_set (&data_ready, 1);
        wake_up_interruptible (&wq);
        return nbytes;
}

static const struct file_operations mycdrv_fops = {
        .owner = THIS_MODULE,
        .read = mycdrv_read,
        .write = mycdrv_write,
        .open = mycdrv_generic_open,
        .release = mycdrv_generic_release,
};

static int __init my_init (void)
{
        spin_lock_init (&nsleepers_lock);
        atomic_set (&data_ready, 0);
        atomic_set (&nsleepers, 0);
        return my_generic_init ();
}

module_init (my_init);
module_exit (my_generic_exit);

MODULE_AUTHOR ("Jerry Cooperstein");
MODULE_DESCRIPTION ("CLDD 1.0: lab1_wait_event_many.c");
MODULE_LICENSE ("GPL v2");
```

lab1_complete.c

```
 /* Copyright 2009, J Cooperstein coop@coopj.com (GPLv2) */

#include <linux/module.h>
#include <linux/completion.h>
#include "lab_char.h"

static DECLARE_COMPLETION (my_wait);

static ssize_t
mycdrv_read (struct file *file, char __user * buf, size_t lbuf, loff_t * ppos)
{
        printk (KERN_INFO "process %i (%s) going to sleep\n", current->pid,
                current->comm);
        wait_for_completion (&my_wait);
        printk (KERN_INFO "process %i (%s) awakening\n", current->pid,
                current->comm);
        return mycdrv_generic_read (file, buf, lbuf, ppos);
}

static ssize_t
mycdrv_write (struct file *file, const char __user * buf, size_t lbuf,
              loff_t * ppos)
{
        int nbytes = mycdrv_generic_write (file, buf, lbuf, ppos);
```

```
    printk (KERN_INFO "process %i (%s) awakening the readers...\n",
            current->pid, current->comm);
    complete (&my_wait);
    return nbytes;
}
static const struct file_operations mycdrv_fops = {
    .owner = THIS_MODULE,
    .read = mycdrv_read,
    .write = mycdrv_write,
    .open = mycdrv_generic_open,
    .release = mycdrv_generic_release,
};

module_init (my_generic_init);
module_exit (my_generic_exit);

MODULE_AUTHOR ("Jerry Cooperstein");
MODULE_DESCRIPTION ("CLDD 1.0: lab1_complete.c");
MODULE_LICENSE ("GPL v2");
```

lab1_semaphore.c

```
 /* Copyright 2009, J Cooperstein coop@coopj.com (GPLv2) */

#include <linux/module.h>
#include <linux/version.h>
#if LINUX_VERSION_CODE < KERNEL_VERSION(2,6,27)
#include <asm/semaphore.h>
#else
#include <linux/semaphore.h>
#endif
#include "lab_char.h"

static DECLARE_MUTEX (my_sem);

static ssize_t
mycdrv_read (struct file *file, char __user * buf, size_t lbuf, loff_t * ppos)
{
    printk (KERN_INFO "process %i (%s) going to sleep\n", current->pid,
            current->comm);
    if (down_interruptible (&my_sem)) {
        printk (KERN_INFO "process %i woken up by a signal\n", current->pid);
        return -ERESTARTSYS;
    }
    printk (KERN_INFO "process %i (%s) awakening\n", current->pid,
            current->comm);
    return mycdrv_generic_read (file, buf, lbuf, ppos);
}

static ssize_t
mycdrv_write (struct file *file, const char __user * buf, size_t lbuf,
              loff_t * ppos)
{
    int nbytes = mycdrv_generic_write (file, buf, lbuf, ppos);
```

```
        printk (KERN_INFO "process %i (%s) awakening the readers...\n",
                current->pid, current->comm);
        up (&my_sem);
        return nbytes;
}
static const struct file_operations mycdrv_fops = {
        .owner = THIS_MODULE,
        .read = mycdrv_read,
        .write = mycdrv_write,
        .open = mycdrv_generic_open,
        .release = mycdrv_generic_release,
};

module_init (my_generic_init);
module_exit (my_generic_exit);

MODULE_AUTHOR ("Jerry Cooperstein");
MODULE_DESCRIPTION ("CLDD 1.0: lab1_semaphore.c");
MODULE_LICENSE ("GPL v2");
```

lab1_semaphore_rw.c

```
 /* Copyright 2009, J Cooperstein coop@coopj.com (GPLv2) */

#include <linux/module.h>
#include <linux/version.h>
#if LINUX_VERSION_CODE < KERNEL_VERSION(2,6,27)
#include <asm/semaphore.h>
#else
#include <linux/semaphore.h>
#endif
#include "lab_char.h"

static DECLARE_RWSEM (my_sem);

static ssize_t
mycdrv_read (struct file *file, char __user * buf, size_t lbuf, loff_t * ppos)
{
        printk (KERN_INFO "process %i (%s) going to sleep\n", current->pid,
                current->comm);
        down_read (&my_sem);
        printk (KERN_INFO "process %i (%s) awakening\n", current->pid,
                current->comm);
        return mycdrv_generic_read (file, buf, lbuf, ppos);
}

static ssize_t
mycdrv_write (struct file *file, const char __user * buf, size_t lbuf,
              loff_t * ppos)
{
        int nbytes = mycdrv_generic_write (file, buf, lbuf, ppos);

        printk (KERN_INFO "process %i (%s) awakening the readers...\n",
                current->pid, current->comm);
```

```
        up_read (&my_sem);
        return nbytes;
}
static const struct file_operations mycdrv_fops = {
        .owner = THIS_MODULE,
        .read = mycdrv_read,
        .write = mycdrv_write,
        .open = mycdrv_generic_open,
        .release = mycdrv_generic_release,
};

module_init (my_generic_init);
module_exit (my_generic_exit);

MODULE_AUTHOR ("Jerry Cooperstein");
MODULE_DESCRIPTION ("CLDD 1.0: lab1_semaphore_rw.c");
MODULE_LICENSE ("GPL v2");
```

lab1_excl.c

```
 /* Copyright 2009, J Cooperstein coop@coopj.com (GPLv2) */

#include <linux/module.h>
#include "lab_char.h"

static DECLARE_WAIT_QUEUE_HEAD (wq);
static atomic_t data_ready, nsleepers;
static spinlock_t nsleepers_lock;

static ssize_t
mycdrv_read (struct file *file, char __user * buf, size_t lbuf, loff_t * ppos)
{
        printk (KERN_INFO "process %i (%s) going to sleep\n", current->pid,
                current->comm);
        atomic_inc (&nsleepers);
        wait_event_interruptible_exclusive (wq, (atomic_read (&data_ready)));
        printk (KERN_INFO "process %i (%s) awakening\n", current->pid,
                current->comm);

        /* need to take spin lock to avoid preemption */

        spin_lock (&nsleepers_lock);
        if (atomic_dec_and_test (&nsleepers))
            atomic_set (&data_ready, 0);
        spin_unlock (&nsleepers_lock);

        return mycdrv_generic_read (file, buf, lbuf, ppos);
}

static ssize_t
mycdrv_write (struct file *file, const char __user * buf, size_t lbuf,
              loff_t * ppos)
{
        int nbytes = mycdrv_generic_write (file, buf, lbuf, ppos);
        printk (KERN_INFO "process %i (%s) awakening the readers...\n",
```

```
                    current->pid, current->comm);
        wake_up_interruptible (&wq);
        atomic_set (&data_ready, 1);
        return nbytes;
}

static const struct file_operations mycdrv_fops = {
        .owner = THIS_MODULE,
        .read = mycdrv_read,
        .write = mycdrv_write,
        .open = mycdrv_generic_open,
        .release = mycdrv_generic_release,
};

static int __init my_init (void)
{
        spin_lock_init (&nsleepers_lock);
        atomic_set (&data_ready, 0);
        atomic_set (&nsleepers, 0);
        return my_generic_init ();
}

module_init (my_init);
module_exit (my_generic_exit);

MODULE_AUTHOR ("Jerry Cooperstein");
MODULE_DESCRIPTION ("CLDD 1.0: lab1_excl.c");
MODULE_LICENSE ("GPL v2");
```

19.2   Lab 2: Killable Sleep

- Modify the `wait_event()` lab to use `wait_event_killable()`. After a reading process goes to sleep, send it a non-fatal signal, such as

  ```
  $ kill -SIGCONT <pid>
  ```

  followed by a kill signal, such as SIGKILL.

lab2_killable.c

```
/* Copyright 2009, J Cooperstein coop@coopj.com (GPLv2) */

#include <linux/module.h>
#include "lab_char.h"

static DECLARE_WAIT_QUEUE_HEAD (wq);

static atomic_t data_ready;

static ssize_t
mycdrv_read (struct file *file, char __user * buf, size_t lbuf, loff_t * ppos)
{
```

```
    printk (KERN_INFO "process %i (%s) going to sleep\n", current->pid,
            current->comm);
    wait_event_killable (wq, (atomic_read (&data_ready)));
    printk (KERN_INFO "process %i (%s) awakening\n", current->pid,
            current->comm);
    atomic_set (&data_ready, 0);
    return mycdrv_generic_read (file, buf, lbuf, ppos);
}

static ssize_t
mycdrv_write (struct file *file, const char __user * buf, size_t lbuf,
            loff_t * ppos)
{
    int nbytes = mycdrv_generic_write (file, buf, lbuf, ppos);
    printk (KERN_INFO "process %i (%s) awakening the readers...\n",
            current->pid, current->comm);
    atomic_set (&data_ready, 1);
    wake_up_interruptible (&wq);
    return nbytes;
}

static const struct file_operations mycdrv_fops = {
    .owner = THIS_MODULE,
    .read = mycdrv_read,
    .write = mycdrv_write,
    .open = mycdrv_generic_open,
    .release = mycdrv_generic_release,
};

static int __init my_init (void)
{
    atomic_set (&data_ready, 0);
    return my_generic_init ();
}

module_init (my_init);
module_exit (my_generic_exit);

MODULE_AUTHOR ("Jerry Cooperstein");
MODULE_DESCRIPTION ("CLDD 1.0: lab2_killable.c");
MODULE_LICENSE ("GPL v2");
```

19.3   Lab 3: Using poll()

- Take the wait_event() solution and extend it to have a poll() entry point.

- You'll need an application that opens the device node and then calls poll() and waits for data
  to be available.

```
lab_char.h
lab3_poll.c
```

```
/* Copyright 2009, J Cooperstein coop@coopj.com (GPLv2) */

#include <linux/module.h>
#include <linux/poll.h>
#include "lab_char.h"

static DECLARE_WAIT_QUEUE_HEAD (wq);

static atomic_t data_ready;

static ssize_t
mycdrv_read (struct file *file, char __user * buf, size_t lbuf, loff_t * ppos)
{
    printk (KERN_INFO "process %i (%s) going to sleep\n", current->pid,
            current->comm);
    wait_event_interruptible (wq, (atomic_read (&data_ready)));
    printk (KERN_INFO "process %i (%s) awakening\n", current->pid,
            current->comm);
    atomic_set (&data_ready, 0);
    return mycdrv_generic_read (file, buf, lbuf, ppos);
}

//if (file->f_flags & O_NDELAY)
//    return -EAGAIN;
static ssize_t
mycdrv_write (struct file *file, const char __user * buf, size_t lbuf,
              loff_t * ppos)
{
    int nbytes = mycdrv_generic_write (file, buf, lbuf, ppos);
    printk (KERN_INFO "process %i (%s) awakening the readers...\n",
            current->pid, current->comm);
    wake_up_interruptible (&wq);
    atomic_set (&data_ready, 1);
    return nbytes;
}

static unsigned int mycdrv_poll (struct file *file, poll_table * wait)
{
    poll_wait (file, &wq, wait);
    printk (KERN_INFO "In poll at jiffies=%ld\n", jiffies);
    if (atomic_read (&data_ready))
        return POLLIN | POLLRDNORM;
    return 0;
}

static const struct file_operations mycdrv_fops = {
    .owner = THIS_MODULE,
    .read = mycdrv_read,
    .write = mycdrv_write,
    .open = mycdrv_generic_open,
    .release = mycdrv_generic_release,
    .poll = mycdrv_poll,
};

static int __init my_init (void)
```

```c
{
    atomic_set (&data_ready, 0);
    return my_generic_init ();
}

module_init (my_init);
module_exit (my_generic_exit);

MODULE_AUTHOR ("Jerry Cooperstein");
MODULE_DESCRIPTION ("CLDD 1.0: lab3_poll.c");
MODULE_LICENSE ("GPL v2");
```

lab3_poll_test.c

```c
/* Copyright 2009, J Cooperstein coop@coopj.com (GPLv2) */

#include <stdio.h>
#include <unistd.h>
#include <fcntl.h>
#include <stdlib.h>
#include <string.h>
#include <poll.h>

int main (int argc, char *argv[])
{
    struct pollfd ufds[1];
    int timeout = 10000;          /* time out for poll */
    int fd, rc, nbytes = 32;
    char *buffer, *filename = "/dev/mycdrv";

    if (argc > 1)
        filename = argv[1];
    if (argc > 2)
        nbytes = atoi (argv[2]);
    buffer = malloc (nbytes);

    fd = open (filename, O_RDONLY);
    printf ("opened file: %s,  with file descriptor = %d\n", filename, fd);

    ufds[0].fd = fd;
    ufds[0].events = POLLIN;

    for (;;) {

        if ((rc = poll (ufds, 1, timeout)) < 0) {
            perror ("Failure in poll\n");
            exit (EXIT_FAILURE);
        }

        if (rc > 0) {

            printf (" poll returns %d, revents = 0x%03x", rc, ufds[0].revents);

            if (ufds[0].revents & POLLIN) {
                rc = read (fd, buffer, nbytes);
```

```
                    printf ("reading %d bytes:%s\n", rc, buffer);
                } else {
                    printf ("POLLIN not set!\n");
                }

            } else {
                printf ("poll timed out in %d milliseconds on %s.\n",
                        timeout, filename);
            }
        }
        close (fd);
        printf ("Shutting down %s\n", argv[0]);
        exit (EXIT_SUCCESS);
}
```

19.4   Lab 4: User-Space Interrupt Handling

- Adapt the character driver with polling to handle a shared interrupt.

- The read method should sleep until events are available and then deal with potentially multiple events.

- The information passed back by the read should include the number of events.

- You can reuse the previously written testing program that opens the device node and then sits on it with poll() until interrupts arrive.

- You can also test it with just using the simple read program, or doing cat < /dev/mycdrv and generating some interrupts.

- You can probably also implement a solution that does not involve poll(), but just a blocking read.

lab_char.h
lab4_interrupt.c

```
/* Copyright 2009, J Cooperstein coop@coopj.com (GPLv2) */

#include <linux/module.h>
#include <linux/interrupt.h>
#include <linux/poll.h>
#include "lab_char.h"

static DECLARE_WAIT_QUEUE_HEAD (wq);

#define SHARED_IRQ 12
static int irq = SHARED_IRQ;
module_param (irq, int, S_IRUGO);

static atomic_t nevents;

static irqreturn_t my_interrupt (int irq, void *dev_id)
```

```
{
    atomic_inc (&nevents);
    wake_up_interruptible (&wq);
    return IRQ_NONE;
}

static ssize_t
mycdrv_read (struct file *file, char __user * buf, size_t lbuf, loff_t * ppos)
{
    char ret_str[32];
    int nev, nc;
    printk (KERN_INFO "waiting for interrupt at jiffies=%ld\n", jiffies);
    wait_event_interruptible (wq, (atomic_read (&nevents) > 0));
    if (signal_pending (current)) {
        printk (KERN_INFO "process %i woken up by a signal\n", current->pid);
        return -ERESTARTSYS;
    }
    nev = atomic_read (&nevents);
    printk (KERN_INFO "Now dealing with %d events\n", nev);
    atomic_sub (nev, &nevents);
    nc = sprintf (ret_str, "%d", nev);
    if (copy_to_user (buf, ret_str, nc))
        return -EIO;
    return nc;
}

static unsigned int mycdrv_poll (struct file *file, poll_table * wait)
{
    poll_wait (file, &wq, wait);
    printk (KERN_INFO "In poll at jiffies=%ld, nevents=%d\n", jiffies,
            atomic_read (&nevents));
    if (atomic_read (&nevents) > 0)
        return POLLIN | POLLRDNORM;
    return 0;
}

static const struct file_operations mycdrv_fops = {
    .owner = THIS_MODULE,
    .read = mycdrv_read,
    .poll = mycdrv_poll,
    .open = mycdrv_generic_open,
    .release = mycdrv_generic_release,
};

static inline int __init my_init (void)
{
    if (request_irq (irq, my_interrupt, IRQF_SHARED, "my_int", my_interrupt))
        return -1;

    atomic_set (&nevents, 0);
    printk (KERN_INFO "successfully loaded\n");
    return my_generic_init ();
}

static inline void __exit my_exit (void)
```

```
{
    synchronize_irq (irq);
    free_irq (irq, my_interrupt);
    printk (KERN_INFO "successfully unloaded\n");
    return my_generic_exit ();
}

module_init (my_init);
module_exit (my_exit);

MODULE_AUTHOR ("Jerry Cooperstein");
MODULE_DESCRIPTION ("CLDD 1.0: lab4_interrupt.c");
MODULE_LICENSE ("GPL v2");
```

Chapter 20

Interrupt Handling and Deferrable Functions

20.1 Lab 1: Deferred Functions

- Write a driver that schedules a deferred function whenever a `write()` to the device takes place.

- Pass some data to the driver and have it print out.

- Have it print out the `current->pid` field when the tasklet is scheduled, and then again when the queued function is executed.

- Implement this using:

  - **tasklets**
  - **work queues**

- You can use the same testing programs you used in the sleep exercises.

- Try scheduling multiple deferred functions and see if they come out in LIFO or FIFO order. What happens if you try to schedule the deferred function more than once?

lab_char.h
lab1_tasklet.c

```
/* Copyright 2009, J Cooperstein coop@coopj.com (GPLv2) */

#include <linux/module.h>
#include <linux/interrupt.h>
#include "lab_char.h"

static struct simp
{
    int len;
} t_data = {
.len = 100};

static void t_fun (unsigned long t_arg)
{
    struct simp *datum;
    datum = (struct simp *)t_arg;
    printk (KERN_INFO "I am in t_fun, jiffies = %ld\n", jiffies);
    printk (KERN_INFO " I think my current task pid is %d\n",
            (int)current->pid);
    printk (KERN_INFO " my data is: %d\n", datum->len);
}

/* initialize tasklet */

static DECLARE_TASKLET (t_name, t_fun, (unsigned long)&t_data);

static ssize_t
mycdrv_write (struct file *file, const char __user * buf, size_t lbuf,
              loff_t * ppos)
{
    printk (KERN_INFO " Entering the WRITE function\n");
    printk (KERN_INFO " my current task pid is %d\n", (int)current->pid);
    printk (KERN_INFO "about to schedule tasklet, jiffies=%ld\n", jiffies);
    tasklet_schedule (&t_name);

    printk (KERN_INFO " i queued the task, jiffies=%ld\n", jiffies);
    t_data.len += 100;
    return lbuf;
}

static const struct file_operations mycdrv_fops = {
    .owner = THIS_MODULE,
    .read = mycdrv_generic_read,
    .write = mycdrv_write,
    .open = mycdrv_generic_open,
    .release = mycdrv_generic_release,
};

module_init (my_generic_init);
module_exit (my_generic_exit);
```

```
MODULE_AUTHOR ("Jerry Cooperstein");
MODULE_DESCRIPTION ("CLDD 1.0: lab1_tasklet.c");
MODULE_LICENSE ("GPL v2");
```

lab1_workqueue.c

```
 /* Copyright 2009, J Cooperstein coop@coopj.com (GPLv2) */

#include <linux/module.h>
#include "lab_char.h"
#include <linux/fs.h>
#include <linux/workqueue.h>

static struct my_dat
{
    atomic_t len;
    struct work_struct work;
} my_data = {
.len = ATOMIC_INIT (100)};

/* initialize workqueue */

static void w_fun (struct work_struct *w_arg)
{
    struct my_dat *data = container_of (w_arg, struct my_dat, work);
    printk (KERN_INFO "I am in w_fun, jiffies = %ld\n", jiffies);
    printk (KERN_INFO " I think my current task pid is %d\n",
            (int)current->pid);
    printk (KERN_INFO " my data is: %d\n", atomic_read (&data->len));
}

static DECLARE_WORK (w, w_fun);

static ssize_t
mycdrv_write (struct file *file, const char __user * buf, size_t lbuf,
            loff_t * ppos)
{
    printk (KERN_INFO " Entering the WRITE function\n");
    printk (KERN_INFO " my current task pid is %d\n", (int)current->pid);
    printk (KERN_INFO "about to schedule workqueue,  jiffies=%ld\n", jiffies);
    schedule_work (&w);
    printk (KERN_INFO " i queued the task, jiffies=%ld\n", jiffies);
    atomic_add (100, &my_data.len);
    return lbuf;
}

static const struct file_operations mycdrv_fops = {
    .owner = THIS_MODULE,
    .read = mycdrv_generic_read,
    .write = mycdrv_write,
    .open = mycdrv_generic_open,
    .release = mycdrv_generic_release,
};

module_init (my_generic_init);
```

```
module_exit (my_generic_exit);

MODULE_AUTHOR ("Jerry Cooperstein");
MODULE_DESCRIPTION ("CLDD 1.0: lab1_workqueue.c");
MODULE_LICENSE ("GPL v2");
```

lab1_write.c

```
/* Copyright 2009, J Cooperstein coop@coopj.com (GPLv2) */

#include <stdio.h>
#include <unistd.h>
#include <fcntl.h>
#include <stdlib.h>
#include <string.h>
#include <stdlib.h>
#include <sys/stat.h>

int main (int argc, char *argv[])
{
    int fd, rc;
    char *buffer = "TESTING CHAR DRIVER WITH A WRITE", *filename =
        "/dev/mycdrv";

    if (argc > 1)
        filename = argv[1];

    fd = open (filename, O_RDWR | O_CREAT | O_TRUNC, S_IRUSR | S_IWUSR);
    rc = write (fd, buffer, strlen (buffer));
    printf ("process %d wrote %d bytes to %s\n", getpid (), rc, filename);
    close (fd);
    exit (EXIT_SUCCESS);
}
```

20.2   Lab 2: Shared Interrupts and Bottom Halves

- Write a module that shares its IRQ with your network card. You can generate some network interrupts either by browsing or pinging.

- Make it use a top half and a bottom half.

- Check /proc/interrupts while it is loaded.

- Have the module keep track of the number of times the interrupt's halves are called.

- Implement the bottom half using:

  - **tasklets**.

  - **work queues**

  - **A background thread** which you launch during the module's initialization, which gets woken up anytime data is available. Make sure you kill the thread when you unload the module, or it may stay in a zombie state forever.

- For any method you use does, are the bottom and top halves called an equal number of times?
  If not why, and what can you do about it?

lab_one_interrupt.h

```
#ifndef _LAB_ONE_INTERRUPT_H
#define _LAB_ONE INTERRUPT_H

#include <linux/module.h>
#include <linux/init.h>
#include <linux/interrupt.h>
#include <linux/delay.h>
#include <linux/workqueue.h>
#include <linux/kthread.h>

#define SHARED_IRQ 19
static int irq = SHARED_IRQ;
module_param (irq, int, S_IRUGO);

/* default delay time in top half -- try 10 to get results */
static int delay = 0;
module_param (delay, int, S_IRUGO);

static atomic_t counter_bh, counter_th;

struct my_dat
{
    unsigned long jiffies;      /* used for timestamp */
    struct tasklet_struct tsk;  /* used in dynamic tasklet solution */
    struct work_struct work;    /* used in dynamic workqueue solution */
};
static struct my_dat my_data;

static irqreturn_t my_interrupt (int irq, void *dev_id);
#ifdef THREADED_IRQ
static irqreturn_t thread_fun (int irq, void *thr_arg);
#endif

static int __init my_generic_init (void)
{
    atomic_set (&counter_bh, 0);
    atomic_set (&counter_th, 0);

    /* use my_data for dev_id */

#ifdef THREADED_IRQ
    if (request_threaded_irq (irq, my_interrupt, thread_fun, IRQF_SHARED,
                              "my_int", &my_data))
#else
    if (request_irq (irq, my_interrupt, IRQF_SHARED, "my_int", &my_data))
#endif
        return -1;

    printk (KERN_INFO "successfully loaded\n");
    return 0;
```

```
}

static void __exit my_generic_exit (void)
{
    synchronize_irq (irq);
    free_irq (irq, &my_data);
    printk (KERN_INFO " counter_th = %d,  counter_bh = %d\n",
            atomic_read (&counter_th), atomic_read (&counter_bh));
    printk (KERN_INFO "successfully unloaded\n");
}

MODULE_AUTHOR ("Jerry Cooperstein");
MODULE_DESCRIPTION ("CLDD 1.0: lab_one_interrupt.h");
MODULE_LICENSE ("GPL v2");
#endif
```

lab2_one_tasklet.c

```
 /* Copyright 2009, J Cooperstein coop@coopj.com (GPLv2) */
#include <linux/module.h>
#include "lab_one_interrupt.h"

static void t_fun (unsigned long t_arg)
{
    struct my_dat *data = (struct my_dat *)t_arg;
    atomic_inc (&counter_bh);
    printk (KERN_INFO
            "In BH: counter_th = %d, counter_bh = %d, jiffies=%ld, %ld\n",
            atomic_read (&counter_th), atomic_read (&counter_bh), data->jiffies,
            jiffies);
}

static DECLARE_TASKLET (t_name, t_fun, (unsigned long)&my_data);

/* initialize tasklet */
static irqreturn_t my_interrupt (int irq, void *dev_id)
{
    struct my_dat *data = (struct my_dat *)dev_id;
    atomic_inc (&counter_th);
    data->jiffies = jiffies;
    tasklet_schedule (&t_name);
    mdelay (delay);              /* hoke up a delay to try to cause pileup */
    return IRQ_NONE;             /* we return IRQ_NONE because we are just observing */
}

module_init (my_generic_init);
module_exit (my_generic_exit);

MODULE_AUTHOR ("Jerry Cooperstein");
MODULE_DESCRIPTION ("CLDD 1.0: lab2_one_tasklet.c");
MODULE_LICENSE ("GPL v2");
```

lab2_one_workqueue.c

```
 /* Copyright 2009, J Cooperstein coop@coopj.com (GPLv2) */
```

```
#include <linux/module.h>
#include "lab_one_interrupt.h"

static void w_fun (struct work_struct *w_arg)
{
    struct my_dat *data = container_of (w_arg, struct my_dat, work);
    atomic_inc (&counter_bh);
    printk (KERN_INFO
            "In BH: counter_th = %d, counter_bh = %d, jiffies=%ld, %ld\n",
            atomic_read (&counter_th), atomic_read (&counter_bh), data->jiffies,
            jiffies);
}

static DECLARE_WORK (w, w_fun);

static irqreturn_t my_interrupt (int irq, void *dev_id)
{
    struct my_dat *data = (struct my_dat *)dev_id;
    atomic_inc (&counter_th);
    data->jiffies = jiffies;
    schedule_work (&w);
    mdelay (delay);              /* hoke up a delay to try to cause pileup */
    return IRQ_NONE;             /* we return IRQ_NONE because we are just observing */
}

module_init (my_generic_init);
module_exit (my_generic_exit);

MODULE_AUTHOR ("Jerry Cooperstein");
MODULE_DESCRIPTION ("CLDD 1.0: lab2_one_workqueue.c");
MODULE_LICENSE ("GPL v2");
```

lab2_one_thread.c

```
 /* Copyright 2009, J Cooperstein coop@coopj.com (GPLv2) */

#include <linux/module.h>
#include "lab_one_interrupt.h"

static DECLARE_WAIT_QUEUE_HEAD (wq);
static atomic_t cond;
static struct task_struct *tsk;

static irqreturn_t my_interrupt (int irq, void *dev_id)
{
    struct my_dat *data = (struct my_dat *)dev_id;
    atomic_inc (&counter_th);
    data->jiffies = jiffies;
    atomic_set (&cond, 1);
    mdelay (delay);              /* hoke up a delay to try to cause pileup */
    wake_up_interruptible (&wq);
    return IRQ_NONE;             /* we return IRQ_NONE because we are just observing */
}
```

```
static int thr_fun (void *thr_arg)
{
    struct my_dat *data = (struct my_dat *)thr_arg;

    /* go into a loop and deal with events as they come */

    do {
        atomic_set (&cond, 0);
        wait_event_interruptible (wq, kthread_should_stop ()
                                  || atomic_read (&cond));
        if (atomic_read (&cond))
            atomic_inc (&counter_bh);
        printk
            (KERN_INFO
             "In BH: counter_th = %d, counter_bh = %d, jiffies=%ld, %ld\n",
             atomic_read (&counter_th), atomic_read (&counter_bh),
             data->jiffies, jiffies);
    } while (!kthread_should_stop ());
    return 0;
}

static int __init my_init (void)
{
    atomic_set (&cond, 1);
    if (!(tsk = kthread_run (thr_fun, (void *)&my_data, "thr_fun"))) {
        printk (KERN_INFO "Failed to generate a kernel thread\n");
        return -1;
    }
    return my_generic_init ();
}

static void __exit my_exit (void)
{
    kthread_stop (tsk);
    my_generic_exit ();
}

module_init (my_init);
module_exit (my_exit);
MODULE_AUTHOR ("Jerry Cooperstein");
MODULE_DESCRIPTION ("CLDD 1.0: lab2_one_thread.c");
MODULE_LICENSE ("GPL v2");
```

20.3   Lab 3: Producer/Consumer

- You may have noticed that you lost some bottom halves. This will happen when more than one interrupt arrives before bottom halves are accomplished. For instance, the same tasklet can only be queued up twice.

- Write a bottom half that can "catch up"b; i.e., consume more than one event when it is called, cleaning up the pending queue. Do this for at least one of the previous solutions.

`lab3_one_tasklet_improved.c`

```
/* Copyright 2009, J Cooperstein coop@coopj.com (GPLv2) */

#include <linux/module.h>
#include "lab_one_interrupt.h"

static atomic_t nevents;        /* number of events to deal with */
static atomic_t catchup;        /* number of 'missed events' */

static void t_fun (unsigned long t_arg)
{
    struct my_dat *data = (struct my_dat *)t_arg;

    /* did we get a spurious interrupt, or was it queued too late? */
    if (atomic_read (&nevents) <= 0)
        return;

    for (;;) {
        atomic_inc (&counter_bh);
        printk
            (KERN_INFO
             "In BH: counter_th = %d, counter_bh = %d, jiffies=%ld, %ld\n",
             atomic_read (&counter_th), atomic_read (&counter_bh),
             data->jiffies, jiffies);
        if (atomic_dec_and_test (&nevents))
            break;
        atomic_inc (&catchup);
        printk (KERN_INFO "****** nevents > 0, catchup=%d\n",
                atomic_read (&catchup));
    }
}

/* initialize tasklet */
static DECLARE_TASKLET (t_name, t_fun, (unsigned long)&my_data);

static irqreturn_t my_interrupt (int irq, void *dev_id)
{
    struct my_dat *data = (struct my_dat *)dev_id;
    atomic_inc (&counter_th);
    atomic_inc (&nevents);
    data->jiffies = jiffies;
    tasklet_schedule (&t_name);
    mdelay (delay);             /* hoke up a delay to try to cause pileup */
    return IRQ_NONE;            /* we return IRQ_NONE because we are just observing */
}

static int __init my_init (void)
{
    atomic_set (&catchup, 0);
    atomic_set (&nevents, 0);
    return my_generic_init ();
}

static void __exit my_exit (void)
{
    my_generic_exit ();
```

```
        printk (KERN_INFO "Final statistics:    catchup = %d\n",
                atomic_read (&catchup));
}

module_init (my_init);
module_exit (my_exit);

MODULE_AUTHOR ("Jerry Cooperstein");
MODULE_DESCRIPTION ("CLDD 1.0: lab3_one_tasklet_improved.c");
MODULE_LICENSE ("GPL v2");
```

lab3_one_tasklet_dynamic.c

```
 /* Copyright 2009, J Cooperstein coop@coopj.com (GPLv2) */

#include <linux/module.h>
#include "lab_one_interrupt.h"

static void t_fun (unsigned long t_arg)
{
    struct my_dat *data = (struct my_dat *)t_arg;
    atomic_inc (&counter_bh);
    printk (KERN_INFO
            "In BH: counter_th = %d, counter_bh = %d, jiffies=%ld, %ld\n",
            atomic_read (&counter_th), atomic_read (&counter_bh), data->jiffies,
            jiffies);
    kfree (data);
}

static irqreturn_t my_interrupt (int irq, void *dev_id)
{
    struct tasklet_struct *t;
    struct my_dat *data;

    data = (struct my_dat *)kmalloc (sizeof (struct my_dat), GFP_ATOMIC);
    t = &data->tsk;
    data->jiffies = jiffies;

    tasklet_init (t, t_fun, (unsigned long)data);

    atomic_inc (&counter_th);
    tasklet_schedule (t);
    mdelay (delay);             /* hoke up a delay to try to cause pileup */
    return IRQ_NONE;            /* we return IRQ_NONE because we are just observing */
}

module_init (my_generic_init);
module_exit (my_generic_exit);

MODULE_AUTHOR ("Jerry Cooperstein");
MODULE_DESCRIPTION ("CLDD 1.0: lab3_one_tasklet_dynamic.c");
MODULE_LICENSE ("GPL v2");
```

lab3_one_workqueue_dynamic.c

```
/* Copyright 2009, J Cooperstein coop@coopj.com (GPLv2) */

#include <linux/module.h>
#include "lab_one_interrupt.h"

static void w_fun (struct work_struct *w_arg)
{
    struct my_dat *data = container_of (w_arg, struct my_dat, work);

    atomic_inc (&counter_bh);
    printk (KERN_INFO
            "In BH: counter_th = %d, counter_bh = %d, jiffies=%ld, %ld\n",
            atomic_read (&counter_th), atomic_read (&counter_bh), data->jiffies,
            jiffies);
    kfree (data);
}

static irqreturn_t my_interrupt (int irq, void *dev_id)
{
    struct my_dat *data =
        (struct my_dat *)kmalloc (sizeof (struct my_dat), GFP_ATOMIC);
    data->jiffies = jiffies;

    INIT_WORK (&data->work, w_fun);
    atomic_inc (&counter_th);
    schedule_work (&data->work);
    mdelay (delay);            /* hoke up a delay to try to cause pileup */
    return IRQ_NONE;           /* we return IRQ_NONE because we are just observing */
}

module_init (my_generic_init);
module_exit (my_generic_exit);

MODULE_AUTHOR ("Jerry Cooperstein");
MODULE_DESCRIPTION ("CLDD 1.0: lab3_one_workqueue_dynamic.c");
MODULE_LICENSE ("GPL v2");
```

lab3_one_thread_improved.c

```
/* Copyright 2009, J Cooperstein coop@coopj.com (GPLv2) */

#include <linux/module.h>
#include "lab_one_interrupt.h"

static atomic_t cond;
static atomic_t nevents;        /* number of events to deal with */
static atomic_t catchup;        /* number of 'missed events' */

static DECLARE_WAIT_QUEUE_HEAD (wq);

static struct task_struct *tsk;

static irqreturn_t my_interrupt (int irq, void *dev_id)
{
    struct my_dat *data = (struct my_dat *)dev_id;
```

```
    atomic_inc (&nevents);
    atomic_inc (&counter_th);
    atomic_set (&cond, 1);
    data->jiffies = jiffies;
    mdelay (delay);                 /* hoke up a delay to try to cause pileup */
    wake_up_interruptible (&wq);
    return IRQ_NONE;                /* we return IRQ_NONE because we are just observing */
}

static int thr_fun (void *thr_arg)
{
    struct my_dat *data;
    data = (struct my_dat *)thr_arg;

    /* go into a loop and deal with events as they come */

    do {
        atomic_set (&cond, 0);
        wait_event_interruptible (wq, kthread_should_stop ()
                                  || atomic_read (&cond));
        /* did we get a spurious interrupt, or was it queued too late? */
        if (kthread_should_stop ())
            return 0;
        if (atomic_read (&nevents) <= 0)
            continue;
        for (;;) {
            atomic_inc (&counter_bh);
            printk
                (KERN_INFO
                 "In BH: counter_th = %d, counter_bh = %d, jiffies=%ld, %ld\n",
                 atomic_read (&counter_th), atomic_read (&counter_bh),
                 data->jiffies, jiffies);
            if (atomic_dec_and_test (&nevents))
                break;
            atomic_inc (&catchup);
            printk (KERN_INFO "****** nevents > 0, catchup=%d\n",
                    atomic_read (&catchup));
        }
    } while (!kthread_should_stop ());
    return 0;
}

static int __init my_init (void)
{
    atomic_set (&cond, 1);
    atomic_set (&catchup, 0);
    atomic_set (&nevents, 0);
    if (!(tsk = kthread_run (thr_fun, (void *)&my_data, "thr_fun"))) {
        printk (KERN_INFO "Failed to generate a kernel thread\n");
        return -1;
    }
    return my_generic_init ();
}

static void __exit my_exit (void)
```

```
{
    kthread_stop (tsk);
    my_generic_exit ();
    printk (KERN_INFO "Final statistics:   catchup = %d\n",
            atomic_read (&catchup));
}

module_init (my_init);
module_exit (my_exit);

MODULE_AUTHOR ("Jerry Cooperstein");
MODULE_DESCRIPTION ("CLDD 1.0: lab3_one_thread_improved.c");
MODULE_LICENSE ("GPL v2");
```

20.4   Lab 4: Sharing All Interrupts, Bottom Halves

- Extend the solution to share all possible interrupts, and evaluate the consumer/producer problem.

lab_all_interrupt.h

```
#ifndef _LAB_ALL_INTERRUPT_H
#define _LAB_ALL_INTERRUPT_H

#include <linux/module.h>
#include <linux/fs.h>
#include <linux/uaccess.h>
#include <linux/init.h>
#include <linux/slab.h>
#include <linux/cdev.h>
#include <linux/delay.h>
#include <linux/interrupt.h>
#include <linux/workqueue.h>
#include <linux/kthread.h>

#define MYDEV_NAME "mycdrv"
#define KBUF_SIZE (size_t)(PAGE_SIZE)
#define MAXIRQS 256
#define NCOPY (MAXIRQS * sizeof(atomic_t))

static char *kbuf;
static dev_t first;
static unsigned int count = 1;
static int my_major = 700, my_minor = 0;
static struct cdev *my_cdev;

static atomic_t *interrupts, *bhs, *nevents;

static int delay = 0;
    /* default delay time in top half -- try 10 to get results */
module_param (delay, int, S_IRUGO);
```

```
static irqreturn_t my_interrupt (int irq, void *dev_id);
#ifdef THREADED_IRQ
static irqreturn_t thread_fun (int irq, void *thr_arg);
#endif

static void freeup_irqs (void)
{
    int irq;
    for (irq = 0; irq < MAXIRQS; irq++) {
        /* if greater than 0, was able to share */
        if (atomic_read (&interrupts[irq]) >= 0) {
            printk
                (KERN_INFO "Freeing IRQ= %4d, which had %10d, %10d events\n",
                 irq, atomic_read (&interrupts[irq]), atomic_read (&bhs[irq]));
            synchronize_irq (irq);
            free_irq (irq, interrupts);
        }
    }
}
static ssize_t
mycdrv_read (struct file *file, char __user * buf, size_t lbuf, loff_t * ppos)
{
    int nbytes, maxbytes, bytes_to_do;
    maxbytes = KBUF_SIZE - *ppos;
    bytes_to_do = maxbytes > lbuf ? lbuf : maxbytes;
    if (bytes_to_do == 0)
        printk (KERN_INFO "Reached end of the device on a read");
    nbytes = bytes_to_do - copy_to_user (buf, kbuf + *ppos, bytes_to_do);
    *ppos += nbytes;
    printk (KERN_INFO "\n Leaving the   READ function, nbytes=%d, pos=%d\n",
            nbytes, (int)*ppos);
    return nbytes;
}

static const struct file_operations mycdrv_fops = {
    .owner = THIS_MODULE,
    .read = mycdrv_read,
};

static int __init my_generic_init (void)
{
    int irq;

    first = MKDEV (my_major, my_minor);

    if (register_chrdev_region (first, count, MYDEV_NAME) < 0) {
        printk (KERN_ERR "failed to register character device region\n");
        return -1;
    }
    if (!(my_cdev = cdev_alloc ())) {
        printk (KERN_ERR "cdev_alloc() failed\n");
        unregister_chrdev_region (first, count);
        return -1;
    }
    nevents = kmalloc (MAXIRQS * sizeof (atomic_t), GFP_KERNEL);
```

```
    kbuf = kmalloc (KBUF_SIZE, GFP_KERNEL);
    cdev_init (my_cdev, &mycdrv_fops);
    if (cdev_add (my_cdev, first, count) < 0) {
        printk (KERN_ERR "cdev_add() failed\n");
        cdev_del (my_cdev);
        unregister_chrdev_region (first, count);
        kfree (kbuf);
        kfree (nevents);
        return -1;
    }

    printk (KERN_INFO "\nSucceeded in registering character device %s\n",
            MYDEV_NAME);
    printk (KERN_INFO "Major number = %d, Minor number = %d\n", MAJOR (first),
            MINOR (first));

    interrupts = (atomic_t *) kbuf;
    bhs = (atomic_t *) (kbuf + NCOPY);

    for (irq = 0; irq < MAXIRQS; irq++) {
        atomic_set (&interrupts[irq], -1);  /* set to -1 as a flag */
        atomic_set (&bhs[irq], 0);
        atomic_set (&nevents[irq], 0);
#ifdef THREADED_IRQ
        if (!request_threaded_irq (irq, my_interrupt, thread_fun,
                                   IRQF_SHARED, "my_int", interrupts))
#else
        if (!request_irq (irq, my_interrupt,
                                   IRQF_SHARED, "my_int", interrupts))
#endif
        {
            atomic_set (&interrupts[irq], 0);
            printk (KERN_INFO "Succeded in registering IRQ=%d\n", irq);
        }
    }
    return 0;
}

static void __exit my_generic_exit (void)
{
    freeup_irqs ();
    cdev_del (my_cdev);
    unregister_chrdev_region (first, count);
    kfree (kbuf);
    kfree (nevents);
    printk (KERN_INFO "\ndevice unregistered\n");
}

MODULE_AUTHOR ("Jerry Cooperstein");
MODULE_DESCRIPTION ("CLDD 1.0: lab_all_interrupt.h");
MODULE_LICENSE ("GPL v2");

#endif
```

lab4_all_getinterrupts.c

```c
/* Copyright 2009, J Cooperstein coop@coopj.com (GPLv2) */
#include <stdlib.h>
#include <stdio.h>
#include <fcntl.h>
#include <unistd.h>
#include <errno.h>

#define DEATH(mess) { perror(mess); exit(errno); };

#define MAXIRQS 256
#define NB (MAXIRQS * sizeof(int))

int main (int argc, char *argv[])
{
    int fd, j;
    char *nodename = "/dev/mycdrv";
    int *interrupts = malloc (NB);
    int *bhs = malloc (NB);

    if (argc > 1)
        nodename = argv[1];

    if ((fd = open (nodename, O_RDONLY)) < 0)
        DEATH ("opening device node");
    if (read (fd, interrupts, NB) != NB)
        DEATH ("reading interrupts");
    if (read (fd, bhs, NB) != NB)
        DEATH ("reading bhs");

    for (j = 0; j < MAXIRQS; j++)
        if (interrupts[j] > 0)
            printf (" %4d %10d%10d\n", j, interrupts[j], bhs[j]);
    exit (0);
}
```

lab4_all_tasklet.c

```c
/* Copyright 2009, J Cooperstein coop@coopj.com (GPLv2) */
#include <linux/module.h>
#include "lab_all_interrupt.h"

static struct my_dat
{
    int irq;
} my_data;

static void t_fun (unsigned long t_arg)
{
    struct my_dat *data = (struct my_dat *)t_arg;
    atomic_inc (&bhs[data->irq]);
}

static DECLARE_TASKLET (t, t_fun, (unsigned long)&my_data);

static irqreturn_t my_interrupt (int irq, void *dev_id)
```

```
{
    struct my_dat *data = (struct my_dat *)&my_data;
    data->irq = irq;
    atomic_inc (&interrupts[irq]);
    tasklet_schedule (&t);
    mdelay (delay);
    /* we return IRQ_NONE because we are just observing */
    return IRQ_NONE;
}

module_init (my_generic_init);
module_exit (my_generic_exit);

MODULE_AUTHOR ("Jerry Cooperstein");
MODULE_DESCRIPTION ("CLDD 1.0: lab4_all_tasklet.c");
MODULE_LICENSE ("GPL v2");
```

lab4_all_workqueue.c

```
 /* Copyright 2009, J Cooperstein coop@coopj.com (GPLv2) */

#include <linux/module.h>
#include "lab_all_interrupt.h"

static struct my_dat
{
    int irq;
    struct work_struct work;
} my_data;

static void w_fun (struct work_struct *w_arg)
{
    struct my_dat *data = container_of (w_arg, struct my_dat, work);
    atomic_inc (&bhs[data->irq]);
}

static irqreturn_t my_interrupt (int irq, void *dev_id)
{
    struct my_dat *data = (struct my_dat *)&my_data;
    data->irq = irq;
    atomic_inc (&interrupts[irq]);
    schedule_work (&data->work);
    mdelay (delay);
    /* we return IRQ_NONE because we are just observing */
    return IRQ_NONE;
}

static int my_init (void)
{
    struct my_dat *data = (struct my_dat *)&my_data;
    INIT_WORK (&data->work, w_fun);
    return my_generic_init ();
}

module_init (my_init);
```

```
module_exit (my_generic_exit);

MODULE_AUTHOR ("Jerry Cooperstein");
MODULE_DESCRIPTION ("CLDD 1.0: lab4_all_workqueue.c");
MODULE_LICENSE ("GPL v2");
```

lab4_all_thread.c

```
 /* Copyright 2009, J Cooperstein coop@coopj.com (GPLv2) */
#include <linux/module.h>
#include "lab_all_interrupt.h"

static atomic_t cond;
static struct task_struct *tsk;

static DECLARE_WAIT_QUEUE_HEAD (wq);

static struct my_dat
{
    int irq;
} my_data;

static irqreturn_t my_interrupt (int irq, void *dev_id)
{
    struct my_dat *data = (struct my_dat *)&my_data;
    data->irq = irq;
    atomic_set (&cond, 1);
    atomic_inc (&interrupts[irq]);
    mdelay (delay);
    wake_up_interruptible (&wq);
    /* we return IRQ_NONE because we are just observing */
    return IRQ_NONE;
}

static int thr_fun (void *thr_arg)
{
    struct my_dat *data = (struct my_dat *)thr_arg;

    /* go into a loop and deal with events as they come */
    printk (KERN_INFO "Beginning the thread loop for name=thr_fun\n");

    do {
        int irq = data->irq;
        atomic_set (&cond, 0);
        wait_event_interruptible (wq, kthread_should_stop ()
                                  || atomic_read (&cond) == 1);
        if (atomic_read (&cond) == 1)
            atomic_inc (&bhs[irq]);
    } while (!kthread_should_stop ());
    return 0;
}
static int __init my_init (void)
{
    atomic_set (&cond, 1);
```

```
    if (!(tsk = kthread_run (thr_fun, (void *)&my_data, "thr_fun"))) {
        printk (KERN_INFO "Failed to generate a kernel thread\n");
        return -1;
    }
    return my_generic_init ();
}

static void __exit my_exit (void)
{
    kthread_stop (tsk);
    my_generic_exit ();
}

module_init (my_init);
module_exit (my_exit);

MODULE_AUTHOR ("Jerry Cooperstein");
MODULE_DESCRIPTION ("CLDD 1.0: lab4_all_thread.c");
MODULE_LICENSE ("GPL v2");
```

20.5   Lab 5:   Sharing All Interrupts, Producer/Consumer Problem

- Find solutions for the producer/consumer problem for the previous lab.

lab5_all_tasklet_dynamic.c

```
/* Copyright 2009, J Cooperstein coop@coopj.com (GPLv2) */

#include <linux/module.h>
#include "lab_all_interrupt.h"

struct my_dat
{
    int irq;
    struct tasklet_struct tsk;
};

static void t_fun (unsigned long t_arg)
{
    struct my_dat *data = (struct my_dat *)t_arg;
    atomic_inc (&bhs[data->irq]);
    kfree (data);
}
static irqreturn_t my_interrupt (int irq, void *dev_id)
{
    struct tasklet_struct *t;
    struct my_dat *data;
    data = (struct my_dat *)kmalloc (sizeof (struct my_dat), GFP_ATOMIC);
    data->irq = irq;
    t = &data->tsk;
    atomic_inc (&interrupts[irq]);
```

```
    tasklet_init (t, t_fun, (unsigned long)data);
    tasklet_schedule (t);
    mdelay (delay);
    /* we return IRQ_NONE because we are just observing */
    return IRQ_NONE;
}

module_init (my_generic_init);
module_exit (my_generic_exit);

MODULE_AUTHOR ("Jerry Cooperstein");
MODULE_DESCRIPTION ("CLDD 1.0: lab5_all_tasklet_dynamic.c");
MODULE_LICENSE ("GPL v2");
```

lab5_all_workqueue_dynamic.c

```
 /* Copyright 2009, J Cooperstein coop@coopj.com (GPLv2) */

#include <linux/module.h>
#include "lab_all_interrupt.h"

struct my_dat
{
    int irq;
    struct work_struct work;
};

static void w_fun (struct work_struct *w_arg)
{
    struct my_dat *data = container_of (w_arg, struct my_dat, work);
    atomic_inc (&bhs[data->irq]);
    kfree (data);
}

static irqreturn_t my_interrupt (int irq, void *dev_id)
{
    struct my_dat *data =
        (struct my_dat *)kmalloc (sizeof (struct my_dat), GFP_ATOMIC);

    INIT_WORK (&data->work, w_fun);
    data->irq = irq;
    atomic_inc (&interrupts[data->irq]);
    schedule_work (&data->work);
    mdelay (delay);

    /* we return IRQ_NONE because we are just observing */
    return IRQ_NONE;
}

module_init (my_generic_init);
module_exit (my_generic_exit);

MODULE_AUTHOR ("Jerry Cooperstein");
MODULE_DESCRIPTION ("CLDD 1.0: lab5_all_workqueue_dynamic.c");
MODULE_LICENSE ("GPL v2");
```

20.6   Lab 6: Threaded Interrupt Handlers

- If you are running a kernel version 2.6.30 or later, solve the producer/consumer problem with a threaded interrupt handler.

- There are two types of solutions presented, one for just one shared interrupt, one sharing them all, with the same delay parameter as used in the earlier exercises.

lab6_one_threaded.c

```
/* Copyright 2009, J Cooperstein coop@coopj.com (GPLv2) */

#include <linux/module.h>
#include <linux/version.h>

#if LINUX_VERSION_CODE < KERNEL_VERSION(2,6,30)
static int __init my_init (void)
{
    printk(KERN_WARNING "Threaded interrupts don't appear until 2.6.30\n");
    return -1;
}
module_init (my_init)

#else

#define THREADED_IRQ

#include "lab_one_interrupt.h"

static atomic_t nevents;

static irqreturn_t my_interrupt (int irq, void *dev_id)
{
    atomic_inc (&counter_th);
    atomic_inc (&nevents);
    mdelay (delay);              /* hoke up a delay to try to cause pileup */
    return IRQ_WAKE_THREAD;
}

static irqreturn_t thread_fun (int irq, void *thr_arg)
{
    do {
        atomic_inc (&counter_bh);
    }
    while (!atomic_dec_and_test (&nevents));
    printk
        (KERN_INFO
         "In BH: counter_th = %d, counter_bh = %d, nevents=%d\n",
         atomic_read (&counter_th), atomic_read (&counter_bh),
         atomic_read (&nevents));

    /* we return IRQ_NONE because we are just observing */
    return IRQ_NONE;
}
```

```
static int __init my_init (void)
{
    atomic_set (&nevents, 0);
    return my_generic_init ();
}
module_init (my_init);
module_exit (my_generic_exit);
#endif

MODULE_AUTHOR ("Jerry Cooperstein");
MODULE_DESCRIPTION ("CLDD 1.0: lab6_one_threaded.c");
MODULE_LICENSE ("GPL v2");
```

lab6_all_threaded.c

```
 /* Copyright 2009, J Cooperstein coop@coopj.com (GPLv2) */

#include <linux/module.h>
#include <linux/version.h>

#if LINUX_VERSION_CODE < KERNEL_VERSION(2,6,30)
static int __init my_init (void)
{
    printk(KERN_WARNING "Threaded interrupts don't appear until 2.6.30\n");
    return -1;
}
module_init (my_init)

#else

#define THREADED_IRQ

#include "lab_all_interrupt.h"

static irqreturn_t my_interrupt (int irq, void *dev_id)
{
    atomic_inc (&interrupts[irq]);
    atomic_inc (&nevents[irq]);
    mdelay (delay);
    return IRQ_WAKE_THREAD;
}

static irqreturn_t thread_fun (int irq, void *thr_arg)
{
    do {
        atomic_inc (&bhs[irq]);
    }
    while (!atomic_dec_and_test (&nevents[irq]));
    if (atomic_read (&bhs[irq]) != atomic_read (&interrupts[irq]))
        printk (KERN_INFO "irq=%5d,th=%6d bh=%6d\n", irq,
                atomic_read (&interrupts[irq]), atomic_read (&bhs[irq]));
    /* we return IRQ_NONE because we are just observing */
    return IRQ_NONE;
}
```

```
module_init (my_generic_init);
module_exit (my_generic_exit);
#endif

MODULE_AUTHOR ("Jerry Cooperstein");
MODULE_DESCRIPTION ("CLDD 1.0: lab6_all_threaded.c");
MODULE_LICENSE ("GPL v2");
```

20.7 Lab 7: Executing in Process Context

- Write a brief module that uses `execute_in_process_context()`. It should do this first in process context (during initialization would be sufficient) and then in an interrupt routine.

- You can adapt the simplest shared interrupt lab module to do this.

- Make sure you print out the return value in order to see whether it just ran the function directly, or from a work queue.

lab7_eipc.c

```
/* Copyright 2009, J Cooperstein coop@coopj.com (GPLv2) */

#include <linux/module.h>
#include <linux/init.h>
#include <linux/interrupt.h>
#include <linux/workqueue.h>

#define SHARED_IRQ 17
static int irq = SHARED_IRQ, my_dev_id, irq_counter = 0;
module_param (irq, int, S_IRUGO);

static struct execute_work ew;
static void tfun (struct work_struct *w)
{
    printk (KERN_INFO "I got into my function\n");
}

static irqreturn_t my_interrupt (int irq, void *dev_id)
{
    int rc;
    irq_counter++;
    printk (KERN_INFO "In the ISR: counter = %d\n", irq_counter);
    rc = execute_in_process_context (tfun, &ew);
    printk (KERN_INFO "rc from execute_in_process_context = %d\n", rc);
    return IRQ_NONE;            /* we return IRQ_NONE because we are just observing */
}

static int __init my_init (void)
{
    int rc;
    if (request_irq
        (irq, my_interrupt, IRQF_SHARED, "my_interrupt", &my_dev_id))
        return -1;
```

```
    printk (KERN_INFO "Successfully loading ISR handler\n");
    rc = execute_in_process_context (tfun, &ew);
    printk (KERN_INFO "rc from execute_in_process_context = %d\n", rc);

    return 0;
}

static void __exit my_exit (void)
{
    synchronize_irq (irq);
    free_irq (irq, &my_dev_id);
    printk (KERN_INFO "Successfully unloading,  irq_counter = %d\n",
            irq_counter);
}

module_init (my_init);
module_exit (my_exit);

MODULE_AUTHOR ("Jerry Cooperstein");
MODULE_DESCRIPTION ("CLDD 1.0: lab7_eipc.c");
MODULE_LICENSE ("GPL v2");
```

Chapter 21

Hardware I/O

21.1   Lab 1: Accessing I/O Ports From User-Space

- Look at **/proc/ioports** to find a free I/O port region. One possibility to use the first parallel port, usually at 0x378, where you should be able to write a 0 to the register at the base address, and read the next port for status information.

- Try reading and writing to these ports by using two methods:

  - ioperm()
  - /dev/port

lab1_ioports.c

```
/* Copyright 2009, J Cooperstein coop@coopj.com (GPLv2) */
#include <stdio.h>
#include <unistd.h>
#include <sys/io.h>
#include <stdlib.h>
#include <fcntl.h>
```

179

```
#define PARPORT_BASE 0x378

/*
  In each method we will:
  1) Clear the data signal -- see parport_pc.h for register info
  2) Sleep for a millisecond
  3) Read the status port
*/

int do_ioperm (unsigned long addr, unsigned long nports)
{
    unsigned char zero = 0, readout = 0;

    if (ioperm (addr, nports, 1))
        return EXIT_FAILURE;

    printf ("Writing: %6d  to  %lx\n", zero, addr);
    outb (zero, addr);

    usleep (1000);

    readout = inb (addr + 1);
    printf ("Reading: %6d from %lx\n", readout, addr + 1);

    if (ioperm (addr, nports, 0))
        return EXIT_FAILURE;

    return EXIT_SUCCESS;
}
int do_read_devport (unsigned long addr, unsigned long nports)
{
    unsigned char zero = 0, readout = 0;
    int fd;

    if ((fd = open ("/dev/port", O_RDWR)) < 0)
        return EXIT_FAILURE;

    if (addr != lseek (fd, addr, SEEK_SET))
        return EXIT_FAILURE;

    printf ("Writing: %6d  to  %lx\n", zero, addr);
    write (fd, &zero, 1);

    usleep (1000);

    read (fd, &readout, 1);
    printf ("Reading: %6d from %lx\n", readout, addr + 1);
    close (fd);

    return EXIT_SUCCESS;

}
int main (int argc, char *argv[])
{
```

```
    unsigned long addr = PARPORT_BASE, nports = 2;

    if (argc > 1)
        addr = strtoul (argv[1], NULL, 0);
    if (argc > 2)
        nports = atoi (argv[2]);

    if (do_read_devport (addr, nports))
        fprintf (stderr, "reading /dev/port method failed");
    if (do_ioperm (addr, nports))
        fprintf (stderr, "ioperm method failed");

    return EXIT_SUCCESS;
}
```

21.2   Lab 2: Accessing I/O Ports

- Look at **/proc/ioports** to find a free I/O port region.

- Write a simple module that checks if the region is available, and requests it.

- Check and see if the region is properly registered in **/proc/ioports**.

- Make sure you release the region when done.

- The module should send some data to the region, and read some data from it. Do the values agree? If not, why?

- Note: there are two solutions given, one for the older *region* API, one for the newer *resource* API.

lab2_region.c

```
/* Copyright 2009, J Cooperstein coop@coopj.com (GPLv2) */

/* IOPORT FROM 0x200 to 0x240 is free on my system (64 bytes) */
#define IOSTART  0x200
#define IOEXTEND 0x40

#include <linux/module.h>
#include <linux/ioport.h>
#include <linux/io.h>
#include <linux/init.h>

static unsigned long iostart = IOSTART, ioextend = IOEXTEND, ioend;
module_param (iostart, ulong, S_IRUGO);
module_param (ioextend, ulong, S_IRUGO);

static int __init my_init (void)
{
    unsigned long ultest = (unsigned long)100;
    ioend = iostart + ioextend;
```

```
    printk (KERN_INFO " requesting the IO region from 0x%lx to 0x%lx\n",
            iostart, ioend);

    if (!request_region (iostart, ioextend, "my_ioport")) {
        printk (KERN_INFO "the IO REGION is busy, quitting\n");
        return -EBUSY;
    }

    printk (KERN_INFO " writing a long=%ld\n", ultest);
    outl (ultest, iostart);

    ultest = inl (iostart);
    printk (KERN_INFO " reading a long=%ld\n", ultest);

    return 0;
}
static void __exit my_exit (void)
{
    printk (KERN_INFO " releasing  the IO region from 0x%lx to 0x%lx\n",
            iostart, ioend);
    release_region (iostart, ioextend);
}

module_init (my_init);
module_exit (my_exit);

MODULE_AUTHOR ("Jerry Cooperstein");
MODULE_DESCRIPTION ("CLDD 1.0: lab2_region.c");
MODULE_LICENSE ("GPL v2");
```

lab2_resource.c

```
 /* Copyright 2009, J Cooperstein coop@coopj.com (GPLv2) */

/* IOPORT FROM 0x200 to 0x240 is free on my system (64 bytes) */
#define IOSTART   0x200
#define IOEXTEND 0x40
#define IOEND     IOSTART+IOEXTEND

#include <linux/module.h>
#include <linux/ioport.h>
#include <linux/io.h>
#include <linux/init.h>

static unsigned long iostart = IOSTART, ioextend = IOEXTEND, ioend;
module_param (iostart, ulong, S_IRUGO);
module_param (ioextend, ulong, S_IRUGO);

static struct resource my_resource;

static int __init my_init (void)
{
    unsigned long ultest = (unsigned long)100;
    ioend = iostart + ioextend;
```

```c
    my_resource.name = "my_ioport";
    my_resource.start = iostart;
    my_resource.end = ioend;

    printk (KERN_INFO " requesting the IO region from 0x%lx to 0x%lx\n",
            iostart, ioend);

    if (request_resource (&ioport_resource, &my_resource)) {
        printk (KERN_INFO "the IO REGION is busy, quitting\n");
        return -EBUSY;
    }

    printk (KERN_INFO " writing a long=%ld\n", ultest);
    outl (ultest, iostart);

    ultest = inl (iostart);
    printk (KERN_INFO " reading a long=%ld\n", ultest);

    return 0;
}

static void __exit my_exit (void)
{
    int rc;
    printk (KERN_INFO " releasing  the IO region from 0x%lx to 0x%lx\n",
            iostart, ioend);
    rc = release_resource (&my_resource);
    printk (KERN_INFO "return value from release_resource is %d\n", rc);
}

module_init (my_init);
module_exit (my_exit);

MODULE_AUTHOR ("Jerry Cooperstein");
MODULE_DESCRIPTION ("CLDD 1.0: lab2_resource.c");
MODULE_LICENSE ("GPL v2");
```

21.3   Lab 3: Remapping I/O Ports

- Alter your solution to use `ioport_map()` and the proper reading and writing functions.

lab3_map.c

```c
/* Copyright 2009, J Cooperstein coop@coopj.com (GPLv2) */

/* IOPORT FROM 0x200 to 0x240 is free on my system (64 bytes) */
#define IOSTART  0x200
#define IOEXTEND 0x40

#include <linux/module.h>
#include <linux/ioport.h>
#include <linux/io.h>
```

```
#include <linux/init.h>

static char __iomem *mapped;
static unsigned long iostart = IOSTART, ioextend = IOEXTEND, ioend;
module_param (iostart, ulong, S_IRUGO);
module_param (ioextend, ulong, S_IRUGO);

static int __init my_init (void)
{

    unsigned long ultest = (unsigned long)100;
    ioend = iostart + ioextend;

    printk (KERN_INFO " requesting the IO region from 0x%lx to 0x%lx\n",
            iostart, ioend);

    if (!request_region (iostart, ioextend, "my_ioport")) {
        printk (KERN_INFO "the IO REGION is busy, quitting\n");
        return -EBUSY;
    }

    mapped = ioport_map (iostart, ioextend);

    printk (KERN_INFO "ioport mapped at %p\n", mapped);
    printk (KERN_INFO " writing a long=%ld\n", ultest);
    iowrite32 (ultest, mapped);

    ultest = ioread32 (mapped);
    printk (KERN_INFO " reading a long=%ld\n", ultest);

    return 0;
}
static void __exit my_exit (void)
{
    printk (KERN_INFO " releasing  the IO region from 0x%lx to 0x%lx\n",
            iostart, ioend);
    release_region (iostart, ioextend);
    ioport_unmap (mapped);

}

module_init (my_init);
module_exit (my_exit);

MODULE_AUTHOR ("Jerry Cooperstein");
MODULE_DESCRIPTION ("CLDD 1.0: lab3_map.c");
MODULE_LICENSE ("GPL v2");
```

21.4   Lab 4: Serial Mouse Driver

- Attach a generic serial mouse using the Microsoft protocol to a free serial port.

- Depending on which serial port you have chosen, you'll have to know the relevant IRQ and base register address; i.e.,

Table 21.1: **Serial mouse nodes and registers**

Port	Node	IRQ	IOPORT
com1	/dev/ttyS0	4	0x03f8-0x03ff
com2	/dev/ttyS1	3	0x02f8-0x02ff
com3	/dev/ttyS2	4	0x03e8-0x03ef
com4	/dev/ttyS3	3	0x02e8-0x02ef

- You will need to view the man page for **mouse**, which says in part:

```
Microsoft protocol

    The  Microsoft  protocol uses 1 start bit, 7 data bits, no
    parity and one stop bit at the  speed  of  1200  bits/sec.
    Data  is  sent  to  RxD  in 3-byte packets. The dx and dy
    movements are sent as two's-complement, lb  (rb)  are  set
    when the left (right) button is pressed:

        byte   d6    d5    d4    d3    d2    d1    d0
           1    1     lb    rb    dy7   dy6   dx7   dx6
           2    0     dx5   dx4   dx3   dx2   dx1   dx0
           3    0     dy5   dy4   dy3   dy2   dy1   dy0
```

- You will also have to take a good look at **/usr/src/linux/include/linux/serial_reg.h** which gives the various UART port assignments (as offsets from the base register) and the symbolic definitions for the various control registers.

- Your driver should contain:

    - An **interrupt** routine which prints out the consecutive number of the interrupt (i.e., keep a counter), the **dx** and **dy** received, and the cumulative **x** and **y** positions.

    - A **read** entry that reports back to user-space the current **x** and **y** positions of the mouse.

    - An **ioctl** entry that can zero out the cumulative **x** and **y** positions.

- You'll have to write a user-space application to interact with your driver, of course.

- The trickiest part here is initialization of the mouse. You will have to initialize the outgoing registers properly to enable interrupts, the FIFO register, the Line Control Register, and the Modem Control Register.

  The worst part of doing this is to set the baud rate. You can do this directly in your driver but it is not easy to figure out. A work around is to run the command (as a script perhaps):

```
gpm -M -D -t ms -m /dev/ttyS0 -V
```

and then kill it, which should set things up ok. (On some PC's this step is unnecessary, either due to **BIOS** differences, or to the way **Linux** has been booted.) It is also possible to do this in other ways, such as using the system command `setserial` or, depending on how you handle the next step, merely opening `/dev/ttyS?` from a user-space application. You can also try

```
stty -F /dev/ttyS0 ospeed 1200 ispeed 1200
```

- If you get hung up on setting the speed, or decoding the bytes, the solutions contain *hint* files that contain the code for doing these steps.

- While you can do this exercise under **X**, it will probably cause fewer headaches to do it at a console, as **X** has some ideas about how to handle the mouse.

- **EXTRA:** Construct a fully functional serial mouse driver, and use it under X. Note to do this you'll have to modify `/etc/X11/xorg.conf` to point to your driver and the protocol. The read entry should deliver the latest raw 3 byte packet, and pad with zeros for any more than 3 bytes requested. You'll have to be careful with things like making sure the packet is not reset while you are reading, etc.

lab4_serial.c

```c
/* Copyright 2009, J Cooperstein coop@coopj.com (GPLv2) */

#include <linux/module.h>
#include <linux/fs.h>
#include <linux/interrupt.h>
#include <linux/ioport.h>
#include <linux/ioctl.h>
#include <linux/serial_reg.h>
#include <linux/init.h>
#include <linux/uaccess.h>
#include <linux/io.h>
#include <linux/cdev.h>
#include <linux/poll.h>
#include <linux/delay.h>

#define MYDEV_NAME "mymouse"

/* Select Serial Port   */

#undef COM1
#undef COM2
#undef COM3
#undef COM4
#define  COM1

/* /dev/ttyS0  com1  */
#ifdef COM1
#define MOUSE_IRQ 4
#define IOSTART  0x03f8
#define IOEXTEND 0x08
#endif

/*  /dev/ttyS1 com2 */
```

```
#ifdef COM2
#define MOUSE_IRQ 3
#define IOSTART  0x02f8
#define IOEXTEND 0x08
#endif

/* /dev/ttyS2 com3 */
#ifdef COM3
#define MOUSE_IRQ 4
#define IOSTART  0x03e8
#define IOEXTEND 0x08
#endif

/* /dev/ttyS3 com4 */
#ifdef COM4
#define MOUSE_IRQ 3
#define IOSTART  0x02e8
#define IOEXTEND 0x08
#endif

#define MY_IOC_TYPE 'k'
#define MY_IOC_Z _IO(MY_IOC_TYPE,1)
static int interrupt_number = 0, xpos = 0, ypos = 0;

static dev_t first;
static unsigned int count = 1;
static int my_major = 700, my_minor = 0;
static struct cdev *my_cdev;

static int my_dev_id;

static int mymouse_open (struct inode *inode, struct file *file)
{
    printk (KERN_INFO " OPENING my_mouse device: %s:", MYDEV_NAME);
    printk (KERN_INFO "  MAJOR number = %d, MINOR number = %d\n",
            imajor (inode), iminor (inode));
    return 0;
}

static int mymouse_release (struct inode *inode, struct file *file)
{
    printk (KERN_INFO " RELEASING my_mouse device: %s:", MYDEV_NAME);
    printk (KERN_INFO "  MAJOR number = %d, MINOR number = %d\n",
            imajor (inode), iminor (inode));
    return 0;
}

static ssize_t
mymouse_read (struct file *file, char __user * buf, size_t lbuf, loff_t * ppos)
{
    printk (KERN_INFO " Entering the  READ function\n");

    if (lbuf < 2 * sizeof (int)) {
        printk (KERN_INFO
                " mymouse_read: buffer not long enough to store x and y\n");
```

```
            return -EFAULT;
    }
    printk (KERN_INFO "xpos=%d, ypos=%d\n", xpos, ypos);
    if (copy_to_user (buf, &xpos, sizeof (int)))
        return -EFAULT;
    if (copy_to_user (buf + sizeof (int), &ypos, sizeof (int)))
        return -EFAULT;
    return 2 * sizeof (int);
}

static ssize_t
mymouse_write (struct file *file, const char __user * buf, size_t lbuf,
               loff_t * ppos)
{
    printk (KERN_INFO " Entering the WRITE function\n");
    return lbuf;
}

static int
mymouse_ioctl (struct inode *inode, struct file *fp,
               unsigned int cmd, unsigned long arg)
{
    switch (cmd) {
    case MY_IOC_Z:
        printk (KERN_INFO " zeroing out x and y, which were x= %d, y= %d\n",
                xpos, ypos);
        xpos = 0;
        ypos = 0;
        break;
    default:
        printk (KERN_INFO " got unknown ioctl, CMD=%d\n", cmd);
        return -EINVAL;
    }
    return 0;
}

static irqreturn_t my_interrupt (int irq, void *dev_id)
{
    /*
     * Note that using static values here is a VERY BAD IDEA. This means that we
     * can only support one mouse at a time with this driver; otherwise their
     * packets can get intermixed and confused! The right thing to do would be
     * to have our byte_in buffer and nbytes_in value held in our device
     * extension.
     */
    static unsigned char byte_in[3];
    static int nbytes_in = 0;
    char byte, left, right;
    int dx, dy;

    interrupt_number++;

    /* Read a byte */

    byte = inb (IOSTART + UART_RX);
```

```
    /*
     * We accept this byte, *UNLESS* it is the first byte of a mouse data
     * packet and it doesn't match the protocol. This lets us resync with the
     * mouse if we somehow get "out of step".
     */
    if ((nbytes_in > 0) || (byte & 0x40)) {
        byte_in[nbytes_in++] = byte;
    }
    /*
     * If we have three bytes, then we have a complete mouse message.
     */
    if (nbytes_in == 3) {

        /* Change in X since last message */
        dx = (signed char)(((byte_in[0] & 0x03) << 6) | (byte_in[1] & 0x3f));
        /* Change in Y since last message */
        dy = (signed char)(((byte_in[0] & 0x0c) << 4) | (byte_in[2] & 0x3f));
        /* Is the left button pressed? */
        left = (byte_in[0] & 0x20 ? 'L' : ' ');
        /* Is the right button pressed? */
        right = (byte_in[0] & 0x10 ? 'R' : ' ');
        /* Increment x and y positions */
        xpos += dx;
        ypos += dy;
        printk (KERN_INFO "mymouse_int %d", interrupt_number);
        printk (KERN_INFO "  Data = %2x:%2x:%2x (buttons[%c%c]), dx=%d, dy=%d",
                byte_in[0], byte_in[1], byte_in[2], left, right, dx, dy);
        printk (KERN_INFO " x=%d, y=%d\n", xpos, ypos);
        nbytes_in = 0;
    }
    /* we return IRQ_NONE because we are just observing */
    return IRQ_NONE;
}

#define BASE_BAUD ( 1843200 / 16 )
#define QUOT ( BASE_BAUD / 1200 )

static void mymouse_turnon (void)
{
    int quot = QUOT;
/* byte 0: Transmit Buffer */
    outb (0x0, IOSTART + UART_TX);
/* byte 1: Interrupt Enable Register */
    outb (UART_IER_RDI, IOSTART + UART_IER);
/* byte 2: FIFO Control Register */
    outb (UART_FCR_ENABLE_FIFO, IOSTART + UART_FCR);
/* byte 3: Line Control Register */
    outb (UART_LCR_WLEN7, IOSTART + UART_LCR);
/* byte 4: Modem Control Register */
    outb (UART_MCR_RTS | UART_MCR_OUT2, IOSTART + UART_MCR);

    /* set baud rate */
    outb (UART_LCR_WLEN7 | UART_LCR_DLAB, IOSTART + UART_LCR);
    outb (quot & 0xff, IOSTART + UART_DLL); /* LS of divisor */
```

```
    outb (quot >> 8, IOSTART + UART_DLM);    /* MS of divisor */
    outb (UART_LCR_WLEN7, IOSTART + UART_LCR);
}

static const struct file_operations mymouse_fops = {
    .owner = THIS_MODULE,
    .read = mymouse_read,
    .write = mymouse_write,
    .open = mymouse_open,
    .release = mymouse_release,
    .ioctl = mymouse_ioctl,
};

static int __init my_init (void)
{
    if (request_irq
        (MOUSE_IRQ, my_interrupt, IRQF_SHARED, "mymouse", &my_dev_id))
        return -1;
    printk (KERN_INFO " my_mouse INTERRUPT %d successfully registered\n",
            MOUSE_IRQ);

    printk (KERN_INFO " requesting the IO region from 0x%x to 0x%x\n",
            IOSTART, IOSTART + IOEXTEND);
    if (!request_region (IOSTART, IOEXTEND, MYDEV_NAME)) {
        printk (KERN_INFO
                "the IO REGION is busy, boldly going forward anyway ! \n");
        /*
            printk (KERN_INFO "the IO REGION is busy, quitting\n");
            synchronize_irq (MOUSE_IRQ);
            free_irq (MOUSE_IRQ, &my_dev_id);
            return -1
        */
    }

    first = MKDEV (my_major, my_minor);
    if (register_chrdev_region (first, count, MYDEV_NAME)) {
        printk (KERN_ERR "Failed registering\n");
        return -1;
    }
    if (!(my_cdev = cdev_alloc ())) {
        printk (KERN_ERR "failed to alloc_cdev\n");
        unregister_chrdev_region (first, count);
        return -1;
    }
    cdev_init (my_cdev, &mymouse_fops);
    cdev_add (my_cdev, first, count);

    printk (KERN_INFO " turning on the mouse\n");
    mymouse_turnon ();
    return 0;
}

static void __exit my_exit (void)
{
    unregister_chrdev_region (first, count);
```

```
        release_region (IOSTART, IOEXTEND);
        synchronize_irq (MOUSE_IRQ);
        free_irq (MOUSE_IRQ, &my_dev_id);
        printk (KERN_INFO " releasing  the IO region from 0x%x to 0x%x\n",
                IOSTART, IOSTART + IOEXTEND);
        printk (KERN_INFO "removing the module\n");
}

module_init (my_init);
module_exit (my_exit);

MODULE_AUTHOR ("Jerry Cooperstein");
MODULE_DESCRIPTION ("CLDD 1.0: lab4_serial.c");
MODULE_LICENSE ("GPL v2");
```

lab4_serial_test.c

```c
 /* Copyright 2009, J Cooperstein coop@coopj.com (GPLv2) */

#include <stdio.h>
#include <unistd.h>
#include <fcntl.h>
#include <malloc.h>
#include <sys/ioctl.h>
#include <string.h>
#include <stdlib.h>

#define MYIOC_TYPE 'k'
#define MYIOC_Z _IO(MYIOC_TYPE,1)

int main (int argc, char *argv[])
{
    int length, fd, rc;
    int buf[2] = { -1000, -1000 };
    ulong MYIOC;

    fd = open ("/dev/mymouse", O_RDWR);
    printf (" opened file descriptor  = %d\n", fd);

    if (argc > 1) {
        if (!strcmp (argv[1], "z")) {
            MYIOC = MYIOC_Z;
            rc = ioctl (fd, MYIOC, "anything");
            printf ("\n\n rc from ioctl = %d \n\n", rc);
        }
    }
    length = 2 * sizeof (int);
    rc = read (fd, buf, length);

    printf ("return code from read  = %d on %d, x = %d, y = %d\n",
            rc, fd, buf[0], buf[1]);
    close (fd);

    exit (0);
}
```

lab4_full_mouse_driver.c

```
/* Copyright 2009, J Cooperstein coop@coopj.com (GPLv2) */

#include <linux/module.h>
#include <linux/fs.h>
#include <linux/interrupt.h>
#include <linux/ioport.h>
#include <linux/ioctl.h>
#include <linux/serial_reg.h>
#include <linux/init.h>
#include <linux/uaccess.h>
#include <linux/io.h>
#include <linux/cdev.h>
#include <linux/poll.h>
#include <linux/delay.h>
#include <linux/device.h>

#define MYDEV_NAME "mymouse"

/* Select Serial Port  */

#undef COM1
#undef COM2
#undef COM3
#undef COM4
#define  COM1

/* /dev/ttyS0  com1  */
#ifdef COM1
#define MOUSE_IRQ 4
#define IOSTART  0x03f8
#define IOEXTEND 0x08
#endif

/*  /dev/ttyS1 com2 */
#ifdef COM2
#define MOUSE_IRQ 3
#define IOSTART  0x02f8
#define IOEXTEND 0x08
#endif

/* /dev/ttyS2 com3 */
#ifdef COM3
#define MOUSE_IRQ 4
#define IOSTART  0x03e8
#define IOEXTEND 0x08
#endif

/* /dev/ttyS3 com4 */
#ifdef COM4
#define MOUSE_IRQ 3
#define IOSTART  0x02e8
#define IOEXTEND 0x08
#endif
```

```
static dev_t first;
static unsigned int count = 1;
static struct cdev *my_cdev;
static struct class *mymouse_class;

static int my_dev_id;

#define MY_NBYTES 3
#define FIRST_BYTE_MAGIC 0x40

static DECLARE_WAIT_QUEUE_HEAD (my_wait);
static struct
{
    unsigned char bytes[5];
    atomic_t ready;
} my_state;

/* save pid for send SIGIO to Xserver */
static long user_pid;

/* send SIGIO to Xserver */
static void t_sendsig (unsigned long unsed)
{
    send_sig (SIGIO,
              pid_task (find_vpid(user_pid),PIDTYPE_PID), 1);
    /* send_sig (SIGIO, find_task_by_vpid (user_pid), 1); */
}

static DECLARE_TASKLET (usersig, t_sendsig, 0);

static int mymouse_open (struct inode *inode, struct file *file)
{
    printk (KERN_INFO " OPENING my_mouse device: %s:", MYDEV_NAME);
    printk (KERN_INFO "  MAJOR number = %d, MINOR number = %d\n",
            imajor (inode), iminor (inode));
    atomic_set (&my_state.ready, 0);

    /* set Xserver pid */
    user_pid = current->tgid;
    return 0;
}

static int mymouse_release (struct inode *inode, struct file *file)
{
    printk (KERN_INFO " RELEASING my_mouse device: %s:", MYDEV_NAME);
    printk (KERN_INFO "  MAJOR number = %d, MINOR number = %d\n",
            imajor (inode), iminor (inode));
    atomic_set (&my_state.ready, 0);

    if (user_pid) {
        tasklet_kill (&usersig);
        user_pid = 0;
    }
    return 0;
```

```
}

static ssize_t mymouse_read (struct file *file, char __user * buf, size_t lbuf,
                              loff_t * ppos)
{
    int r;
    /* int flags; */

    /* Must be a request for at least 3 bytes */
    if (lbuf < 3)
        return -EINVAL;

    /* go into a loop until a packet is ready, unless O_NODELAY is specified */

    while (!atomic_read (&my_state.ready)) {
        if (file->f_flags & O_NDELAY)
            return -EAGAIN;

        /* to sleep until a packet is ready */

        wait_event_interruptible (my_wait, atomic_read (&my_state.ready));

        /* Maybe a signal has arrived? */

        if (signal_pending (current))
            return -ERESTARTSYS;
    }

    /* disable this irq while processing */

    disable_irq (MOUSE_IRQ);

    /* just send the raw packet */
    if (copy_to_user (buf, my_state.bytes, 3))
        return -EFAULT;

    /* pad out the rest of the read request with zeros */

    if (lbuf > 3) {
        for (r = 3; r < lbuf; r++)
            put_user (0x00, buf + r);
    }

    /* Ok, we are ready to get a new packet  */

    atomic_set (&my_state.ready, 0);

    /* Let interrupts begin again for the mouse */

    enable_irq (MOUSE_IRQ);

    return lbuf;
}

static ssize_t
```

```
mymouse_write (struct file *file, const char __user * buf, size_t lbuf,
            loff_t * ppos)
{
    /* in case we want to turn on a real write:
        int r;
        char byte;
        printk (KERN_INFO " Entering the WRITE function, shouldn't be here\n");
        for (r = 3; r < lbuf; r++) {
        get_user (byte, buf + r);
        outb (byte, IOSTART + UART_TX);
        }
        return lbuf;
     */

    /*
     * Should not be here!
     */

    return -EINVAL;
}


/* poll for mouse input */

static unsigned int mymouse_poll (struct file *file, poll_table * wait)
{
    poll_wait (file, &my_wait, wait);
    if (atomic_read (&my_state.ready))
        return POLLIN | POLLRDNORM;
    return 0;
}

static int
mymouse_ioctl (struct inode *inode, struct file *fp,
            unsigned int cmd, unsigned long arg)
{
    switch (cmd) {
    default:
        printk (KERN_INFO " got unknown ioctl, CMD=%d\n", cmd);
        return -EINVAL;
    }
    return 0;
}

static irqreturn_t my_interrupt (int irq, void *dev_id)
{
    static int numByteIn = 0;
    char byte;

    /* Check the LSR register; do we have data ready to read? */

    while (inb (IOSTART + UART_LSR) & UART_LSR_DR) {

        /*
         * We have at least one byte waiting on the UART for us to read it.
         */
```

```
        byte = inb (IOSTART + UART_RX);
        /*      printk("byte = %0x\n", byte); */


        /*
           We accept this byte, *UNLESS* it is the first byte of a
           my_mouse data packet and it doesn't match the protocol. This
           lets us resync with the mouse if we somehow get "out of
           step".
         */

        if ((numByteIn > 0) || (byte & FIRST_BYTE_MAGIC)) {
            my_state.bytes[numByteIn++] = byte;
        }


        /*
         * If we have five bytes, then we have a complete my_mouse message.
         */

        if (numByteIn == MY_NBYTES) {
            atomic_set (&my_state.ready, 1);
            numByteIn = 0;
            wake_up_interruptible (&my_wait);

            /* schedule tasklset for SIGIO */
            if (user_pid)
                tasklet_schedule (&usersig);

        }
    }
    return IRQ_HANDLED;
}


#define BASE_BAUD ( 1843200 / 16 )
#define QUOT ( BASE_BAUD / 1200 )

static void mymouse_turnon (void)
{
    int quot = QUOT;
/* byte 0: Transmit Buffer */
    outb (0x0, IOSTART + UART_TX);
/* byte 1: Interrupt Enable Register */
    outb (UART_IER_RDI, IOSTART + UART_IER);
/* byte 2: FIFO Control Register */
    outb (UART_FCR_ENABLE_FIFO, IOSTART + UART_FCR);
/* byte 3: Line Control Register */
    outb (UART_LCR_WLEN7, IOSTART + UART_LCR);
/* byte 4: Modem Control Register */
    outb (UART_MCR_RTS | UART_MCR_OUT2, IOSTART + UART_MCR);

    /* set baud rate */
    outb (UART_LCR_WLEN7 | UART_LCR_DLAB, IOSTART + UART_LCR);
    outb (quot & 0xff, IOSTART + UART_DLL); /* LS of divisor */
    outb (quot >> 8, IOSTART + UART_DLM);   /* MS of divisor */
    outb (UART_LCR_WLEN7, IOSTART + UART_LCR);
```

```
}

static const struct file_operations mymouse_fops = {
    .owner = THIS_MODULE,
    .read = mymouse_read,
    .write = mymouse_write,
    .open = mymouse_open,
    .release = mymouse_release,
    .ioctl = mymouse_ioctl,
    .poll = mymouse_poll,
};

static int __init my_init (void)
{
    if (request_irq
        (MOUSE_IRQ, my_interrupt, IRQF_SHARED, "mymouse", &my_dev_id))
        return -1;
    printk (KERN_INFO " my_mouse INTERRUPT %d successfully registered\n",
            MOUSE_IRQ);

    printk (KERN_INFO " requesting the IO region from 0x%x to 0x%x\n",
            IOSTART, IOSTART + IOEXTEND);
    if (!request_region (IOSTART, IOEXTEND, MYDEV_NAME)) {
        printk (KERN_INFO
                "the IO REGION is busy, boldly going forward anyway ! \n");
        /*
            printk (KERN_INFO "the IO REGION is busy, quitting\n");
            synchronize_irq (MOUSE_IRQ);
            free_irq (MOUSE_IRQ, &my_dev_id);
            return -1
        */
    }
#if 0
    first = MKDEV (my_major, my_minor);
    if (register_chrdev_region (first, count, MYDEV_NAME)) {
        printk (KERN_ERR "Failed registering\n");
        return -1;
    }
#else
    if (!(my_cdev = cdev_alloc ())) {
        printk (KERN_ERR "failed to alloc_cdev\n");
        unregister_chrdev_region (first, count);
        return -1;
    }
    cdev_init (my_cdev, &mymouse_fops);
    cdev_add (my_cdev, first, count);
#endif

    if (alloc_chrdev_region (&first, 0, count, MYDEV_NAME) < 0) {
        printk (KERN_ERR "failed to allocate character device region\n");
        return -1;
    }
    if (!(my_cdev = cdev_alloc ())) {
        printk (KERN_ERR "cdev_alloc() failed\n");
        unregister_chrdev_region (first, count);
```

```
            return -1;
    }
    cdev_init (my_cdev, &mymouse_fops);
    if (cdev_add (my_cdev, first, count) < 0) {
        printk (KERN_ERR "cdev_add() failed\n");
        cdev_del (my_cdev);
        unregister_chrdev_region (first, count);
        return -1;
    }

    mymouse_class = class_create (THIS_MODULE, "mymouse");
    device_create (mymouse_class, NULL, first, "%s", "mymouse");

    printk (KERN_INFO " turning on the mouse\n");
    mymouse_turnon ();
    atomic_set (&my_state.ready, 0);
    return 0;
}

static void __exit my_exit (void)
{
    device_destroy (mymouse_class, first);
    class_destroy (mymouse_class);
    unregister_chrdev_region (first, count);
    release_region (IOSTART, IOEXTEND);
    synchronize_irq (MOUSE_IRQ);
    free_irq (MOUSE_IRQ, &my_dev_id);
    printk (KERN_INFO " releasing  the IO region from 0x%x to 0x%x\n",
            IOSTART, IOSTART + IOEXTEND);
    printk (KERN_INFO "removing the module\n");
}

module_init (my_init);
module_exit (my_exit);

MODULE_AUTHOR ("Tatsuo Kawasaki");
MODULE_AUTHOR ("Jerry Cooperstein");
MODULE_DESCRIPTION ("CLDD 1.0: lab4_full_mouse_driver.c");
MODULE_LICENSE ("GPL v2");
```

Chapter 22

PCI

22.1 Lab 1: PCI Utilities

- The **pciutils** package (**http://mj.ucw.cz/pciutils.html**) contains the following utilities:

  - **lspci** displays information about **PCI** buses and connected devices, with many options.
  - **setpci** can interrogate and configure properties of **PCI** devices.
  - **update-pciids** obtains the most recent copy of the **PCI ID** database and installs it on your system.

- Run **update-pciids** to update your database. If it fails because the URL pointed to in the script is down or obsolete try obtaining it directly from **http://pci-ids.ucw.cz/**. The location of the downloaded file (`pci.ids`) depends on your distribution, but will be somewhere under `/usr/share`. (Entering `locate pci.ids` will tell you.)

- Get more than basic information from **lspci**. You can get details from `man lspci` or `lspci -help`. For example, to get very verbose information about all **Intel** devices on your system you could type `lspci -vv -d 0x8086:*`, or for **AMD** devices, `lspci -vv -d 0x1022:*`. Experiment with the `-x(xx)` options to get detailed dumps of the configuration registers.

- Use `setpci` to evaluate or change specific values in the configuration register. For example you could find out the device identifier for all **Intel** devices on your system with `setpci -vD -d 0x1022:*` `DEVICE_ID`, where the `-D` option prevents actual changes from happening. See the **man** pages for examples of changing various configuration register entries.

22.2   Lab 2: PCI Devices

- Write a module that scans your **PCI** devices, and gathers information about them.

- For each found device, read some information from its configuration register. (Make sure you read **/usr/src/linux/include/linux/pci_regs.h** and **/usr/src/linux/include/linux/pci_ids.h** to get symbolic names.) Fields you may wish to obtain could include: `PCI_VENDOR_ID`, `PCI_DEVICE_ID`, `PCI_REVISION_ID`, `PCI_INTERRUPT_LINE`, `PCI_LATENCY_TIMER`, `PCI_COMMAND`.

- The information you obtain should agree with that obtained from **lspci**.

lab2_pci.c

```
/* Copyright 2009, J Cooperstein coop@coopj.com (GPLv2) */

#include <linux/module.h>
#include <linux/pci.h>
#include <linux/errno.h>
#include <linux/init.h>

static int __init my_init (void)
{
    u16 dval;
    char byte;
    int j = 0;
    struct pci_dev *pdev = NULL;

    printk (KERN_INFO "LOADING THE PCI_DEVICE_FINDER\n");

    /* either of the following looping constructs will work */

    for_each_pci_dev (pdev) {

        /*    while ((pdev = pci_get_device
            (PCI_ANY_ID, PCI_ANY_ID, pdev))) { */

        printk (KERN_INFO "\nFOUND PCI DEVICE # j = %d, ", j++);
        printk (KERN_INFO "READING CONFIGURATION REGISTER:\n");

        printk (KERN_INFO "Bus,Device,Function=%s", pci_name (pdev));

        pci_read_config_word (pdev, PCI_VENDOR_ID, &dval);
        printk (KERN_INFO " PCI_VENDOR_ID=%x", dval);

        pci_read_config_word (pdev, PCI_DEVICE_ID, &dval);
        printk (KERN_INFO " PCI_DEVICE_ID=%x", dval);
```

```
        pci_read_config_byte (pdev, PCI_REVISION_ID, &byte);
        printk (KERN_INFO " PCI_REVISION_ID=%d", byte);

        pci_read_config_byte (pdev, PCI_INTERRUPT_LINE, &byte);
        printk (KERN_INFO " PCI_INTERRUPT_LINE=%d", byte);

        pci_read_config_byte (pdev, PCI_LATENCY_TIMER, &byte);
        printk (KERN_INFO " PCI_LATENCY_TIMER=%d", byte);

        pci_read_config_word (pdev, PCI_COMMAND, &dval);
        printk (KERN_INFO " PCI_COMMAND=%d\n", dval);

        /* decrement the reference count and release */
        pci_dev_put (pdev);

    }
    return 0;
}

static void __exit my_exit (void)
{
    printk (KERN_INFO "UNLOADING THE PCI DEVICE FINDER\n");
}

module_init (my_init);
module_exit (my_exit);

MODULE_AUTHOR ("Jerry Cooperstein");
MODULE_DESCRIPTION ("CLDD 1.0: lab2_pci.c");
MODULE_LICENSE ("GPL v2");
```

Chapter 23

Direct Memory Access (DMA)

23.1 Lab 1: DMA Memory Allocation

- Write a module that allocates and maps a suitable **DMA** buffer, and obtains the bus address handle.

- Do this in three ways:

    - Using dma_alloc_coherent().
    - Using dma_map_single()
    - Using a **DMA Pool**.

    You can use NULL for the device and/or pci_dev structure arguments since we don't actually have a physical device.

- Compare the resulting kernel and bus addresses; how do they differ? Compare with the value of PAGE_OFFSET.

- In each case copy a string into the buffer and make sure it can be read back properly.

- In the case of dma_map_single(), you may want to compare the use of different direction arguments.

- We give two solutions, one with the bus-independent interface, and one with the older **PCI API**.

lab1_dma.c

```
/* Copyright 2009, J Cooperstein coop@coopj.com (GPLv2) */

#include <linux/module.h>
#include <linux/init.h>
#include <linux/pci.h>
#include <linux/slab.h>
#include <linux/dma-mapping.h>
#include <linux/dmapool.h>

// int direction = PCI_DMA_TODEVICE ;
// int direction = PCI_DMA_FROMDEVICE ;
static int direction = PCI_DMA_BIDIRECTIONAL;
//int direction = PCI_DMA_NONE;

static char *kbuf;
static dma_addr_t handle;
static size_t size = (10 * PAGE_SIZE);
static struct dma_pool *mypool;
static size_t pool_size = 1024;
static size_t pool_align = 8;

static void output (char *kbuf, dma_addr_t handle, size_t size, char *string)
{
    unsigned long diff;
    diff = (unsigned long)kbuf - handle;
    printk (KERN_INFO "kbuf=%12p, handle=%12p, size = %d\n", kbuf,
            (unsigned long *)handle, (int)size);
    printk (KERN_INFO
            "(kbuf-handle)= %12p, %12lu, PAGE_OFFSET=%12lu, compare=%lu\n",
            (void *)diff, diff, PAGE_OFFSET, diff - PAGE_OFFSET);
    strcpy (kbuf, string);
    printk (KERN_INFO "string written was, %s\n", kbuf);
}

static int __init my_init (void)
{

    /* dma_alloc_coherent method */

    printk (KERN_INFO "Loading DMA allocation test module\n");
    printk (KERN_INFO "\nTesting dma_alloc_coherent()..........\n\n");
    kbuf = dma_alloc_coherent (NULL, size, &handle, GFP_KERNEL);
    output (kbuf, handle, size, "This is the dma_alloc_coherent() string");
    dma_free_coherent (NULL, size, kbuf, handle);

    /* dma_map/unmap_single */
```

```
    printk (KERN_INFO "\nTesting dma_map_single().................\n\n");
    kbuf = kmalloc (size, GFP_KERNEL);
    handle = dma_map_single (NULL, kbuf, size, direction);
    output (kbuf, handle, size, "This is the dma_map_single() string");
    dma_unmap_single (NULL, handle, size, direction);
    kfree (kbuf);

    /* dma_pool method */

    printk (KERN_INFO "\nTesting dma_pool_alloc()..........\n\n");
    mypool = dma_pool_create ("mypool", NULL, pool_size, pool_align, 0);
    kbuf = dma_pool_alloc (mypool, GFP_KERNEL, &handle);
    output (kbuf, handle, size, "This is the dma_pool_alloc() string");
    dma_pool_free (mypool, kbuf, handle);
    dma_pool_destroy (mypool);

    return 0;
}
static void __exit my_exit (void)
{
    printk (KERN_INFO "Module Unloading\n");
}

module_init (my_init);
module_exit (my_exit);

MODULE_AUTHOR ("Jerry Cooperstein");
MODULE_DESCRIPTION ("CLDD 1.0: lab1_dma.c");
MODULE_LICENSE ("GPL v2");
```

lab1_dma_PCI_API.c

```
 /* Copyright 2009, J Cooperstein coop@coopj.com (GPLv2) */

#include <linux/module.h>
#include <linux/init.h>
#include <linux/pci.h>
#include <linux/slab.h>

// int direction = PCI_DMA_TODEVICE ;
// int direction = PCI_DMA_FROMDEVICE ;
static int direction = PCI_DMA_BIDIRECTIONAL;
//int direction = PCI_DMA_NONE;

static void output (char *kbuf, dma_addr_t handle, size_t size, char *string)
{
    unsigned long diff;
    diff = (unsigned long)kbuf - handle;
    printk (KERN_INFO "kbuf=%12p, handle=%12p, size = %d\n", kbuf,
            (unsigned long *)handle, (int)size);
    printk (KERN_INFO "diff=%12p, %12lu, PAGE_OFFSET=%12lu, compare=%lu\n",
            (void *)diff, diff, PAGE_OFFSET, diff - PAGE_OFFSET);
    strcpy (kbuf, string);
    printk (KERN_INFO "string written was, %s\n", kbuf);
}
```

```
static int __init my_init (void)
{
    char *kbuf;
    dma_addr_t handle;
    size_t size = (10 * PAGE_SIZE);

    /* pci_alloc_consistent method */

    printk (KERN_INFO "Loading DMA allocation test module\n");
    printk (KERN_INFO "\nTesting pci_alloc_consistent()..........\n\n");
    kbuf = pci_alloc_consistent (NULL, size, &handle);
    output (kbuf, handle, size, "This is the pci_alloc_consistent() string");
    pci_free_consistent (NULL, size, kbuf, handle);

    /* pci_map/unmap_single */

    printk (KERN_INFO "\nTesting pci_map_single()...............\n\n");
    kbuf = kmalloc (size, GFP_KERNEL);
    handle = pci_map_single (NULL, kbuf, size, direction);
    output (kbuf, handle, size, "This is the pci_map_single() string");
    pci_unmap_single (NULL, handle, size, direction);
    kfree (kbuf);

    /* let it fail all the time! */

    return 0;
}
static void __exit my_exit (void)
{
    printk (KERN_INFO "Module Unloading\n");
}

module_init (my_init);
module_exit (my_exit);

MODULE_AUTHOR ("Jerry Cooperstein");
MODULE_DESCRIPTION ("CLDD 1.0: lab1_dma_PCI_API.c");
MODULE_LICENSE ("GPL v2");
```

Chapter 24

Network Drivers I: Basics

24.1 Lab 1: Building a Basic Network Driver Stub

- Write a basic network device driver.

- It should register itself upon loading, and unregister upon removal.

- Supply minimal open() and stop() methods.

- You should be able to exercise it with:

  ```
  insmod lab1_network.ko
  ifconfig mynet0 up 192.168.3.197
  ifconfig
  ```

  Make sure your chosen address is not being used by anything else.

- **Warning:** Depending on kernel version, your stub driver may crash if you try to bring it up or ping it. If you put in a trivial transmit function, such as

  ```
  static int stub_start_xmit(struct sk_buff *skb,struct net_device *dev)
  {
    dev_kfree_skb (skb);
  ```

```
    return 0;
    }
```

this should avoid the problems.

lab1_network.c

```c
/* Copyright 2009, J Cooperstein coop@coopj.com (GPLv2) */
#include <linux/module.h>
#include <linux/netdevice.h>
#include <linux/init.h>

static struct net_device *dev;

static int my_open (struct net_device *dev)
{
    printk (KERN_INFO "Hit: my_open(%s)\n", dev->name);

    /* start up the transmission queue */

    netif_start_queue (dev);
    return 0;
}
static int my_close (struct net_device *dev)
{
    printk (KERN_INFO "Hit: my_close(%s)\n", dev->name);

    /* shutdown the transmission queue */

    netif_stop_queue (dev);
    return 0;
}

/* Note this method is only needed on some; without it
   module will fail upon removal or use. At any rate there is a memory
   leak whenever you try to send a packet through in any case*/

static int stub_start_xmit (struct sk_buff *skb, struct net_device *dev)
{
    dev_kfree_skb (skb);
    return 0;
}

#ifdef HAVE_NET_DEVICE_OPS
static struct net_device_ops ndo = {
    .ndo_open = my_open,
    .ndo_stop = my_close,
    .ndo_start_xmit = stub_start_xmit,
};
#endif

static void my_setup (struct net_device *dev)
{
    int j;
    printk (KERN_INFO "my_setup(%s)\n", dev->name);
```

```
    /* Fill in the MAC address with a phoney */

    for (j = 0; j < ETH_ALEN; ++j) {
        dev->dev_addr[j] = (char)j,
    }

    ether_setup (dev);

#ifdef HAVE_NET_DEVICE_OPS
    dev->netdev_ops = &ndo;
#else
    dev->open = my_open;
    dev->stop = my_close;
    dev->hard_start_xmit = stub_start_xmit;
#endif
}
static int __init my_init (void)
{
    printk (KERN_INFO "Loading stub network module:....");
    dev = alloc_netdev (0, "mynet%d", my_setup);
    if (register_netdev (dev)) {
        printk (KERN_INFO " Failed to register\n");
        free_netdev (dev);
        return -1;
    }
    printk (KERN_INFO "Succeeded in loading %s!\n\n", dev_name (&dev->dev));
    return 0;
}
static void __exit my_exit (void)
{
    printk (KERN_INFO "Unloading stub network module\n\n");
    unregister_netdev (dev);
    free_netdev (dev);
}

module_init (my_init);
module_exit (my_exit);

MODULE_AUTHOR ("Bill Shubert");
MODULE_AUTHOR ("Jerry Cooperstein");
MODULE_AUTHOR ("Tatsuo Kawasaki");
MODULE_DESCRIPTION ("CLDD 1.0: lab1_network.c");
MODULE_LICENSE ("GPL v2");
```

Chapter 25

Network Drivers II: Data Structures

25.1   Lab 1: Examining Network Devices

- All network devices are linked together in a list. You can get a pointer to the head of the list and then walk through it using:

```
struct net_device *first_net_device (struct net *net);
struct net_device *next_net_device(struct net_device *dev);
```

- Write a module that works its way down the list and prints out information about each driver.

- This should include the name, any associated irq, and various other parameters you may find interesting.

- Try doing this with your previous simple network module loaded.

`lab1_devices.c`

```c
/* Copyright 2009, J Cooperstein coop@coopj.com (GPLv2) */

#include <linux/module.h>
#include <linux/init.h>
#include <linux/netdevice.h>

static int __init my_init (void)
{
    struct net_device *dev;
    printk (KERN_INFO "Hello: module loaded at 0x%p\n", my_init);
    dev = first_net_device (&init_net);
    printk (KERN_INFO "Hello: dev_base address=0x%p\n", dev);
    while (dev) {
        printk (KERN_INFO
                "name = %6s irq=%4d trans_start=%12lu last_rx=%12lu\n",
                dev->name, dev->irq, dev->trans_start, dev->last_rx);
        dev = next_net_device (dev);
    }
    return 0;
}
static void __exit my_exit (void)
{
    printk (KERN_INFO "Module Unloading\n");
}

module_init (my_init);
module_exit (my_exit);

MODULE_AUTHOR ("Jerry Cooperstein");
MODULE_DESCRIPTION ("CLDD 1.0: lab1_devices.c");
MODULE_LICENSE ("GPL v2");
```

Chapter 26

Network Drivers III: Transmission and Reception

26.1 Lab 1: Building a Transmitting Network Driver

- Extend your stub network device driver to include a transmission function, which means supplying a method for dev->hard_start_xmit().

- While you are at it, you may want to add other entry points to see how you may exercise them.

- Once again, you should be able to exercise it with:

```
insmod lab1_network.ko
ifconfig mynet0 up 192.168.3.197
ping -I mynet0 localhost
    or
ping -bI mynet0 192.168.3
```

Make sure your chosen address is not being used by anything else.

`lab1_transmit_simple.c`

```c
/* Copyright 2009, J Cooperstein coop@coopj.com (GPLv2) */
#include <linux/module.h>
#include <linux/netdevice.h>
#include <linux/init.h>

static struct net_device *dev;

static int my_hard_start_xmit (struct sk_buff *skb, struct net_device *dev)
{
    int i;

    printk (KERN_INFO "my_hard_start_xmit(%s)\n", dev->name);

    dev->trans_start = jiffies;
    printk (KERN_INFO "Sending packet :\n");

    /* print out 16 bytes per line */
    for (i = 0; i < skb->len; ++i) {
        if ((i & 0xf) == 0)
            printk (KERN_INFO "\n  ");
        printk (KERN_INFO "%02x ", skb->data[i]);
    }
    printk (KERN_INFO "\n");

    dev_kfree_skb (skb);
    return 0;
}
static int my_open (struct net_device *dev)
{
    printk (KERN_INFO "Hit: my_open(%s)\n", dev->name);

    /* start up the transmission queue */

    netif_start_queue (dev);
    return 0;
}
static int my_close (struct net_device *dev)
{
    printk (KERN_INFO "Hit: my_close(%s)\n", dev->name);

    /* shutdown the transmission queue */

    netif_stop_queue (dev);
    return 0;
}

#ifdef HAVE_NET_DEVICE_OPS
static struct net_device_ops ndo = {
    .ndo_open = my_open,
    .ndo_stop = my_close,
    .ndo_start_xmit = my_hard_start_xmit,
};
#endif

static void my_setup (struct net_device *dev)
```

```c
{
    int j;
    printk (KERN_INFO "my_setup(%s)\n", dev->name);

    /* Fill in the MAC address with a phoney */

    for (j = 0; j < ETH_ALEN; ++j) {
        dev->dev_addr[j] = (char)j;
    }

    ether_setup (dev);

#ifdef HAVE_NET_DEVICE_OPS
    dev->netdev_ops = &ndo;
#else
    dev->open = my_open;
    dev->stop = my_close;
    dev->hard_start_xmit = my_hard_start_xmit;
#endif
    dev->flags |= IFF_NOARP;
}
static int __init my_init (void)
{
    printk (KERN_INFO "Loading transmitting network module:....");
    dev = alloc_netdev (0, "mynet%d", my_setup);
    if (register_netdev (dev)) {
        printk (KERN_INFO " Failed to register\n");
        free_netdev (dev);
        return -1;
    }
    printk (KERN_INFO "Succeeded in loading %s!\n\n", dev_name (&dev->dev));
    return 0;
}
static void __exit my_exit (void)
{
    printk (KERN_INFO "Unloading transmitting network module\n\n");
    unregister_netdev (dev);
    free_netdev (dev);
}

module_init (my_init);
module_exit (my_exit);

MODULE_AUTHOR ("Bill Shubert");
MODULE_AUTHOR ("Jerry Cooperstein");
MODULE_DESCRIPTION ("CLDD 1.0: lab1_transmit_simple.c");
MODULE_LICENSE ("GPL v2");
```

lab1_transmit.c

```c
/* Copyright 2009, J Cooperstein coop@coopj.com (GPLv2) */
#include <linux/module.h>
#include <linux/netdevice.h>
#include <linux/init.h>
```

```
static struct net_device *dev;
static struct net_device_stats *stats;

static int my_hard_start_xmit (struct sk_buff *skb, struct net_device *dev)
{
    int i;

    printk (KERN_INFO "my_hard_start_xmit(%s)\n", dev->name);

    dev->trans_start = jiffies;
    printk (KERN_INFO "Sending packet :\n");

    /* print out 16 bytes per line */
    for (i = 0; i < skb->len; ++i) {
        if ((i & 0xf) == 0)
            printk (KERN_INFO "\n  ");
        printk (KERN_INFO "%02x ", skb->data[i]);
    }
    printk (KERN_INFO "\n");

    dev_kfree_skb (skb);
    ++stats->tx_packets;

    return 0;
}
static int my_do_ioctl (struct net_device *dev, struct ifreq *ifr, int cmd)
{
    printk (KERN_INFO "my_do_ioctl(%s)\n", dev->name);
    return -1;
}
static struct net_device_stats *my_get_stats (struct net_device *dev)
{
    printk (KERN_INFO "my_get_stats(%s)\n", dev->name);
    return stats;
}

/*
 * This is where ifconfig comes down and tells us who we are, etc.
 * We can just ignore this.
 */
static int my_config (struct net_device *dev, struct ifmap *map)
{
    printk (KERN_INFO "my_config(%s)\n", dev->name);
    if (dev->flags & IFF_UP) {
        return -EBUSY;
    }
    return 0;
}
static int my_change_mtu (struct net_device *dev, int new_mtu)
{
    printk (KERN_INFO "my_change_mtu(%s)\n", dev->name);
    return -1;
}
static int my_open (struct net_device *dev)
{
```

```
    printk (KERN_INFO "Hit: my_open(%s)\n", dev->name);

    /* start up the transmission queue */

    netif_start_queue (dev);
    return 0;
}
static int my_close (struct net_device *dev)
{
    printk (KERN_INFO "Hit: my_close(%s)\n", dev->name);

    /* shutdown the transmission queue */

    netif_stop_queue (dev);
    return 0;
}

#ifdef HAVE_NET_DEVICE_OPS
static struct net_device_ops ndo = {
    .ndo_open = my_open,
    .ndo_stop = my_close,
    .ndo_start_xmit = my_hard_start_xmit,
    .ndo_do_ioctl = my_do_ioctl,
    .ndo_get_stats = my_get_stats,
    .ndo_set_config = my_config,
    .ndo_change_mtu = my_change_mtu,
};
#endif
static void my_setup (struct net_device *dev)
{
    int j;
    printk (KERN_INFO "my_setup(%s)\n", dev->name);

    /* Fill in the MAC address with a phoney */

    for (j = 0; j < ETH_ALEN; ++j) {
        dev->dev_addr[j] = (char)j;
    }

    ether_setup (dev);

#ifdef HAVE_NET_DEVICE_OPS
    dev->netdev_ops = &ndo;
#else
    dev->open = my_open;
    dev->stop = my_close;
    dev->hard_start_xmit = my_hard_start_xmit;
    dev->do_ioctl = my_do_ioctl;
    dev->get_stats = my_get_stats;
    dev->set_config = my_config;
    dev->change_mtu = my_change_mtu;
#endif
    dev->flags |= IFF_NOARP;
    stats = &dev->stats;
```

```
    /*
     * Just for laughs, let's claim that we've seen 50 collisions.
     */
    stats->collisions = 50;
}
static int __init my_init (void)
{
    printk (KERN_INFO "Loading transmitting network module:....");
    dev = alloc_netdev (0, "mynet%d", my_setup);
    if (register_netdev (dev)) {
        printk (KERN_INFO " Failed to register\n");
        free_netdev (dev);
        return -1;
    }
    printk (KERN_INFO "Succeeded in loading %s!\n\n", dev_name (&dev->dev));
    return 0;
}
static void __exit my_exit (void)
{
    printk (KERN_INFO "Unloading transmitting network module\n\n");
    unregister_netdev (dev);
    free_netdev (dev);
}

module_init (my_init);
module_exit (my_exit);

MODULE_AUTHOR ("Bill Shubert");
MODULE_AUTHOR ("Jerry Cooperstein");
MODULE_DESCRIPTION ("CLDD 1.0: lab1_transmit.c");
MODULE_LICENSE ("GPL v2");
```

26.2   Lab 2: Adding Reception

- Extend your transmitting device driver to include a reception function.

- You can do a **loopback** method in which any packet sent out is received.

- Be careful not to create memory leaks!

lab2_receive.c

```
 /* Copyright 2009, J Cooperstein coop@coopj.com (GPLv2) */
#include <linux/module.h>
#include <linux/netdevice.h>
#include <linux/init.h>

static struct net_device *dev;
static struct net_device_stats *stats;

static void my_rx (struct sk_buff *skb, struct net_device *dev)
{
    /* just a loopback, already has the skb */
```

```
        printk (KERN_INFO "I'm receiving a packet\n");
        ++stats->rx_packets;
        netif_rx (skb);
}
static int my_hard_start_xmit (struct sk_buff *skb, struct net_device *dev)
{
        int i;
        printk (KERN_INFO "my_hard_start_xmit(%s)\n", dev->name);

        dev->trans_start = jiffies;
        printk (KERN_INFO "Sending packet :\n");

        /* print out 16 bytes per line */
        for (i = 0; i < skb->len; ++i) {
            if ((i & 0xf) == 0)
                printk (KERN_INFO "\n  ");
            printk (KERN_INFO "%02x ", skb->data[i]);
        }
        printk (KERN_INFO "\n");

        ++stats->tx_packets;

        /* loopback it */
        my_rx (skb, dev);

        return 0;
}
static int my_do_ioctl (struct net_device *dev, struct ifreq *ifr, int cmd)
{
        printk (KERN_INFO "my_do_ioctl(%s)\n", dev->name);
        return -1;
}
static struct net_device_stats *my_get_stats (struct net_device *dev)
{
        printk (KERN_INFO "my_get_stats(%s)\n", dev->name);
        return stats;
}


/*
 * This is where ifconfig comes down and tells us who we are, etc.
 * We can just ignore this.
 */
static int my_config (struct net_device *dev, struct ifmap *map)
{
        printk (KERN_INFO "my_config(%s)\n", dev->name);
        if (dev->flags & IFF_UP) {
            return -EBUSY;
        }
        return 0;
}
static int my_change_mtu (struct net_device *dev, int new_mtu)
{
        printk (KERN_INFO "my_change_mtu(%s)\n", dev->name);
        return -1;
}
```

```
static int my_open (struct net_device *dev)
{
    printk (KERN_INFO "Hit: my_open(%s)\n", dev->name);

    /* start up the transmission queue */

    netif_start_queue (dev);
    return 0;
}
static int my_close (struct net_device *dev)
{
    printk (KERN_INFO "Hit: my_close(%s)\n", dev->name);

    /* shutdown the transmission queue */

    netif_stop_queue (dev);
    return 0;
}

#ifdef HAVE_NET_DEVICE_OPS
static struct net_device_ops ndo = {
    .ndo_open = my_open,
    .ndo_stop = my_close,
    .ndo_start_xmit = my_hard_start_xmit,
    .ndo_do_ioctl = my_do_ioctl,
    .ndo_get_stats = my_get_stats,
    .ndo_set_config = my_config,
    .ndo_change_mtu = my_change_mtu,
};
#endif
static void my_setup (struct net_device *dev)
{
    int j;
    printk (KERN_INFO "my_setup(%s)\n", dev->name);

    /* Fill in the MAC address with a phoney */

    for (j = 0; j < ETH_ALEN; ++j) {
        dev->dev_addr[j] = (char)j;
    }

    ether_setup (dev);

#ifdef HAVE_NET_DEVICE_OPS
    dev->netdev_ops = &ndo;
#else
    dev->open = my_open;
    dev->stop = my_close;
    dev->hard_start_xmit = my_hard_start_xmit;
    dev->do_ioctl = my_do_ioctl;
    dev->get_stats = my_get_stats;
    dev->set_config = my_config;
    dev->change_mtu = my_change_mtu;
#endif
    dev->flags |= IFF_NOARP;
```

```
    stats = &dev->stats;

    /*
     * Just for laughs, let's claim that we've seen 50 collisions.
     */
    stats->collisions = 50;

}
static int __init my_init (void)
{
    printk (KERN_INFO "Loading transmitting network module:....");
    dev = alloc_netdev (0, "mynet%d", my_setup);
    if (register_netdev (dev)) {
        printk (KERN_INFO " Failed to register\n");
        free_netdev (dev);
        return -1;
    }
    printk (KERN_INFO "Succeeded in loading %s!\n\n", dev_name (&dev->dev));
    return 0;
}
static void __exit my_exit (void)
{
    printk (KERN_INFO "Unloading transmitting network module\n\n");
    unregister_netdev (dev);
    free_netdev (dev);
}

module_init (my_init);
module_exit (my_exit);

MODULE_AUTHOR ("Bill Shubert");
MODULE_AUTHOR ("Jerry Cooperstein");
MODULE_DESCRIPTION ("CLDD 1.0: lab2_receive.c");
MODULE_LICENSE ("GPL v2");
```

Chapter 28

USB Drivers

28.1   Lab 1: Installing a USB device.

- We are going to write a simple **USB** device driver.

- The driver should register itself with the **USB** subsystem upon loading and unregister upon unloading.

- The `probe()` and `disconnect()` functions should issue printout whenever the device is added or removed from the system.

- Your instructor will pass around one or more **USB** devices, such as web cameras, keyboards and mice.

- By proper use of the `usb_device_id` table, you can configure your driver either to sense any device plugged, or only a specific one. You can obtain the vendor and device ID's by noting the output when the **USB** subsystem senses device connection.

- You will have to make sure your kernel has the proper **USB** support compiled in, and that no driver for the device is already loaded, as it may interfere with your driver claiming the device.

- **Hint:** You'll probably want to do a `make modules_install` to get automatic loading to work properly.

lab1_usb.c

```
/* Copyright 2009, J Cooperstein coop@coopj.com (GPLv2) */

#include <linux/module.h>
#include <linux/init.h>
#include <linux/usb.h>
#include <linux/slab.h>

struct my_usb_info
{
    int connect_count;
};

static int
my_usb_probe (struct usb_interface *intf, const struct usb_device_id *id)
{

    struct my_usb_info *usb_info;

    struct usb_device *dev = interface_to_usbdev (intf);
    static int my_counter = 0;

    printk (KERN_INFO "\nmy_usb_probe\n");
    printk (KERN_INFO "devnum=%d, speed=%d\n", dev->devnum, (int)dev->speed);
    printk (KERN_INFO "idVendor=0x%hX, idProduct=0x%hX, bcdDevice=0x%hX\n",
            dev->descriptor.idVendor,
            dev->descriptor.idProduct, dev->descriptor.bcdDevice);
    printk (KERN_INFO "class=0x%hX, subclass=0x%hX\n",
            dev->descriptor.bDeviceClass, dev->descriptor.bDeviceSubClass);
    printk (KERN_INFO "protocol=0x%hX, packetsize=%hu\n",
            dev->descriptor.bDeviceProtocol, dev->descriptor.bMaxPacketSize0);
    printk (KERN_INFO "manufacturer=0x%hX, product=0x%hX, serial=%hu\n",
            dev->descriptor.iManufacturer, dev->descriptor.iProduct,
            dev->descriptor.iSerialNumber);

    usb_info = kmalloc (sizeof (struct my_usb_info), GFP_KERNEL);
    usb_info->connect_count = my_counter++;
    usb_set_intfdata (intf, usb_info);
    printk (KERN_INFO "connect_count=%d\n\n", usb_info->connect_count);

    return 0;
}

static void my_usb_disconnect (struct usb_interface *intf)
{
    struct my_usb_info *usb_info;
    usb_info = usb_get_intfdata (intf);
    printk (KERN_INFO "\nmy_usb_disconnect\n");
    kfree (usb_info);
}

static struct usb_device_id my_usb_table[] = {
    {USB_DEVICE (0x0545, 0x808a)},  // Veo USB camera
    {USB_DEVICE (0x046D, 0x870)},   // Labtec WebCam
```

```
    {USB_DEVICE (0x204, 0x6025)},   // Via USB PEN
    {USB_DEVICE (0x0ace, 0x1215)},  // Zonet Wireless
    {}                              // Null terminator (required)
};

MODULE_DEVICE_TABLE (usb, my_usb_table);

static struct usb_driver my_usb_driver = {
    .name = "usb-hotplug",
    .probe = my_usb_probe,
    .disconnect = my_usb_disconnect,
    .id_table = my_usb_table,
};

static int __init my_init_module (void)
{
    int err;
    printk (KERN_INFO "Hello USB\n");
    err = usb_register (&my_usb_driver);
    return err;
}

static void my_cleanup_module (void)
{
    printk (KERN_INFO "Goodbye USB\n");
    usb_deregister (&my_usb_driver);
}

module_init (my_init_module);
module_exit (my_cleanup_module);

MODULE_AUTHOR ("Terry Griffin");
/* revisions by Bill Kerr */
/* upgrade to work with kernel 2.6 by Jerry Cooperstein and other changes*/
MODULE_DESCRIPTION ("CLDD 1.0: lab1_usb.c");
MODULE_LICENSE ("GPL v2");
```

Chapter 29

Memory Technology Devices

29.1   Lab 1: Emulating MTD in memory

- Even if you don't have any **MTD** devices on your system, you can emulate them in memory, using some built-in kernel features.

- First you'll have to make sure you have all the right facilities built into the kernel. Go to the kernel source directory, run `make xconfig` and turn on the appropriate **MTD** options, as well as including the **jffs2** filesystem.

- The important ones here are: under **MTD**, turn on *Memory Technology Device Support*, pick a level of debugging (3 should show all), turn on *Direct char device access...*, etc. Also turn on *Test driver using RAM* and *MTD emulation using block device*. By default you'll get a disk of 4 MB with 128 KB erase block size. Under *Filesystems*, turn on **JFFS(2)** and pick a verbosity level.

- If you have done everything as modules you *may* get away without a reboot, as long as you run `depmod`. At any rate, recompile, reboot, etc., into the kernel that now includes **MTD** and **JFFS2**.

- First we'll test the character emulation interface. To do this you have to make sure you create the device node:

```
mknod -m 666 /dev/mtd0 c 90 0
```

- Before or after this, you'll have to make sure to do

```
modprobe mtdram total_size=2048 erase_size=8
```

  (or leave out the options to get the default values you compiled into the kernel.) You won't have to run modprobe if you haven't done this as modules.

- You can now use this as a raw character ram disk, reading and writing to it. Experiment using **dd, cat, echo**, etc.

29.2   Lab 2: jffs2 filesystem and MTD block interface.

- In order to place a **jffs2** filesystem on a **MTD** device it is easiest to first make a filesystem **image** on another filesystem, and then copy it over. To do this you must have the **mkfs.jffs2** utility, which you can download in source or binary form from **http://sources.redhat.com/jffs2**.

- You'll need to do

```
modprobe mtdblock
```

  if you haven't built this into the kernel.

- You'll also have to make the proper device node:

```
mknod -m 666 /dev/mtdblock0 b 31 0
```

- Populate a directory tree (say ./dir_tree) with some files and subdirectories; the total size should be less then or equal to the size of **MTD** ram disk. Then put a filesystem on it **and** copy it over to the **MTD** block device emulator with:

```
mkfs.jffs2 -d ./dir_tree -o /dev/mtdblock0
```

  (You may want to separate out these steps so you can keep the initial filesystem image; i.e., do something like

```
mkfs.jffs2 -d ./dir_tree -o jfs.image
dd if=jfs.image of=/dev/mtdblock0
```

- Now you can mount the filesystem and play with it to your heart's content:

```
mkdir ./mnt_jffs2
mount -t jffs2 /dev/mtdblock0 ./mnt_jffs2
```

- Note that you can change the contents of the filesystem as you would like, but the updates will be lost when you unload the **MTD** modules or reboot. However, you can copy the contents to an image file and save that for a restore.

- Note that if you have turned on some verbosity you will see messages like

```
Feb 20 09:02:48 p3 kernel: ram_read(pos:520192, len:4096)
Feb 20 09:02:48 p3 kernel: ram_write(pos:393216, len:12)
Feb 20 09:02:48 p3 kernel: ram_read(pos:262144, len:4096)
Feb 20 09:02:48 p3 kernel: ram_read(pos:266240, len:4096)
Feb 20 09:02:48 p3 kernel: ram_read(pos:270336, len:4096)
```

and other such diagnostic information which will help you examine what is going on in the disk.

- Notice that because **jffs2** is a compressed filesystem, you can accommodate much more than nominal size, depending on your actual contents.

Chapter 30

Power Management

30.1   Lab 1: Monitoring Power Usage with powertop

- A tool for assessing power consumption can be obtained from **http://www.lesswatts.org/ projects/powertop/**.

- **powertop** can monitor how many times CPU's are being woken up every second, and help curtail unnecessary activity in order to save power. It can also keep track of total power consumption and suggest methods of reduction.

- To make **powertop** work `CONFIG_TIMER_STATS` must be set in the kernel configuration.

Chapter 31

Notifiers

31.1   Lab 1: Joining the USB Notifier Chain

- To register and unregister with the already existing notifier chain for hot-plugging of **USB** devices, use the exported functions:

```
void usb_register_notify   (struct notifier_block *nb);
void usb_unregister_notify (struct notifier_block *nb);
```

- You should be able to trigger events by plugging and unplugging a **USB** device, such as a mouse, pendrive, or keyboard.

- Print out the event that triggers your callback function. (Note that definitions of events can be found in **/usr/src/linux/include/linux/usb.h**.).

```
lab1_usb_notifier.c
```

```
#include <linux/module.h>
#include <linux/init.h>
```

```
#include <linux/notifier.h>
#include <linux/usb.h>

static int my_notifier_call (struct notifier_block *b, unsigned long event,
                             void *data)
{
    printk (KERN_INFO "\nRECEIVING USB event = %ld\n", event);
    switch (event) {
    case USB_DEVICE_ADD:
        printk (KERN_INFO "Adding a USB device, event=USB_DEVICE_ADD\n");
        break;
    case USB_DEVICE_REMOVE:
        printk (KERN_INFO "Removing a USB device, event=USB_DEVICE_REMOVE\n");
        break;
    case USB_BUS_ADD:
        printk (KERN_INFO "Adding a USB bus, event=USB_BUS_ADD\n");
        break;
    case USB_BUS_REMOVE:
        printk (KERN_INFO "Removing a USB bus, event=USB_BUS_REMOVE\n");
        break;
    default:
        printk (KERN_INFO "Receiving an unknown USB event\n");
        break;
    }

    return NOTIFY_OK;
}

static struct notifier_block my_nh_block = {
    .notifier_call = my_notifier_call,
    .priority = 0,
};

static int __init my_init (void)
{
    usb_register_notify (&my_nh_block);
    printk (KERN_INFO "USB Notifier module successfully loaded\n");

    return 0;
}
static void __exit my_exit (void)
{
    usb_unregister_notify (&my_nh_block);
    printk (KERN_INFO "USB Notifier module successfully unloaded\n");
}

module_init (my_init);
module_exit (my_exit);

MODULE_AUTHOR ("Jerry Cooperstein");
MODULE_DESCRIPTION ("CLDD 1.0: lab1_usb_notifier.c");
MODULE_LICENSE ("GPL v2");
```

31.2   Lab 2: Installing and Using a Notifier Chain

- Write a brief module that implements its own notifier chain.

- The module should register the chain upon insertion and unregister upon removal.

- The callback function should be called at least twice, with different event values, which should be printed out.

- You may want to make use of the data pointer, modifying the contents in the callback function.

lab2_notifier.c

```
/* Copyright 2009, J Cooperstein coop@coopj.com (GPLv2) */

#include <linux/module.h>
#include <linux/init.h>
#include <linux/notifier.h>

static BLOCKING_NOTIFIER_HEAD (my_nh);
static int my_notifier_call (struct notifier_block *b, unsigned long event,
                             void *data)
{
    long *c = (long *)data;
    *c += 100;
    printk (KERN_INFO "\n ..... I was called with event = %ld data=%ld\n",
            event, *c);
    return NOTIFY_OK;
}

static struct notifier_block my_nh_block = {
    .notifier_call = my_notifier_call,
    .priority = 0,
};
static long counter = 0;

static int __init my_init (void)
{
    int rc;
    if (blocking_notifier_chain_register (&my_nh, &my_nh_block)) {
        printk (KERN_INFO "Failed to register with notifier\n");
        return -1;
    }

    rc = blocking_notifier_call_chain (&my_nh, 1000, &counter);
    printk (KERN_INFO " rc from call chain = %d\n", rc);
    printk (KERN_INFO "Notifier module successfully loaded\n");

    return 0;
}
static void __exit my_exit (void)
{
    int rc;
    rc = blocking_notifier_call_chain (&my_nh, -1000, &counter);
    printk (KERN_INFO " rc from call chain = %d\n", rc);
```

```
    if (blocking_notifier_chain_unregister (&my_nh, &my_nh_block))
        printk (KERN_INFO " Failed to unregister from notifier\n");
    printk (KERN_INFO "Notifier module successfully unloaded\n");
}

module_init (my_init);
module_exit (my_exit);

MODULE_AUTHOR ("Jerry Cooperstein");
MODULE_DESCRIPTION ("CLDD 1.0: lab2_notifier.c");
MODULE_LICENSE ("GPL v2");
```

Chapter 32

CPU Frequency Scaling

32.1 Lab 1: CPU Frequency Notifiers

- Write a module that registers callback functions for the CPU frequency transition and policy notifier chains.

- Print out what event is causing the callback, and some information from the data structures delivered to the callback functions.

- You can test this by echoing values to some of the entries in **/sys/devices/system/cpu/cpu0 /cpufreq**. Even easier you can add the **CPU Frequency Scaling Monitor** applet to your taskbar, and easily switch governors and frequencies.

lab1_cpufreq.c

```
/* Copyright 2009, J Cooperstein coop@coopj.com (GPLv2) */
#include <linux/module.h>
#include <linux/init.h>
#include <linux/notifier.h>
#include <linux/cpufreq.h>
```

```
static int my_transition_notifier_call (struct notifier_block *b,
                                        unsigned long event, void *data)
{
    struct cpufreq_freqs *cf = data;
    printk (KERN_INFO "\nRECEIVING CPUFREQ TRANSITION event = %ld\n", event);
    switch (event) {
    case CPUFREQ_PRECHANGE:
        printk (KERN_INFO "event=CPUFREQ_PRECHANGE\n");
        break;
    case CPUFREQ_POSTCHANGE:
        printk (KERN_INFO "event=CPUFREQ_POSTCHANGE\n");
        break;
    case CPUFREQ_RESUMECHANGE:
        printk (KERN_INFO "event=CPUFREQ_RESUMECHANGE\n");
        break;
    case CPUFREQ_SUSPENDCHANGE:
        printk (KERN_INFO "event=CPUFREQ_SUSPENDCHANGE\n");
        break;
    default:
        printk (KERN_INFO "Receiving an unknown CPUFREQ TRANSITION event\n");
        break;
    }

    printk (KERN_INFO "        cpu=%d, old=%d, new=%d, flags=%d\n",
            cf->cpu, cf->old, cf->new, cf->flags);

    return NOTIFY_OK;
}
static int my_policy_notifier_call (struct notifier_block *b,
                                    unsigned long event, void *data)
{
    struct cpufreq_policy *cp = data;
    printk (KERN_INFO "\nRECEIVING CPUFREQ POLICY event = %ld\n", event);
    switch (event) {
    case CPUFREQ_ADJUST:
        printk (KERN_INFO "event=CPUFREQ_ADJUST\n");
        break;
    case CPUFREQ_INCOMPATIBLE:
        printk (KERN_INFO "event=CPUFREQ_INCOMPATIBLE\n");
        break;
    case CPUFREQ_NOTIFY:
        printk (KERN_INFO "event=CPUFREQ_NOTIFY\n");
        break;
    default:
        printk (KERN_INFO "Receiving an unknown CPUFREQ POLICY event\n");
        break;
    }
    printk (KERN_INFO "        cpu=%d, min=%d, max=%d, cur=%d, policy=%d\n",
            cp->cpu, cp->min, cp->max, cp->cur, cp->policy);
    return NOTIFY_OK;
}

static struct notifier_block my_transition_nh_block = {
    .notifier_call = my_transition_notifier_call,
```

```
        .priority = 0,
};

static struct notifier_block my_policy_nh_block = {
    .notifier_call = my_policy_notifier_call,
    .priority = 0,
};

static int __init my_init (void)
{
    cpufreq_register_notifier (&my_transition_nh_block,
                              CPUFREQ_TRANSITION_NOTIFIER);
    cpufreq_register_notifier (&my_policy_nh_block, CPUFREQ_POLICY_NOTIFIER);
    printk (KERN_INFO "\nCPUFREQ Notifier module successfully loaded\n");

    return 0;
}
static void __exit my_exit (void)
{
    cpufreq_unregister_notifier (&my_transition_nh_block,
                                CPUFREQ_TRANSITION_NOTIFIER);
    cpufreq_unregister_notifier (&my_policy_nh_block, CPUFREQ_POLICY_NOTIFIER);
    printk (KERN_INFO "\nCPUFREQ Notifier module successfully unloaded\n");
}

module_init (my_init);
module_exit (my_exit);

MODULE_AUTHOR ("Jerry Cooperstein");
MODULE_DESCRIPTION ("CLDD 1.0: lab1_cpufreq.c");
MODULE_LICENSE ("GPL v2");
```

Chapter 33

Asynchronous I/O

33.1 Lab 1: Adding Asynchronous Entry Points to a Character Driver

- Take one of your earlier character drivers and add new entry points for `aio_read()` and `aio_write()`.

- To test this you'll need to write a user-space program that uses the native **Linux API**. Have it send out a number of write and read requests and synchronize properly.

- We also present a solution using the **Posix API** for the user application; note that this will never hit your driver unless you comment out the normal read and write entry points in which case the kernel will fall back on the asynchronous ones.

- Make sure you compile by linking with the right libraries; use `-laio` for the **Linux API** and `-lrt` for the **Posix API**. (You can use both in either case as they don't conflict.)

```
lab_char.h
lab1_aio.c
```

```
/* Copyright 2009, J Cooperstein coop@coopj.com (GPLv2) */

#include <linux/module.h>
#include "lab_char.h"

#include <linux/aio.h>            /* for aio stuff */

static ssize_t mycdrv_aio_read (struct kiocb *iocb, const struct iovec *iov,
                                unsigned long niov, loff_t offset)
{
    printk (KERN_INFO "entering mycdrv_aio_read\n");
    return mycdrv_generic_read (iocb->ki_filp, iov->iov_base, iov->iov_len,
                                &offset);
}

static ssize_t mycdrv_aio_write (struct kiocb *iocb, const struct iovec *iov,
                                 unsigned long niov, loff_t offset)
{
    printk (KERN_INFO "entering mycdrv_aio_write\n");
    return mycdrv_generic_write (iocb->ki_filp, iov->iov_base, iov->iov_len,
                                 &offset);
}

static const struct file_operations mycdrv_fops = {
    .owner = THIS_MODULE,
    .read = mycdrv_generic_read,
    .write = mycdrv_generic_write,
    .open = mycdrv_generic_open,
    .release = mycdrv_generic_release,
    .llseek = mycdrv_generic_lseek,
    .aio_read = mycdrv_aio_read,
    .aio_write = mycdrv_aio_write,
};

module_init (my_generic_init);
module_exit (my_generic_exit);

MODULE_AUTHOR ("Jerry Cooperstein");
MODULE_DESCRIPTION ("CLDD 1.0: lab1_aio.c");
MODULE_LICENSE ("GPL v2");
```

lab1_aio_test.c

```
/* Copyright 2009, J Cooperstein coop@coopj.com (GPLv2) */
#include <stdio.h>
#include <stdlib.h>
#include <unistd.h>
#include <string.h>
#include <fcntl.h>
#include <errno.h>
#include <libaio.h>
#include <sys/stat.h>

#define NBYTES 32
#define NBUF   100
```

```c
void printbufs (char **buf, int nbytes)
{
    int j;
    fflush (stdout);
    for (j = 0; j < NBUF; j++) {
        write (STDOUT_FILENO, buf[j], nbytes);
        printf ("\n");
    }
    printf ("\n");
}

int main (int argc, char *argv[])
{
    int fd, rc, j, k, nbytes = NBYTES, maxevents = NBUF;
    char *buf[NBUF], *filename = "/dev/mycdrv";
    struct iocb *iocbray[NBUF], *iocb;
    off_t offset;
    io_context_t ctx = 0;
    struct io_event events[2 * NBUF];
    struct timespec timeout = { 0, 0 };

    /* open or create the file and fill it with a pattern */

    if (argc > 1)
        filename = argv[1];

    printf ("opening %s\n", filename);

    /* notice opening with these flags won't hurt a device node! */

    if ((fd = open (filename, O_RDWR | O_CREAT | O_TRUNC,
                    S_IRUSR | S_IWUSR | S_IRGRP | S_IWGRP)) < 0) {
        printf ("couldn't open %s, ABORTING\n", filename);
        exit (-1);
    }

    /* write initial data out, clear buffers, allocate iocb's */

    for (j = 0; j < NBUF; j++) {
        /* no need to zero iocbs; will be done in io_prep_pread */
        iocbray[j] = malloc (sizeof (struct iocb));
        buf[j] = malloc (nbytes);
        sprintf (buf[j], "%4d%4d%4d%4d%4d%4d%4d%4d", j, j, j, j, j, j, j, j);
        write (fd, buf[j], nbytes);
        memset (buf[j], 0, nbytes);
    }
    printf ("\n");

    /* prepare the context */

    rc = io_setup (maxevents, &ctx);
    printf (" rc from io_setup = %d\n", rc);

    /* (async) read the data from the file */
```

```
    printf (" reading initial data from the file:\n");

    for (j = 0; j < NBUF; j++) {
        iocb = iocbray[j];
        offset = j * nbytes;
        io_prep_pread (iocb, fd, (void *)buf[j], nbytes, offset);
        rc = io_submit (ctx, 1, &iocb);
    }

    /* sync up and print out the readin data */

    while ((rc = io_getevents (ctx, NBUF, NBUF, events, &timeout)) > 0) {
        printf (" rc from io_getevents on the read = %d\n\n", rc);
    }

    printbufs (buf, nbytes);

    /* filling in the buffers before the write */

    for (j = 0; j < NBUF; j++) {
        char *tmp = buf[j];
        for (k = 0; k < nbytes; k++) {
            sprintf ((tmp + k), "%1d", j);
        }
    }

    /* write the changed buffers out */

    printf (" writing new data to the file:\n");
    for (j = 0; j < NBUF; j++) {
        iocb = iocbray[j];
        offset = j * nbytes;
        io_prep_pwrite (iocb, fd, buf[j], nbytes, offset);
        rc = io_submit (ctx, 1, &iocb);
    }

    /* sync up again */

    while ((rc = io_getevents (ctx, NBUF, NBUF, events, &timeout)) > 0) {
        printf (" rc from io_getevents on the write = %d\n\n", rc);
    }

    printbufs (buf, nbytes);

    /* clean up */
    rc = io_destroy (ctx);
    close (fd);
    exit (0);
}
```

lab1_posix_test.c

```
/* Copyright 2009, J Cooperstein coop@coopj.com (GPLv2) */
#include <stdio.h>
```

```c
#include <stdlib.h>
#include <unistd.h>
#include <string.h>
#include <fcntl.h>
#include <errno.h>
#include <aio.h>
#include <sys/stat.h>

#define NBYTES 32
#define NBUF   100

void printbufs (char **buf, int nbytes)
{
    int j;
    fflush (stdout);
    for (j = 0; j < NBUF; j++) {
        write (STDOUT_FILENO, buf[j], nbytes);
        printf ("\n");
    }
    printf ("\n");
}

int main (int argc, char *argv[])
{
    int fd, rc, j, k, nbytes = NBYTES;
    char *tmp, *buf[NBUF], *filename = "/dev/mycdrv";
    struct aiocb *cbray[NBUF], *cb;

    /* create the file and fill it with a pattern */

    if (argc > 1)
        filename = argv[1];

    /* notice opening with these flags won't hurt a device node! */

    if ((fd = open (filename, O_RDWR | O_CREAT | O_TRUNC,
                    S_IRUSR | S_IWUSR | S_IRGRP | S_IWGRP)) < 0) {
        printf ("couldn't open %s, ABORTING\n", filename);
        exit (-1);
    }

    /* write initial data out, clear buffers, allocate aiocb's */

    for (j = 0; j < NBUF; j++) {

        buf[j] = malloc (nbytes);
        sprintf (buf[j], "%4d%4d%4d%4d%4d%4d%4d%4d", j, j, j, j, j, j, j, j);
        write (fd, buf[j], nbytes);
        memset (buf[j], 0, nbytes);

        cb = malloc (sizeof (struct aiocb));
        cbray[j] = cb;
        memset (cb, 0, sizeof (struct aiocb));

        cb->aio_fildes = fd;
```

```
        cb->aio_nbytes = nbytes;
        cb->aio_offset = j * nbytes;
        cb->aio_buf = (void *)buf[j];
}
printf ("\n");

/* (async) read the data from the file */

printf (" reading initial data from the file:\n");

for (j = 0; j < NBUF; j++) {
    cb = cbray[j];
    rc = aio_read (cb);
}

/* sync up and print out the readin data */

for (j = 0; j < NBUF; j++) {
    cb = cbray[j];
    while (aio_error (cb) == EINPROGRESS) {
    };
    printf ("%d:  aio_error=%d  aio_return=%d\n  ",
            j, aio_error (cb), (int)aio_return (cb));
}

printbufs (buf, nbytes);

/* filling in the buffers before the write */

for (j = 0; j < NBUF; j++) {
    tmp = buf[j];
    for (k = 0; k < nbytes; k++) {
        sprintf ((tmp + k), "%1d", j);
    }
    /*      printf ("%d, %s\n", j, buf[j]); */
}
printf ("\n");

/* write the changed buffers out */

printf (" writing new data to the file:\n");
for (j = 0; j < NBUF; j++) {
    cb = cbray[j];
    rc = aio_write (cb);
}

/* sync up again */

for (j = 0; j < NBUF; j++) {
    cb = cbray[j];
    while (aio_error (cb) == EINPROGRESS) {
    };
    printf ("%d:  aio_error=%d  aio_return=%d\n  ",
            j, aio_error (cb), (int)aio_return (cb));
}
```

```
    printbufs (buf, nbytes);

    close (fd);
    exit (0);
}
```

lab1_testloop.sh

```
#!/bin/bash

# 2/2008 J. Cooperstein (coop@coopj.com) License:GPLv2

file="/dev/mycdrv" && [ "$1" != "" ] && file=$1
reps=1000            && [ "$2" != "" ] && reps=$2

echo DOING $reps iterations on $file with ../lab1_aio_test:
time   ( n=0 ; \
while [ $n -lt $reps ]
  do ./lab1_aio_test $file > /dev/null
  n=$(($n+1))
done )

echo DOING $reps iterations on $file with ../lab1_posix_test:
time   ( n=0; \
while [ $n -lt $reps ]
  do ./lab1_posix_test $file > /dev/null
  n=$(($n+1))
done )
```

Chapter 34

I/O Scheduling

34.1   Lab 1: Comparing I/O schedulers

- Write a script (or program if you prefer) that cycles through available I/O schedulers on a hard disk and does a configurable number of parallel reads and writes of files of a configurable size. You'll probably want to test reads and writes as separate steps.

- To test reads you'll want to make sure you're actually reading from disk and not from cached pages of memory; you can flush out the cache by doing

  ```
  $ echo 3 > /proc/sys/vm/drop_caches
  ```

  before doing the reads. You can **cat** into **/dev/null** to avoid writing to disk. To make sure all reads are complete before you get timing information, you can issue a **wait** command under the shell.

- To test writes you can simply copy a file (which will be in cached memory after the first read) multiple times simultaneously. To make sure you wait for all writes to complete before you get timing information you can issue a **sync** call.

`lab1_iosched.sh`

```bash
#!/bin/bash

NMAX=8
NMEGS=100
[ "$1" != "" ] && NMAX=$1
[ "$2" != "" ] && NMEGS=$2

echo Doing: $NMAX parallel read/writes on: $NMEGS MB size files

TIMEFORMAT="%R    %U    %S"

################################################################
# simple test of parallel reads
do_read_test(){
    for n in $(seq 1 $NMAX) ; do
        cat file$n > /dev/null &
    done
# wait for previous jobs to finish
    wait
}

# simple test of parallel writes
do_write_test(){
    for n in $(seq 1 $NMAX) ; do
        [ -f fileout$n ] && rm -f fileout$n
        (cp file1 fileout$n && sync) &
    done
# wait for previous jobs to finish
    wait
}

# create some files for reading, ok if they are the same
create_input_files(){
    [ -f file1 ] || dd if=/dev/urandom of=file1 bs=1M count=$NMEGS
    for n in $(seq 1 $NMAX) ; do
        [ -f file$n ] || cp file1 file$n
    done
}

echo -e "\ncreating as needed random input files"
create_input_files

################################################################
# begin the aectual work

# do parallel read test
echo -e "\ndoing timings of parallel reads"
echo -e " REAL    USER    SYS\n"
for iosched in noop deadline anticipatory cfq ; do
    echo testing IOSCHED = $iosched
    echo $iosched > /sys/block/sda/queue/scheduler
#   cat /sys/block/sda/queue/scheduler
#    echo -e "\nclearing the memory caches\n"
    echo 3 > /proc/sys/vm/drop_caches
    time do_read_test
```

```
done
##################################################################
# do parallel write test
echo -e "\ndoing timings of parallel writes"
echo -e " REAL    USER    SYS\n"
for iosched in noop deadline anticipatory cfq ; do
    echo testing IOSCHED = $iosched
#    echo $iosched > /sys/block/sda/queue/scheduler
#    cat /sys/block/sda/queue/scheduler
    time  do_write_test
done
##################################################################
```

Chapter 35

Block Drivers

35.1   Lab 1: Building a Block Driver

- Write a basic block device driver.

- You'll need to implement at least the `open()` and `release()` entry points, and include a request function.

- You can safely use 254 for the major device number and select a minor device number. For an added exercise try getting a major number dynamically. Assuming you are using **udev**, the node should be made automatically when you load the driver; otherwise you will have to actually add the node with the `mknod` command.

- Keep track of the number of times the node is opened. Try permitting multiple opens, or exclusive use.

- Write a program to read (and/or write) from the node, using the standard **Unix** I/O functions (`open()`, `read()`, `write()`, `close()`). After loading the module with `insmod` use this program to access the node.

- **NOTE**: Make sure you have enough memory to handle the ram disk you create; The solution has 128 MB allocated.

35.2   Lab 2: Mountable Read/Write Block Driver

- Extend the previous exercise in order to put an **ext3** file system (or another type) on your device.

- You can place a filesystem on the device with

  ```
  mkfs.ext3 /dev/mybdrv
  mount /dev/mybdrv mnt
  ```

  where you give the appropriate name of the device node and mount point.

- For an additional enhancement, try partitioning the device with **fdisk**. For this you may need an additional ioctl() for HDIO_GETGEO, and you'll have to include: linux/hdreg.h. This **ioctl** returns a pointer to the following structure:

  ```
  struct hd_geometry {
        unsigned char heads;
        unsigned char sectors;
        unsigned short cylinders;
        unsigned long start;
  };
  ```

  Remember the total capacity is (sector size) x (sectors/track) x (cylinders) x (heads). You also want to use a value of 4 for the starting sector.

- If you are using a recent kernel and version of **udev**, the partition nodes should be made automatically when you load the driver; otherwise you will have to actually add them manually.

lab2_block.c

```
/* Copyright 2009, J Cooperstein coop@coopj.com (GPLv2) */

#include <linux/fs.h>
#include <linux/module.h>
#include <linux/moduleparam.h>
#include <linux/init.h>
#include <linux/vmalloc.h>
#include <linux/blkdev.h>
#include <linux/genhd.h>
#include <linux/errno.h>
#include <linux/hdreg.h>
#include <linux/version.h>

#define MY_DEVICE_NAME "mybdrv"

static int mybdrv_ma_no = 0, diskmb = 128;
static int disk_size = 0;
static char *my_dev;
static struct gendisk *my_gd;
static spinlock_t lock;
static unsigned short sector_size = 512;

module_param_named (size, diskmb, int, 0);
```

```
static struct request_queue *my_request_queue;

#if LINUX_VERSION_CODE < KERNEL_VERSION(2,6,31)
static void my_request (struct request_queue *q)
{
    struct request *rq;
    int size;
    char *ptr;
    unsigned nr_sectors, sector;

    printk (KERN_INFO "entering request routine\n");

    while ((rq = elv_next_request (q))) {
        if (!blk_fs_request (rq)) {
            printk (KERN_WARNING "This was not a normal fs request, skipping\n");
            end_request (rq, 0);
            continue;
        }

        nr_sectors = rq->current_nr_sectors;
        sector = rq->sector;
        ptr = my_dev + sector * sector_size;
        size = nr_sectors * sector_size;

        if ((ptr + size) > (my_dev + disk_size)) {
            printk (KERN_WARNING " tried to go past end of device\n");
            end_request (rq, 0);
            continue;
        }

        if (rq_data_dir (rq)) {
            printk (KERN_INFO "writing at sector %d, %ud sectors \n",
                    sector, nr_sectors);
            memcpy (ptr, rq->buffer, size);
        } else {
            printk (KERN_INFO "reading at sector %d, %ud sectors \n",
                    sector, nr_sectors);
            memcpy (rq->buffer, ptr, size);
        }

        end_request (rq, 1);
    }
    printk (KERN_INFO "leaving request\n");
}
#else
static void my_request (struct request_queue *q)
{
    struct request *rq;
    int size, res=0;
    char *ptr;
    unsigned nr_sectors, sector;
    printk (KERN_INFO "entering request routine\n");

    rq = blk_fetch_request(q);
```

```
    while (rq){
        if (!blk_fs_request (rq)) {
            printk (KERN_WARNING "This was not a normal fs request, skipping\n");
            goto done;
        }
        nr_sectors = blk_rq_cur_sectors(rq);
        sector = blk_rq_pos(rq);

        ptr = my_dev + sector * sector_size;
        size = nr_sectors * sector_size;

        if ((ptr + size) > (my_dev + disk_size)) {
            printk (KERN_WARNING " tried to go past end of device\n");
            goto done;
        }

        if (rq_data_dir (rq)) {
            printk (KERN_INFO "writing at sector %d, %ud sectors \n",
                    sector, nr_sectors);
            memcpy (ptr, rq->buffer, size);
        } else {
            printk (KERN_INFO "reading at sector %d, %ud sectors \n",
                    sector, nr_sectors);
            memcpy (rq->buffer, ptr, size);
        }
    done:
        if (!__blk_end_request_cur(rq, res))
            rq = blk_fetch_request(q);
    }
    printk (KERN_INFO "leaving request\n");
}
#endif

#if LINUX_VERSION_CODE < KERNEL_VERSION(2,6,28)
static int my_ioctl (struct inode *i, struct file *f,
                     unsigned int cmd, unsigned long arg)
#else
static int my_ioctl (struct block_device *bdev, fmode_t mode,
                     unsigned int cmd, unsigned long arg)
#endif
{
    long size;
    struct hd_geometry geo;

    printk (KERN_INFO "cmd=%d\n", cmd);

    switch (cmd) {
    case HDIO_GETGEO:
        printk (KERN_INFO "HIT HDIO_GETGEO\n");
        /*
         * get geometry: we have to fake one...  trim the size to a
         * multiple of 64 (32k): tell we have 16 sectors, 4 heads,
         * whatever cylinders. Tell also that data starts at sector. 4.
         */
```

```
            size = disk_size;
            size &= ~0x3f;            /* multiple of 64 */
            geo.cylinders = size >> 6;
            geo.heads = 4;
            geo.sectors = 16;
            geo.start = 4;

            if (copy_to_user ((void __user *)arg, &geo, sizeof (geo)))
                return -EFAULT;

            return 0;
        }
        printk (KERN_WARNING "return -ENOTTY\n");

        return -ENOTTY;              /* unknown command */
}

static struct block_device_operations mybdrv_fops = {
    .owner = THIS_MODULE,
    .ioctl = my_ioctl,
};

static int __init my_init (void)
{
    disk_size = diskmb * 1024 * 1024;
    spin_lock_init (&lock);

    if (!(my_dev = vmalloc (disk_size)))
        return -ENOMEM;

    if (!(my_request_queue = blk_init_queue (my_request, &lock))) {
        vfree (my_dev);
        return -ENOMEM;
    }

#if LINUX_VERSION_CODE < KERNEL_VERSION(2,6,31)
    blk_queue_hardsect_size (my_request_queue, sector_size);
#else
    blk_queue_logical_block_size (my_request_queue, sector_size);
#endif

    mybdrv_ma_no = register_blkdev (mybdrv_ma_no, MY_DEVICE_NAME);
    if (mybdrv_ma_no < 0) {
        printk (KERN_ERR "Failed registering mybdrv, returned %d\n",
                mybdrv_ma_no);
        vfree (my_dev);
        return mybdrv_ma_no;
    }

    if (!(my_gd = alloc_disk (16))) {
        unregister_blkdev (mybdrv_ma_no, MY_DEVICE_NAME);
        vfree (my_dev);
        return -ENOMEM;
    }
```

```c
    my_gd->major = mybdrv_ma_no;
    my_gd->first_minor = 0;
    my_gd->fops = &mybdrv_fops;
    strcpy (my_gd->disk_name, MY_DEVICE_NAME);
    my_gd->queue = my_request_queue;
    set_capacity (my_gd, disk_size / sector_size);
    add_disk (my_gd);

    printk (KERN_INFO "device successfully   registered, Major No. = %d\n",
            mybdrv_ma_no);
    printk (KERN_INFO "Capacity of ram disk is: %d MB\n", diskmb);

    return 0;
}

static void __exit my_exit (void)
{
    del_gendisk (my_gd);
    put_disk (my_gd);
    unregister_blkdev (mybdrv_ma_no, MY_DEVICE_NAME);
    printk (KERN_INFO "module successfully unloaded, Major No. = %d\n",
            mybdrv_ma_no);
    blk_cleanup_queue (my_request_queue);
    vfree (my_dev);
}

module_init (my_init);
module_exit (my_exit);

MODULE_AUTHOR ("Jerry Cooperstein");
MODULE_DESCRIPTION ("CLDD 1.0: lab2_block.c");
MODULE_LICENSE ("GPL v2");
```

lab2_block_test.c

```c
 /* Copyright 2009, J Cooperstein coop@coopj.com (GPLv2) */

#include <stdio.h>
#include <fcntl.h>
#include <sys/types.h>
#include <unistd.h>
#include <stdlib.h>

#define SIZE 2122
#define CHK   250

int main ()
{
    int j, length, fd, rc;
    int vector[SIZE];
    off_t offset;

    length = sizeof (int) * SIZE;
    offset = sizeof (int) * CHK;
```

```
    fd = open ("/dev/mybdrv", O_RDWR);

    for (j = 0; j < SIZE; j++) {
        vector[j] = j;
    }

    rc = write (fd, vector, length);
    printf ("\n **** return code from write = %d\n", rc);

    rc = lseek (fd, offset, SEEK_SET);
    printf ("\n **** retrun code from lseek(%d) = %d \n", (int)offset, rc);

    rc = read (fd, vector + CHK, sizeof (int));
    printf ("\n **** retrun code from read vec[%d] = %d, vec[%d] = %d \n",
            CHK, rc, CHK, vector[CHK]);

    close (fd);

    exit (0);

}
```

17260106R00144

Made in the USA
Lexington, KY
07 September 2012